Contents

Acknowledgments

In researching this book, I often traveled far from home, and more than once I found myself depending upon the kindness of strangers. The following people were both helpful and gracious: Anne Whelpley, research librarian at the Beinecke Library at Yale University; Ann Allen Shockley, head of Special Collections at the Fisk University Library; Thomas Battle, curator of manuscripts in the Moorland-Spingarn Collection at Howard University; Charles Cooney, former research librarian at the Library of Congress; John Stinson, research librarian at the New York Public Library at 42nd Street; Robert Morris, research librarian for the Schomburg Collection at the New York Public Library at 135th Street; Neda Westlake, curator of the Rare Book Collection at the Charles Van Pelt Library at the University of Pennsylvania; and Edwin Castagna, former head librarian at the Enoch Pratt Free Library of Baltimore. And closer to home, I would especially like to thank Lois Olsrud, central reference librarian at the University of Arizona, for unselfishly giving me so much of her time when I failed miserably at tracking down an obscure article or book. I would also like to thank the NAACP and the following libraries for giving me permission to use unpublished material: Fisk University Library, Howard University Library, the Library of Congress, the New York Public Libraries, and the Beinecke Library at Yale University. I am especially grateful to Carl Cowl and to Carolyn Mitchell for allowing me to quote from the unpublished letters of Claude McKay and George Schuyler, respectively.

Around eight years ago, I first began thinking of writing a book on the Harlem Renaissance, that marvelous burst of black creativity that we associate with the 1920s. How the thought came to me of connecting Mencken to this literary movement I don't quite recall. I do remember collaring many of my friends and springing my ideas upon them with the same sense of urgency that prompted the ancient mariner to latch onto the wedding guest. I remember having an idea at the time that the Harlem Renaissance could be "solved," as a mystery is solved, if one could only find the right pieces to the puzzle. It may have been that I heard Mencken's laughter in the background as I thought of various solutions to the mystery of the Harlem Renaissance, for he was a man who did not put much stock in pat solutions. It may have been, too, that I was continually being reminded, by my notes from the unpublished correspondence and black newspapers of the period, that Mencken's presence dominated the early years of the 1920s. The number of times I saw his name in the columns of the black newspapers or heard the tone of his voice in the utterances of the black intellectuals—these specific memories slowly began to assume an importance that I could not ignore. I soon began to pester my friends with my ideas about Mencken and the Harlem Renaissance, and I wish to thank the following people who had the patience to listen to me: Tom Anderson, Roger Bowen, Ardner Cheshire, Brian Fay, Linc Keiser, Fred Kiefer, Lawrence Clark Powell, Teresa Scruggs, Lee Van deMarr, and Ed Waldron. I am especially indebted to Mr. Van deMarr, who served as Mencken to my rather clumsy Dreiser. He read the rough drafts of this present manuscript and made many valuable suggestions. The least that I can say of his help is that he saved me from getting lost down too many side roads; the best, that he made this book a much better one than it was when I first showed it to him.

I would also like to thank Professor Walter Rideout for reading my book in manuscript; his judicious criticism forced me to shape the final product into something reasonably coherent. In addition, I would like to pay tribute to Professor Edwin H. Cady for his warm encouragement over the last several years; when I told him that I wanted to write about Mencken, he gave me some sage Menckenian advice—he said to do it before somebody else does.

I am grateful to both Boleyn Baylor McLane and Majill Weber for typing my manuscript with meticulous care, and to Nancy Mairs and Ron and Joan Stottlemyer for proofreading it with the concentration of a desert owl getting ready to pounce on a pack rat.

My wife, Teresa, deserves more than my gratitude. As I was writing this book, she was both an incisive critic and my most loyal supporter.

Finally, I am indebted to the American Philosophical Society, the University of Arizona, and the National Endowment for the Humanities for financial assistance while I was writing this book. Without their help, I would still be shuffling my notecards.

THE SAGE IN HARLEM

What thou lovest well, remains American.

—Richard Hugo

CHAPTER ONE

Why Mencken?

It has been said of Americans that they have short memories, and if there is any truth to this generalization, the case of H. L. Mencken seems to bear it out. Once "the most powerful personal influence on this whole generation of educated people,"[1] as Walter Lippmann called him in 1926, he is now remembered primarily by professors of English literature (an ironical fate, given Mencken's low opinion of them). True, Mencken has survived in popular folklore, but this folk Mencken is hardly the real man. The distortion that has occurred in his character over the years is similar to one that metamorphosed Dr. Johnson into a humorous eccentric in the nineteenth-century mind. Bertrand Bronson has shown that the English historian Thomas Macaulay provided the text for that metamorphosis, and one could just as easily argue that Charles Angoff is Mencken's Macaulay.[2] His portrait of Mencken did not exactly create the folk Mencken, but it did provide evidence for the image of him that people had already begun to accept—if they thought of him at all in 1956. That this image of Mencken as the cigar-waving, bigoted escapee from a vaudeville show still exists, even among intellectuals, is given proof by Robert Brustein's recent sobriquet: "The W. C. Fields of journalism."[3]

As Lippmann's comment suggests, however, it was not just Mencken's personal image that suffered after 1930 or so; it was also his reputation as a literary critic and as an observer of American life. Contemporary critics should remind themselves of Mencken's past stature in the world of American literature. Frank Turaj puts it succinctly:

It is still difficult to appreciate the immense influence that Mencken exerted as a literary man. That he was an important figure and taste maker in American letters is incontestable. Sinclair Lewis dedicated *Elmer Gantry*

to him, and he was perhaps responsible for the central ideas in others of
Lewis' novels. He served Dreiser as confidant, proof-reader, advisor, and
champion. F. Scott Fitzgerald cared more to please Mencken than any
other critic. Ezra Pound longed for Mencken to join the expatriates. New-
ton Arvin thought of him as America's first literary dictator.[4]

Yet because he seemed so much in tune with the *Zeitgeist* of the 1920s
—perhaps creating much of it—later critics saw him as a symbol of the
era's most glaring superficialities. And certainly there was a comic appropriateness to Mencken's fall from grace. Although the Depression
damaged his reputation, the professors dealt it the final blow. What
Mencken had done to them in the first two decades of the twentieth
century (witness Paul Elmer More, Stuart Sherman, and others), they
now did to him with a vengeance. Even good critics such as Alfred Kazin
in *On Native Grounds* (1942) and Frederick Hoffman in *The Twenties*
(1949) tended to denigrate his worth and the positive effects of his influence. To Kazin, Mencken is merely a clever comic: "Mencken's gaiety
was the secret of his charm, and his charm was everything."[5] To Hoffman,
his sociological insights are false: "He never lied; he never actually told
the truth."[6] (Hoffman neglects to say that this is what satirists have
always done.) And despite the scholarly interest in Mencken over the last
two decades, it is still not uncommon to find a professor today who will
denounce Mencken as though the man had personally offended him.
Thus, John McCormick in *The Middle Distance* (1971) sniffs at Mencken's
ignorance: His "preparation for his career as literary dictator was limited
to completion of work in a technical high school in Baltimore."[7] (Mencken
would have loved this last ad hominem attack; it represented the same
lofty disdain that the professors had assumed toward him from the
beginning.)
    In light of these prejudices against Mencken, a man who took a
delight in having quite a few himself, it is not surprising that he has been
generally neglected by modern critics of the Harlem Renaissance. They
have simply forgotten, or not known of, Mencken's enormous presence
in American culture—that, in fact, to quote Isaac Goldberg in 1925, he
once "compelled the discussion of every theme that [was] of vital concern
to him."[8] Mencken is usually mentioned briefly whenever the Jazz Age is
discussed (another irony, since he did not especially like jazz), and
sometimes his iconoclastic wit, vitriolic style, and contempt for the American "booboisie" are duly noted as sources for the irreverent side of the
Harlem Renaissance, but at the same time these generalizations are meant
to exhaust his importance.[9] Occasionally, he is praised for some special
service to a black writer. Charles Cooney, Edward Waldron, Robert C.
Hart, and David Levering Lewis all note his "midwifery" of Walter White's

novel *The Fire in the Flint* (1924)[10] and Fenwick Anderson observes how often Mencken published black writers in the *American Mercury*. Yet Anderson's attitude toward Mencken could stand for that of most critics. He is somewhat surprised by Mencken's generosity, and although he can imagine Mencken shaking hands with black America, "like a gentleman," he cannot imagine Mencken going out of his way to help a whole genera-tion of black writers or his being seriously interested in their literary movement.[11] Why not? This question brings us to a second reason that Mencken's influence on the Harlem Renaissance has been overlooked.

An obvious reason for ignoring Mencken is Mencken himself. How can anyone take a man seriously who often referred to the Negro as a "coon," a "blackamoor," a "darkey," and even a "niggero"? Today people are extremely sensitive about matters of race and minorities, and writers who use words like these are quite readily rejected. Yet this very sensitivity may carry its own burden of obtuseness: Such overreaction may prevent contemporary critics from seeing what an author in the past actually said. Whenever the subject of Mencken and race is mentioned, the old bugaboo of his racial slurs is dutifully brought up and lamented over, and all discussion stops right there. Furthermore, this obligatory condem-nation is rhetorical; it is meant to show the audience that the critic is a good, right-thinking man or woman. In a recent book review of an anthology of Mencken's writings, even so excellent a critic as Justin Kaplan scolds Mencken for the following metaphor, overlooking the fact that Mencken has identified with the lowly "blackamoor": "More than once I have slipped out of daily journalism to dally in its meretricious suburbs, but I have always returned repentent and relieved, like a blackamoor coming back in Autumn to a warm and sociable jail."[12] So too Alan Dundes reprints Mencken's scholarly essay "Designations for Colored Folk" in his collection of Afro-American folklore (*Mother Wit From the Laughing Barrel*), but he feels compelled to add, "No doubt some readers will find some of the discussion distasteful"—as if Mencken is somehow tainted by those terms whose etymologies he discusses.[13] So common is this view of Mencken's insensitivity to blacks that more than one critic has misread what Mencken has actually said. In an otherwise entertaining portrait of Harlem in the 1920s, Jervis Anderson in the *New Yorker* (13 July 1981) totally misinterprets Mencken's attitude in the famous *Mercury* editorial, "A Coon Age." Mencken's point is that the cultural contributions of Negroes *are* a welcome addition to the "cultural mosaic" of America (and if they are not always a welcome addition, they are a fait accompli, and he portrays them as such). Anderson, however, projects upon Mencken a disapproval of the gaiety he describes and a general dislike of the cultural pluralism that it symbolizes. No doubt Mencken's language affected Anderson's judgment, for Anderson ends his paragraph complaining that "in a journal of reasonable civility, one might have wished for racial terminology that was not so degrading and primitive."[14]

A third reason for Mencken's neglect, especially among recent black critics, is explained by the omnipresence of white author Carl Van Vechten. His soirees for black artists, his efforts to help them find publishers and to spotlight the literary movement in magazines such as *Vanity Fair,* and his sensational best-selling novel, *Nigger Heaven* (1926) — all these were highly publicized in the 1920s. From Sterling Brown to the present, black and white critics have quarreled over how much good or evil Van Vechten accomplished for the Harlem Renaissance. During the late 1960s, as one might expect, the scales clearly registered on the side of evil — at least as far as the black critics were concerned.[15] Since one white influence was already one too many (and much critical energy was expended in showing just how pernicious Van Vechten's influence actually was), Mencken's presence naturally got shoved into the background. Actually, as editor of the *American Mercury* (1924-1933) and as a personal friend of Alfred Knopf, Mencken was able to do more for black writers than could Van Vechten, but rarely is he remembered in that light. Rather, his name became associated with a *Mercury* that satirized the follies and knaveries of the white citizens of the Republic. Hence, in Nathan Huggins's well-known study of the intellectual backgrounds of the Harlem Renaissance, Mencken is mentioned only one time — and that in a brief reference to a character in *Nigger Heaven.*

However, the episode to which Huggins refers reflects Van Vechten's knowledge of just how much the black writers of the 1920s owed Mencken, for it is the pivotal point in Byron Kasson's moral and intellectual pilgrimage. As editor of the *American Mars* (*American Mercury*), Russett Durwood (Mencken) has received a manuscript from a young Negro, a college graduate who has learned all the wrong things about life and literature. A hard man (Dur-wood), the editor nevertheless has a soft heart, especially for black writers. Hence, he summons Kasson to his offices and, all the while pretending complete indifference, roundly chastizes him for writing a cliché-ridden story about an interracial love affair gone awry. "I am very much interested in Negro literature," the somewhat embarrassed Durwood says; "that's why I sent for you. . . . When I see a fellow with talent going the wrong way, I try to be honest." Then he adds, "Why in hell don't you write about something you know about?" And without waiting for an answer, he proceeds to lecture Byron about the untold riches of Harlem:

The whole place, contrary to the general impression, is overrun with fresh, unused material. Nobody has yet written a good gambling story; nobody has touched the outskirts of cabaret life; nobody has gone into the curious subject of the divers tribes of the region. Why, there are West Indians and Abyssinian Jews, religious Negroes, pagan Negroes, and Negro intellectuals, all living together more or less amicably in the same community, each group with its own opinions and atmosphere and manner of living; each individual with his own opinions and atmosphere and manner of living. But I find that Negroes don't write about these matters; they continue to employ all the old clichés and formulas that have been worried to death by Nordic blonds who, after all, never did know anything about the subject from the inside.[16]

The key for Durwood lies in being an acute observer: "Good God, man, of you object to dulness in literature, look around you. Harlem life isn't dull. It has more aspects than a diamond has facets." Take Marcus Garvey, Durwood continues, "I'd like to find a good character study of *him.*"

Van Vechten probably did not agree with everything *his* Mencken says here (one theme in *Nigger Heaven* is that hardly anyone lived together "amicably" in Harlem),[17] but his portrait is no gratuitous bit of name-dropping. He is reminding his readers that the dean of literary critics has given this advice in real life and that he, Van Vechten, plans to follow it in his own novel. Furthermore, his picture of Mencken has been painted with scrupulous accuracy; he has caught both Mencken's manner and his matter. The episode with Kasson, for instance, Van Vechten probably borrowed from an account given him by his good friend James Weldon Johnson, who as a young black artist (musician and author) had sought out Mencken. The tale Johnson tells of this event in his autobiography (*Along This Way*) is a bit different from Van Vechten's version. Johnson had come to Mencken uninvited.

Around 1915, said Johnson, "Mencken had made a sharper impression on my mind than any other American then writing, and I wanted to know him." Having the audacity of youth, he went to the offices of the *Smart Set* and sent in his name. Mencken appeared "promptly" and the two chatted for "thirty, forty, perhaps, forty-five minutes." Johnson was impressed that "a man as busy as he could give so much time to a mere stranger." And he added:

> I had never been so fascinated at hearing anyone talk. He talked about literature, about Negro literature, the Negro problem, and Negro music. He declared that Negro writers in writing about their own race made a mistake when they indulged in pleas for justice and mercy, when they prayed indulgence for shortcomings, when they based their protests against unjust treatment on the Christian or moral or ethical code, when they argued to prove that they were as good as anybody else. "What they

should do," he said, "is to single out the strong points of the race and emphasize them over and over and over; asserting, at least on these points, that they are *better* than anybody else."

Johnson said that when he left Mencken, he "felt buoyed up, exhilarated. It was as though I had taken a mental cocktail."[18]

Before looking at the implications of this conversation, it is important to remember that in 1915 Negro letters were not exactly flourishing. At this time, the Harlem Renaissance was not even a name; and the "New Negro," not even a fond dream. Charles Chesnutt had published his last novel in 1905; Dunbar had stopped writing; Sutton Griggs was unheard of; and DuBois had buried himself in polemics as editor of the *Crisis* and as author of *The Quest of the Silver Fleece* (1911). True, there were signs of life in Chicago with Fenton Johnson's poetry magazine, but by and large, 1905 to 1915 were not very good years for black literature. That James Weldon Johnson published his fine novel, *The Autobiography of an Ex-Colored Man* (1912), anonymously is perhaps symbolic of the uncertainties of the time. (Too, Carl Van Vechten had not yet discovered Negroes.)

From his conversation with Johnson, I can make several generalizations about Mencken's associations with the black writers of the 1920s. First, Mencken was a good talker, and when he was not actually goring people (*comme* Dr. Johnson), he tended to inspire them. (James Weldon Johnson later confessed that Mencken's writings had the same alcoholic effect on him as did his conversation.) Second, Mencken knew what he was talking about. At times he seemed to be a fund of information on black life, though he was capable of making some flagrant mistakes when the prejudicial fit was upon him. Third, implicit in Mencken's message to Johnson was the idea that the tangible signs of excellence would do more to benefit the race than would a thousand complaints (a major theme of the Harlem Renaissance). Explicit in Mencken's message was that the Negro (as Mencken firmly believed) was in some ways superior to the America in which he lived.

Yet it would be a mistake to take this theme of Negro superiority as an indication that Mencken sentimentalized Negro writers. He was not, to use Zora Neale Hurston's felicitous coinage, a "Negrotarian"—a white do-gooder. He simply did not fit the pattern in any way: He was contemptuous of the patronage system as it was practiced in the 1920s; he resisted the temptation (if he ever felt any) to go slumming in Harlem with the white aficionados; and he stayed away from the interracial literary gatherings that were so popular at the time. For Mencken, the black writer was a writer like anybody else; if he wrote a good book, Mencken praised him; if he wrote a bad one, Mencken called him a blockhead. It could even be argued that more than any other critic in American letters, black or white, Mencken made it possible for the black writer to be treated as a fellow laborer in the vineyard. Before Mencken, the idea of a Negro writing was akin to Dr. Johnson's remark about a woman preaching: It is not done very well, but one is surprised to see it done at all. Mencken simply refused to speak down to the Negro writer. In review after review, he kept insisting that the Negro had the same obligations to craft, to honesty, to life as he knew it, as did all other writers. Accordingly, the "New Negroes" responded to Mencken if only for the simple fact that he treated them as men and women, not as trained dogs.

If Mencken was not a "Negrotarian," if he refused to go the way of other "concerned" white critics and authors, he nevertheless had a strong curiosity about the future of Negro arts and letters. And although he never invited black intellectuals to his home in Baltimore for literary soirees (as did Van Vechten), he may have been hospitable to these men and women in a more important sense: He opened the pages of the *American Mercury* to them. In fact, if one wanted to find out what both black and white America were thinking in the 1920s vis-à-vis the Negro, a good place to begin would be Mencken's *Mercury*. Every possible aspect of Negro culture, from art to Negro newspapers to Pullman porters, was discussed in its pages. Not only was Mencken interested in Negro life but he tried to help Negro writers whenever he had the chance. He continually threw out hints to them encouraging this or that article on this or that subject, for he rarely resisted the opportunity of telling them what they should be writing about.

Perhaps the essay that best illustrates Mencken's brand of intelligent meddling is a book review that he penned for the *Smart Set* in 1920, three years before the Harlem Renaissance showed any signs of life. This article was only one of the many since 1917 in which he had touched on the subject of black literature, but it was certainly his most significant to date. The occasion of his comments was a review of Mary White Ovington's novel *The Shadow*. Assuming that Ovington was a Negro (a natural enough mistake, since she was a high-ranking official in the NAACP), Mencken used her book as a platform to explain his own ideas for writing the Great Negro Novel.

The Shadow is not a good book, said Mencken, but it does indicate what might be done in the future if the right author with the right attitude wielded the right weapons. Overlooking Chesnutt, Dunbar, and a few nineteenth-century novelists, Mencken made the pontifical pronouncement that Ovington's book is "a first attempt by a colored writer to plunge into fiction in the grand manner." To her everlasting credit, added Mencken, Ovington "shows skill, observation, a civilized point of view," virtues that are usually absent in most American novelists. Nevertheless, her novel is marred by an unbelievable story and an equally unbelievable heroine. That the events she describes may have actually happened is no defense: "I once knew a German saloon-keeper who drank sixty glasses of beer every day of his life, but a novel celebrating his life and eminent attainments would have been grossly false. The serious novel does not deal with prodigies; it deals with normalities." Mencken's strictures were not new (he may have been thinking of Fielding's prefaces to *Tom Jones*), but concerning Negro life, they certainly had the ring of novelty about them. Mencken was simply asking the black novelist to practice "realism," the same advice he had been giving the American novelist since 1908, the year he started writing book reviews for the *Smart Set*.

As Mencken continued his assessment of *The Shadow*, he digressed into the subject of the Negro's qualifications for the job of novelist. He noted that the darker brother is a "shrewd observer." He knows much more about the white man than the latter knows about him. What is curious is that the white man claims to know the Negro, yet "knows next to nothing of [his] inner life."[19] Here the Negro author has his work cut out for him; here is terra incognita that only the Negro can explore:

> The thing we need is a realistic picture of this inner life of the negro by one who sees the race from within—a self-portrait as vivid and accurate as Dostoyevsky's portrait of the Russian or Thackeray's of the Englishman. The action should be kept within the normal range of negro experience. It should extend over a long enough range of years to show some development in character and circumstance. It should be presented against a background made vivid by innumerable small details. The negro author who makes such a book will dignify American literature and accomplish more for his race than a thousand propagandists and theorists. He will force the understanding that now seems so hopeless. He will blow up nine-tenths of the current poppycock. But let him avoid the snares that fetched Mrs. Ovington. She went to Kathleen Norris and Gertrude Atherton for her model. The place to learn how to write novels is in the harsh but distinguished seminary kept by Prof. Dr. Dreiser.

Packed into this passage are many of the themes that came to dominate critical discussion in the Harlem Renaissance: (1) art as a panacea—almost at times a secular religion; (2) the novel as the foremost literary form, with the corollary strongly stated that the Great Negro Novel would be written by a Negro; (3) realism as the appropriate mode for dealing with black life—perhaps the only mode; (4) the novelist as an observer, from the vantage points of both "insider" and "outsider." If he functions as an insider, he will treat (as Mencken told Walter White) "the drama within the race, so far scarcely touched."[20] If he functions as an outsider, he will write satire upon the smug, cocksure master race. Either way, as Dreiser or Swift, the road lies wide before him, for nobody, Mencken kept insisting, has been this way before.

Mencken, of course, was exaggerating. Actually, Chesnutt had practiced a kind of realism before Mencken had begun promoting it. In his Uncle Julius stories, some of which were collected in *The Conjure Woman* (1899), he had debunked the myth of the loyal retainer; and in *The Wife of His Youth and Other Stories of the Color Line* (1899), he had successfully bypassed the stereotype of the tragic mulatto. A friend and admirer of William Dean Howells, Chesnutt was obviously influenced by Howells's plea for realism in American letters, and Howells in return had championed Chesnutt as a realist.[21] As Frank Turaj notes, Mencken always gave the impression that realism had not existed in American literature before he had discovered it in Dreiser. In fact, he simply ignored a native tradition of literary realism in order to emphasize the difference between the Dark Ages (the "genteel tradition") and the Age of Light, which he was ushering in: The Age of Light looked that much brighter set against a background of unrelieved darkness. Thus, the "father of them all" was not William Dean Howells but Emile Zola; if there had to be an antecedent to Dreiser, it was rhetorically necessary to find that antecedent abroad. Mencken practiced a similar sleight of hand, of course, when it came to Afro-American letters. In 1920, he pretended that no black writer had escaped the aesthetic arenas of the dime novel and the stage melodrama.[22] Either he had forgotten Chesnutt and Dunbar, or he had not read them. He also neglected to mention that Gertrude Stein, Stephen Crane, George Washington Cable, and even Dreiser himself had ventured into the unexplored terrain of Negro life.

Yet it is important to remember that his assessment of the literary situation in America was more or less correct; and if one considers the general cultural climate around 1920, it is possible to get some idea of Mencken's boldness and prescience. The history of America's racial attitudes from 1900 to 1920 has been told many times, so I need not dwell upon the obvious: the crippling effect that the Jim Crow laws had upon the mind of the South, the sensationalism of *The Birth of a Nation* (1915), the revival of the Ku Klux Klan, and the racial intolerance that led to the terrible riots of 1919. Asking writers to quit treating Negroes as though they were inhuman was comparable to asking the pilots of the airplanes hovering around King Kong to shut off their machine guns. Lest this metaphor sound like an exaggeration, we need only watch again *The Birth of a Nation* (the cinematic epic of the New South) to remind ourselves how myopic American views of the Negro could be. Silas Lynch, Lydia Brown, Gus the renegade—one could not find more villainous villains in the penny dreadfuls. We may also recall that this movie had an opening run of seven months at Clune's Theater in Los Angeles (unprecedented even for a play), and that critics still conjecture that it may have been seen by more people than any other film.[23] Even the novel upon which it was based, *The Clansman* (1905) by Thomas Dixon, was made into a popular play.

As we know, the stereotype of the "black beast" was not the only one that dominated the American mind. The docile, watermelon-eating, lazy, crap-shooting "darkey" was another favorite, and although modern critics have discussed this character at length, there is a dimension to his appearance in American literature which has not yet been mentioned. The writers who created this character and the milieu in which he lived kept insisting (or at least their publishers did) that they were the Negro's officially recognized chroniclers. For instance, for Octavus Roy Cohen's *Polished Ebony* (1919), the advertisement in *Publishers Weekly* read, "If you have been reading the *Saturday Evening Post* this year you are familiar with Mr. Cohen's extremely clever stories of the 'sassiety' negro of the South. The best of these stories are in this book. Mr. Cohen has been termed 'the negro's O. Henry.'"

In the same issue of *Publishers Weekly*, an advertisement for a collection of short stories by E. K. Means claimed that the author had a "perfect comprehension of the negro's turn of thought, his love of laughter, his shiftlessness, his love of music, his superstition." And in addition to this "perfect" understanding of the Negro's character, Means also "caught with an accuracy" the Negro's "picturesque idiom of speech." This eulogy ended with a comparison of Means's stories to "the work of Synge and Lady Gregory."[24] A year earlier, the cover of *Publishers Weekly* put forth an even broader claim for Means's artistry: "The author, a Louisiana pastor, who has made himself so completely THE writer of negro stories that it is enough to call the book E. K. Means."[25]

In the same year as Mencken's review of *The Shadow* (1920), two more collections of darkey stories were published, *Further E. K. Means* and Cohen's *Come Seven*, and one picaresque novel, Hugh Wiley's *Wildcat*. In the next five years—that is, until the publication of Alain Locke's *New Negro* (1925), the anthology of Negro arts and letters which heralded the presence of the Harlem Renaissance—works by white humorists appeared with some regularity: Cohen's *Highly Colored* (1921), *Assorted Chocolates* (1922), *Dark Days and Black Knights* (1923), and *Bigger and Blacker* (1925); Irvin Cobb's *J. Poindexter, Colored* (1922); and Hugh Wiley's *Lady Luck* (1921), *Lily* (1922), and *The Prowler* (1924). In fact, these caricatures of the Negro were popular throughout the 1920s. Wiley's J. Vitus Marsden ("the Wildcat"), Cohen's Florian Slappey, and Cobb's J. Poindexter all became household names, and they were the immediate antecedents for the Amos 'n Andy radio show, which occurred later in the decade. Although Wiley's last book on "the Wildcat" appeared in 1927 (*Fo' Meals a Day*), Cohen published his stories about crap-shooters and con artists right up until the 1930s: *Black and Blue* (1926), *Florian Slappey* (1927), *Florian Slappey Goes Abroad* (1928), *Epic Peters*, and *Pullman Porter* (1930). In addition to the picturesque and picaresque Negro, the plantation Negro (loyal, self-deprecating, motherly) was also present in the novels of Emma Speed Sampson: *Billy and the Major* (1918), *The Shorn Lamb* (1922), and *Miss Minerva on the Old Plantation* (1923). Furthermore, the delight of the nineteenth-century melodrama, the tragic mulatto, also made her tearful, distressed appearance in many popular novels of the 1920s, the most sensational being Frances Mocatta's *Forbidden Woman* (1928).

Thus, when Mencken called for "normalities," he was undoubtedly thinking of the strange grotesques of popular fiction which had tried to pass themselves off as realistic portraiture. His indictment of the South in the Ovington review is both ethical and aesthetic: "What the average Southerner believes about the negroes who surround him is chiefly nonsense. His view of them is moral and indignant, or worse still, sentimental and idiotic." On the one hand, storytellers such as E. K. Means and Octavus Roy Cohen saw the darkey as living in a world of pastoral innocence ("sentimental and idiotic"); on the other hand, a novelist such as Thomas Dixon saw the Negro as a diabolical atavist ("moral and indignant"). Such a Manichean conception of human nature was repugnant to Mencken for two reasons: (1) It smacked of the very "puritanism" in American literature with which he was currently at war (and had been for the last fifteen years), and (2) it was a denial of the world that he perceived around him. People are just not that simple, he would consistently argue in the *Smart Set*, and although he himself was sometimes guilty of oversimplifying the American character (for example, the American farmer), he was a battler for honesty, accuracy, and, above all, acute observation. It is for this reason that Van Vechten's Mencken is so angry with Byron: The young man doesn't see what is right in front of him, even though, because he himself is a Negro, he is in a perfect position to do so.

Mencken remained entirely consistent on this theme—that the Negro had a privileged view. In *Nigger Heaven*, Van Vechten is speaking (for obvious reasons), not Mencken, when Russett Durwood tells Byron that "if you young Negro intellectuals don't get busy, a new crop of Nordics is going to spring up who will take the trouble to become better informed and will exploit this material before the Negro gets around to it."[26] (*Nigger Heaven* is indirectly telling its readers that its author *has* taken the trouble.) Like Van Vechten, Mencken believed that white authors could write good books on Negro life; in fact, he thought it absolutely necessary that they do so. Nevertheless, it was one thing to "exploit" colorful material, but quite another to know what to make of it. Because the Negro writer could "see the race from within," the chances were better that he would know what to make of it. That Mencken believed the Negro had the inside track when it came to understanding his own life and that of his people is revealed in a letter he wrote to W.E.B. DuBois in 1935. He told the fiery editor of the *Crisis* that "an encyclopedia of the Negro is badly needed and the time for doing it is as soon as possible": "I am, of course, interested in the subject, but I know of no detail of it in which the information of other men is not greater than my own. I suggest that, if possible, it ought to be done principally by Negroes—indeed, it would be best if it could be done wholly by Negroes."[27]

That he further believed that the Negro should publish his own books as well as tell his own story is revealed in a letter he wrote to Walter White regarding the proposed publication of a manuscript:

> The race is still trying to hang on to the Caucasian tailgate. It should be standing alone. There should be a Negro publisher to do such books, and he should do them as well as a white publisher. A colored clergyman down here (Pratt by name: an old acquaintance of mine) lately wrote a history of the colored parishes in the Protestant Episcopal Church—an accurate and valuable work. Instead of having it published by a white publisher, he went to two young colored fellows who had set up a printing business here and got them to print it. It turned out that they had a lot to learn about the printing of books, but in the end they finished the job, and the result was doubly creditable to the race. No white man touched the thing from beginning to end.[28]

Not only does Mencken pay deference in these two letters to the Negro's superior knowledge, but he also has an implicit faith in the Negro's ability to stand on his own. His antipathy toward white patronage is made clear, as well as a side of his character that has rarely been appreciated, his interest in scholarship. He wanted accurate and encyclopedic coverage of Negro life, and this desire to get the truth out into the open was to be his greatest strength and greatest weakness as a critic of Negro letters in the 1920s.

Two months after *Nigger Heaven* appeared in the bookstores, Mencken once again assumed his pedagogical pose (one he was always assuming despite his dislike of pedagogues), and he proceeded to lecture the Harlem Renaissance novelists. The occasion for this reproof was a review of a collection of Negro work songs (put together by white sociologist Howard Odum). Mencken singled out "an amusing and instructive chapter on a typical Negro minstrel of the present day, by name Left Wing Gordon," and then attacked the black writer:

It is astonishing that none of the Negro novelists who now practise among us has ever put such a character into a book. He and his brothers are immensely closer to the racial norm than any of the idealistic doctors, daredevil lawyers and other such illuminati who now figure in colored fiction, and moreover they are very much more charming as men. Nearly all the heavy work of the South—the building of roads and bridges, the leveling of forests and the mining of iron and coal—is done by just such gay wanderers. They come in over the vague horizon, they work stupendously for a month or two, and then they vanish between days, leaving fingers, ears or maybe widows as souvenirs. John Henry, the Negro Paul Bunyan, was of their merry company, though he stood above the common run, for he was an expert at his art of wielding a ten-pound sledge. The others are mainly dubious and almost anonymous fellows, usually bearing fantastic sobriquets or palpably made-up names. They are all young, for the death rate in their order is truly staggering.[29]

Mencken typically distinguishes between believable and unbelievable human beings ("illuminati"), but he also expresses several other aesthetic views. For Mencken, Left Wing Gordon both represents the "racial norm" and transcends it. As a member of a unique social milieu, he belongs to a race of men who build America and then "vanish." These people have their own codes of behavior and inhabit their own strange world; for all we know about them, they might as well be creatures from another planet. Yet Left Wing Gordon has risen above the average because he has left his mark behind him. He is the unknown bard of the Negro spirituals that Mencken will praise in his review of James Weldon Johnson's *Book of American Negro Spirituals*.[30] Thus he is a natural aristocrat because, like John Henry, he stands "above the common run." Yet unlike the illuminati, who are superhuman, he is a real man with real human weaknesses.

In view of his preference for Negro lowlife (and his implication that the black bourgeoisie had lost its racial identity), it is tempting to charge Mencken with succumbing to primitivism—which, if one is to believe the critics, is the cardinal sin that all white meddlers in Negro culture were guilty of. Certainly, it would be easy to find evidence for such a thesis. In 1928, Howard Odum wrote a documentary novel (*Rainbow Round My Shoulder*), which featured a roustabout hero, probably a composite of many individuals Odum had interviewed, whom he called Black Ulysses. In a *Mercury* review, Mencken said of Odum's work, "For the first time the low-down coon of the South—not the gaudy Aframerican intellectual of Harlem and the universities, but the low-down, no-account, dirty and thieving, but infinitely rakish and picturesque coon—has found his poet. It is a curious irony that that poet is a white man, a college professor—and a Georgian."[31] Although this comment was another ploy by Mencken to stir up the hornet's nest—to sting black writers into activity by insulting them—words like "dirty and thieving" and "rakish and picturesque" remind us of Van Vechten, not only of some of his characters in *Nigger Heaven* but also of his advice to Negro authors in the famous *Crisis* symposium of 1926: "The squalor of Negro life," said Van Vechten, "the vice of Negro life, offer a wealth of novel, exotic, picturesque material to the artist."[32]

Yet, as I shall show, it would be a mistake to pin the fuzzy label of primitivism upon Mencken's thought. Perhaps Arthur O. Lovejoy's category of "hard" primitivism might be more properly applied,[33] if one were to use the term at all, because Mencken was convinced that Negroes lived in a universe that was often harsh and austere. If they were "thieving," it only meant that they had to be; if they were "picturesque and rakish," it only meant that they survived with a modicum of dignity. As Mencken noted in his remarks on Left Wing Gordon, John Henry, and men of that ilk, their "death rate" was "truly staggering." That the gods were hostile to man was a theorem in which Mencken long believed, and it helps to explain his aesthetic delight in novelists as diverse as Hardy, Zola, Conrad, and Arnold Bennett. It also explains his encouragement of white author Julia Peterkin, who wrote novels and short stories about Negro peasant life. He urged her to continue to write her grim tales of black folkways despite her family's opposition to her work, and he probably persuaded Knopf to publish her first collection of short stories, *Green Thursday* (1924).[34] The heroes of Peterkin's fictional world—Killdee in *Green Thursday*, April in *Black April* (1927), and Mary in *Scarlet Sister Mary* (1928)—were the kind that would have appealed to Mencken. They were both realistic and true: realistic because they were portrayed as products of a stark environment and true because they illustrated the human being's eternal warfare with the gods. They were men and women pitted against a cruel universe that defined them, hardened them, and, often as not, broke them.

Yet even to limit Mencken to this perspective is to be unjust to him. He wanted black writers to treat their world as would an anthropologist—not as a series of glittering picturesque fragments but as a distinct culture. In this case, he would not be against a novelist investigating the lives of the black bourgeoisie, if their world could be clearly distinguished from that of the white middle class. Like Van Vechten, he was somewhat skeptical of novelists who dwelt upon "genteel" Negro life—not because it was less colorful (*Nigger Heaven* showed it was not) but because it was imitative. For this reason, however, he saw it as a fit subject for satire—and said so.

Of course, Mencken's advice to the Negro novelist was only part of a larger aesthetic program that he laid out for the American writer. He kept reminding the latter that the novelist by definition is "only half an artist; the other half of him is a scientist."[35] Furthermore, the "Americano" as a distinct type had never been thoroughly examined. In this light, he praised Sinclair Lewis and Sherwood Anderson for studying the American in his milieu with the exactitude of the scientist (*Main Street, Babbitt,* and *Winesburg, Ohio*), and he singled out George Babbitt in particular as "a genuine museum piece."[36] When *Middletown* was published in 1931, he recommended this sociological study of a small Indiana town to "all persons who have any genuine interest in the life of the American people"; and in the same review he called for an "explorer" of Kansas, for the "anthropology" of the region had never been done: "The great masses of Kansans have never been studied."[37] He especially urged the ethnic artist to study the subcultures of minorities and immigrants, as Abraham Cahan had done in *The Rise of David Levinsky,* because the lives of these people had no other chronicler. "More than anyone else perhaps," Van Wyck Brooks recalled of the years before World War I, "Mencken broke the way for writers who were descended from 'foreign' stocks and who were not yet assured of their place in the sun."[38]

Before the 1920s ended, more than one black writer found his or her place in the sun, doing so by taking Mencken's advice: to reveal the race from within. Sometimes black writers depicted its seamier side (Claude McKay); sometimes, its respectable side (Jessie Fauset). Sometimes they tried to use the character sketch (Mencken's favorite ploy) to show a side of Negro life never before seen. Arna Bontemps's Little Augie in *God Sends Sunday* (1931), for example, is an attempt to show the black smart set of the 1890s through the portrait of a black jockey. So too his Gabriel Prosser (*Black Thunder,* 1936) is a historical picture of an unknown black hero (Denmark Vesey), painted with care from within. An example of a black author who explored the racial soil of Kansas two years before Mencken said it should be done was Langston Hughes. In *Not Without Laughter* (1929) he presented the "anthropology" of a small black community, and focused specifically upon the social matrix of a black family. And Zora Neale Hurston made a specialty of this anthropological approach in all her fiction.[39]

Other examples of this desire to explore black life could be found, but the important point here is that the Harlem Renaissance did not sacrifice realism for exotic romanticism, as has sometimes been assumed.[40] The black novelists of the 1920s wanted to depict heroes and nonheroes who had previously gone unrecognized by American literature. This was the realism that held forth in the 1920s, whereas for the writers of the 1930s, the Depression created a new kind of realism. In a capitalist society, these writers felt, all men and women were victims of an intolerable system. This was the realism that replaced the exploration of Negro life, and for a long time it seemed the only realism worthy of the name.

When one thinks of Dreiser in connection with black literature, one thinks of *An American Tragedy* (1925) because of its similarity to Richard Wright's *Native Son*, but the Dreiser Mencken had in mind was the author of *Sister Carrie* (1900), *Jennie Gerhardt* (1911), and *The Titan* (1914). Those were Mencken's favorite Dreiser novels in 1920, and although no black novelist in the 1920s rewrote *The Titan*, several wrote about women who, like Carrie and Jennie, suffered from their own inchoate desires and from the world's incomprehensibility. Walter White's Mimi Daquin (*Flight*, 1926) was a composite of both Dreiser heroines, together with Carol Kennicott in Lewis's *Main Street*. Both Joanna Marshall in *There Is Confusion* (1924) and Angela Murray in *Plum Bun* (1929), novels by Jessie Fauset, are Carrie-like in their ambitions, though they are rescued from Carrie's restless fate. Wallace Thurman's Emma Lou Morgan (*The Blacker the Berry*, 1929) painfully learns Jennie's lesson at the novel's end when she stoically decides to "find—not seek."[41] So too the heroine of Nella Larsen's *Quicksand* (1928), Helga Crane, illustrates "the primary theme of every sound novelist ever heard of," according to Mencken: "human character in disintegration."[42] Larsen's delineation of Helga's fall in *Quicksand*—a combination of character and fate—certainly got its inspiration from those authors whom Mencken most admired: Conrad, Zola, and Dreiser.

Like others of her generation, Nella Larsen read Mencken's literary criticism, and she may even have been influenced by his remarks on technique as well as character. She was definitely aware of his hints to American novelists,[43] and she probably read the same review of *The Moon and Sixpence* that had inspired F. Scott Fitzgerald to write *The Great Gatsby*. In this piece, Mencken praised Somerset Maugham for getting the "colors of life" into his central character "by leaving him a bit out of focus—by constantly insisting, in the midst of every discussion of him, upon his pervasive mystery."[44] Maugham probably learned this device from Conrad, Mencken continued, for Conrad had used Marlow in *Lord Jim* and *Heart of Darkness* to keep Jim and Kurtz at a distance. Nella Larsen employed a similar technique in *Passing* (1929), a novel whose conventional melodrama is offset by an oblique narrative point of view. Seen through the eyes of obtuse, biased Irene Redfield, Clare Kendry—Larsen's heroine—is left "a bit out of focus." As with Jay Gatsby, a "pervasive mystery" surrounds both her life and death.

I mention these specific instances of Mencken's influence, not to prove them beyond all doubt (they probably can't be proven in any scholarly sense), but rather to indicate a wide range of possibilities. For instance, Mencken may have influenced Zora Neale Hurston through Julia Peterkin, the one white writer of black life who was generally admired by the black intellectuals. The heroine of Hurston's *Their Eyes Were Watching God* (1937) bears a striking resemblance to the protagonist of Peterkin's prize-winning novel, *Scarlet Sister Mary* (1928). Both Janie and Mary are tough, independent women who are nevertheless rooted in the life of a small, autonomous community. (Their strong personalities, expressed especially through their sexual drives, remind us of the heroine of Toni Morrison's contemporary novel *Sula* [1973].) Both are hedonistic in a Menckenian sense, refusing to close down their souls because others ask them to, and both survive a succession of marriages and men. And as in a typical Menckenian universe, each woman must pay a price for the happiness she seeks.

While all of the above is admittedly conjectural, Mencken's actual influence was at once more direct and more subtle. Many black intellectuals—James Weldon Johnson, Walter White, Kelly Miller, W.E.B. DuBois, George Schuyler, J. A. Rogers, Theophilus Lewis, Wallace Thurman, Eugene Gordon—read Mencken with care and in turn recommended him to black America. In fact, nearly every black intellectual read him. Even someone like Alain Locke, whose temperament differed radically from Mencken's, learned from him. Furthermore, the diversity of Mencken's influence is a testament to the different roles that he played between 1908 and 1930: literary critic, social pundit, and acid-tongued satirist. His writing touched upon nearly every aspect of American life, and the folly and vice that he uncovered could not help but fire the enthusiasm of a race of people who were burning to prove that they were the intellectual equals of the white folk who had once enslaved them. Every week, in his books and articles, Mencken seemed to show that the historical arrangement of slave to master should have been reversed.

Mencken not only compelled a discussion of every theme important to him, he also defined the approach that should be taken to that theme. Certainly his brand of realism helped to make it imperative that the novel become the major literary form in the period between 1910 and 1930. In fact, when Mencken talked about literature, he meant the novel; he thought poetry an expression of artistic immaturity and the drama a poor substitute for the novel—having all of its vices (for instance, popular sentiment) but none of its virtues. It is not accidental, I believe, that all the major poets of the Harlem Renaissance—Claude McKay, Countee Cullen, Jean Toomer, and Langston Hughes—wrote novels. Mencken's dominance in the field of literary criticism may also provide an answer to that knotty question concerning the scarcity of Negro playwrights during the 1920s. Nathan Huggins's explanation for the failure of a native theatrical movement to develop during the Harlem Renaissance is clever but unconvincing. According to Huggins, the blame can be placed on the white public. Unwilling to give up the stereotypes that neatly contrasted with their conception of their own humanity, white people could not abide the presence of "real" Negro life on stage.[45] Yet are we to believe that the readers of the *American Mercury*, who constituted a large share of the literate public, were not ready for the Negro's view of himself? Almost every month, Mencken had the New Negro holding forth *his* view of the universe; or if not a New Negro, an anthropologist debunking racial myths or an acute white observer (such as L. M. Hussey) deflating white egos. The truth may be that Negro writers stayed away from the theater because Mencken told them that their future lay with the novel, with prose satire, or with journalistic pieces for the *Mercury*. Even as late as 1945, Arna Bontemps could quote Mencken to Langston Hughes on the theater and take his comments quite seriously. Like Hughes, Bontemps loved the stage but saw the sense in Mencken's complaint about the mob's "hysteria": "Maybe that's why Mencken said that the theatre rots the brains," he lamented to Hughes.[46]

Mencken not only helped determine what literary forms would dominate the Harlem Renaissance, his literary prejudices also point to a contradiction that beset many of its spokesmen—that curious marriage of High Culture and "paganism." Mencken, as we know, fought on all fronts against the genteel tradition—a sort of tyrannical Victorianism in the arts which he felt smothered all creativity under its blanket of academic stuffiness and moralism. By and large, Mencken argued, Americans do not believe in the arts, and so the best minds go into business;[47] the artists that we do have reduce literature to the level of religious tracts or soap operas. But "art," said Mencken grandly, is "not a device for improving the mind. It is wholly a magnificent adventure."[48] Civilizations in the past, for example, did not restrict the flights of the human imagination as ours has: "In the history of every other literature there have been periods of what might be called moral innocence—periods in which a naif *joie de vivre* has broken through all concepts of duty and responsibility, and the wonder and glory of the universe have been hymned with unashamed zest."[49] Americans robbed art of its magnificence and "unashamed zest" by confining it to the moral realm. They wanted literature to map out life for them, to put up warning signs for the uncharted territory. They wanted to know what roads to travel and what roads to avoid because they were afraid of all detours. Any book that reminded Americans that life could not be neatly organized like a YMCA picnic, that it was in fact an unmapped mess of confusion and tragedy, was a book to be condemned. Such intellectual timidity, Mencken thought, was the reason for America's failure as a civilization.

For Mencken the idea of a civilization took precedence over a society that was simply moral; and the truly civilized man, as Mencken defined him, had catholic tastes, not a stricken conscience. That is, he took a broad view, had refined sensibilities, saw life whole. As Mencken said of the New American writers that he approved of, what they "all . . . have in common is a sort of new-found elasticity or goatishness, a somewhat exaggerated sense of aliveness, a glowing delight in the spectacle before them, a vigorous and naive self-consciousness."[50] These qualities—elasticity, naïveté, and goatishness—are all positive because they suggest the novelist's openness to experience; they suggest a return to a period of "moral innocence" such as the Elizabethan Age. Of the novelists of whom he disapproved, those who wrote the "staple fiction" of the Republic, he said that the real horror of what they wrote was "not that it is addressed primarily to shoe-drummers and shop-girls; the worst of it is that it is written by authors who *are*, to all intellectual intents and purposes, shoe-drummers and shop-girls."[51]

The problem with being a shoe-drummer, as Mencken saw it, is that there is always the temptation to put one's soul in a shoe box. This is what the Puritan had done, and he was a man who was eternally present in American society. Mencken linked him with the savage ("the most meticulously moral of men"),[52] and he conversely associated the hedonist with civilization. This distinction was more than just whimsy on Mencken's part; it was one that he had taken from Nietzsche, a distinction that he thought could explain the differences between cultures. America, after all, had produced the nay-saying God of the Puritans but almost no artists, whereas ancient Greece had worshipped Dionysus and had produced great artists. There was a lesson to be learned here, and Mencken was quick to pounce upon it. The hedonist did not simply pursue pleasure; he pursued life. He tried to capture its essence in art, and when he succeeded, he gave the world something that was a reflection of himself and of his country. Mencken once compared the whole of Christian culture to what Beethoven had done for Germany: "What did Rome ever produce to match the Fifth Symphony?"[53] Someone like Henry Adams might have answered with one word, "Chartres"; but both men's answers would be based on a certain unstated premise: that the spiritual health of a culture is in some ways dependent upon the state of its art.

So while Mencken was attacking the boy scout morality of the genteel tradition, he was to a certain extent substituting one kind of moral enthusiasm for another. He complained that the genteel tradition reduced literature to a simplified form of Christianity, but he himself often expressed a quasi-religious attitude toward the books he admired. It might take an irreverent form, but it was there nonetheless: "As for *Lord Jim*," he once said, "I would not swap it for all the children born in Trenton, N.J."[54] Swiftian humor aside, Mencken's point is clear—babies come and go, but works of art endure (*ars longa, vita brevis*), and a culture is sustained by what endures. Ironically, the idea that great art creates a great culture can easily lead to the notion that *refined* art creates a great culture. As we shall see, despite Mencken's quarrel with the genteel tradition he occasionally let the enemy in through the back door. A similar confusion also hounded the Harlem Renaissance, for it too believed that the pursuit of art was a spiritual pilgrimage. Mencken always gave the impression that art was a kind of secular Holy Grail, because the value of the very culture one lived in depended upon it.

There is no doubt that the black writers of the 1920s responded to this theme. Here is James Weldon Johnson, a man who read Mencken religiously, in his introduction to *The Book of American Negro Poetry* (1922):

> A people may become great through many means, but there is only one measure by which its greatness is recognized and acknowledged. The final measure of the greatness of all peoples is the amount and standard of the literature and art they have produced. The world does not know that a people is great until that people produces great literature and art. No people that has produced great literature and art has ever been looked upon by the world as distinctly inferior.[55]

Johnson was not just speaking of the challenge to his own people; his inference was that American artists needed to turn to black life for those pagan elements that were lacking in the outer, puritan culture. Only in this way could America rid itself of the intellectual sterility which kept it, in Mencken's words, "a third-rate culture." That Mencken's influence spread far and wide can be seen in the dichotomy that Alain Locke used to describe his own character. When he once called himself more "a pagan than a Puritan,"[56] he may perhaps have been thinking of a Menckenian distinction; but when he noted in 1926 that the contemporary interest in the "primitive and pagan and emotional aspects of Negro life" sprang from "the revolt against Puritanism,"[57] he most certainly was. For both Johnson and Locke, the truly civilized man, if he were a Negro, would react to the antics of white folk with Rabelaisian laughter. He would shun the temptation to accuse, for overt didacticism of any kind in art was a manifestation of incivility and puritanism.

Mencken also appealed to the intellectuals of the Harlem Renaissance because he symbolized an attempt to be free of the lies of the past, and for these Negroes the biggest lies were told during the Great War. When the reality behind President Wilson's pious bilge about democratic ideals came to be known—that secret agreements had been signed discriminating against black troops, that Jim Crowism had been encouraged, that none of the prewar promises concerning equality were ever intended to be honored—then the black men and women of the postwar world realized that if they were ever to get anywhere in these "United Snakes" (as the wag George Schuyler called them), some serious truth telling was in order. There were to be no more lies told about Negroes by either whites or blacks. Negro authors had always complained of literary distortion, but a general revulsion against wartime propaganda was necessary to make this complaint into a principal aesthetic tenet. "The truth, whether it hurts or not" (to quote Alain Locke),[58] became the battle cry of this new generation of black writers, and their one hope was that both white and black audiences would accept it.

Because Mencken was also discriminated against during the war, because he began to identify with Negroes in their pursuit of truth, these men and women who were trying to forge a new literature read him. They all found different things to respond to in Mencken, but upon one subject they all agreed: He would never give them conventional liberal mush in answer to a difficult question. In 1934, for example, Walter White (then head of the NAACP) asked Mencken to write an article on Negro strategy for the *Crisis*. By this time he and Mencken had been friends for over fifteen years, and White knew what kind of article he would get: surly, funny, and uncompromisingly honest. Typically, Mencken replied to White that his solution to the Negro problem was that there was none, that he believed many of the Negro's problems in America to be "insoluble."[59] Instead of being put off by such an answer, Roy Wilkins—then managing editor of the *Crisis*—was delighted; he told Mencken to tackle the subject anyway, to treat the whole issue of strategy just as he saw it, Mencken style. "What a sweet bomb-shell to drop among the hip-and-thigh smoting 'race' campaigners," Wilkins added.[60] Mencken took him at his word and wrote an article that informed the readers of the *Crisis* that they should expect no quarter from a society mired in its own stupidity. Furthermore, it was probably better for Negroes in the long run that things were that way.[61] Such an answer probably did not win him any votes among the general Negro populace, but it was this kind of straightforwardness which gave Mencken a distinct credibility in the eyes of Negro intellectuals.

In fact, as early as 1910, Mencken had been campaigning for intellectual honesty when it came to describing Negroes in literature. In that year he praised Howard Odum for the "scientific spirit" shown in the pamphlet "Social and Mental Traits of the Negro."[62] Odum refused to moralize about the Negro, and he wasted "no time upon miraculous negroes ('all that is worth hearing about them we have already heard')." Instead, Odum "sought out the common every-day darkey of the villages and small towns, who makes up fully 95 per cent of the black population of the South. Of this darkey, the professional negromaniacs know nothing whatever." But it wasn't enough to dispense with the southerner's "nonsense" on the Negro question; those myths that were flattering to the Negro should be challenged. In the same essay in which he reviewed *The Shadow*, Mencken had also reviewed *The Negro Faces America*, by Herbert Seligmann. Here he took a different tack from the one he had taken in the Ovington review. He complained that Seligmann had created a few fictions of his own in his attempt to debunk others. It is true, Mencken said, that "balderdash" about the Negro "originates in the South, where gross ignorance of the actual negro of today is combined with a great cocksureness."[63] However, "*all* of the prevailing generalizations, even in the South, are not dubious," and to insist that they are is to do the Negro a real disservice. In Seligmann's book, the Negro is no longer a human but a saint, "an innocent who never was on land or sea." What is needed, Mencken concluded, is "honest and relentless criticism," or, as he said in another context, "all races have some defects and to pretend that they don't exist is absurd."

One can see why the writers of the Harlem Renaissance took to Mencken. He was their cup of tea precisely because he was a bitter brew; they wanted to be toughminded, antisentimental, and honest, and they found a man who told them, with zest and humor, that these attitudes were necessary for writing great literature. Yet as it turns out, these qualities may not have been enough. When we look back upon the Harlem Renaissance from the perspective of the 1980s, we find only a few novels and poems (no plays) that have endured. To be sure, extravagant claims have been made for the literature, but usually by those who have been swept away by their own enthusiasms or by their desires to justify their own intellectual efforts. Appropriately, the two best books on the Harlem Renaissance—Nathan Huggins's *Harlem Renaissance* and David Levering Lewis's *When Harlem Was In Vogue*—have been written by historians, not literary critics. Unquestionably, intelligent analyses of the period's literature exist, but few would dare claim that the movement matched the creative excellence of the Irish Renaissance.

There are also those who insist that the Harlem Renaissance was nothing more than a puff of smoke in a Harlem cabaret. The music was real; the cabarets were real; the white people slumming in Harlem were real; but the literary movement was not. Critics like Imamu Amiri Baraka (LeRoi Jones) and Harold Cruse have simply written off its literature as papier-mâché, fake products of a white culture and not a black one. This attitude, I think, is as mistaken as the first one; the literary movement was simply not as bankrupt or as insubstantial as some of its harsher critics claim. Moreover, in assessing the merits of the Renaissance's litera- ture, critics consider only the novels, poems, and plays (or lack of plays). The satirical impulse, which Mencken inspired (and the black writers of the 1920s acknowledged this inspiration), resulted in essays that appeared in Mencken's *Mercury* and elsewhere, and these have never been given their proper due. In fact, the satire of the period can be viewed as one facet of the Renaissance's claim to an immortality of sorts; this impulse never manifested itself in a *Gulliver's Travels* or a *Candide*, but there were many minor fireworks that positively dazzled.

Still the question remains why, armed with such good intentions and with such a pragmatic aesthetic, did the Harlem Renaissance not live up to its own aspirations? Perhaps there is no answer to this question, although we might look to Mencken's influence for a partial answer. In his review of Ovington's novel, Mencken had confined realism for the black writer to "normalities." Although Mencken had been talking about the nature of art in general (truth in art is different from truth in life), his emphasis upon normalities suggested a backward look. Against the stereo- types of the past—the black beast, the docile darkey, the matronly mammy—Mencken had posited the distinctly human as an ideal. The Negro was now to be treated as a human being, a creature made up of faults and virtues, and the black writer was urged to depict him in the fullness of his humanity. Naturally such a perspective appealed to Negro writers because of its honesty, but it also had another appeal considerably less honest. Realism could be interpreted in such a way that the black character might never be seen as abnormal, for such a deviation from the norm, it would be argued, was a return to those unreal stereotypes. Thus, certain kinds of black characters would be excluded from realism on the grounds that they were unreal.

It would be a mistake to suggest that Mencken's view of realism ever became this inflexible—or, for that matter, that all Harlem Renaissance writers took the position described above. In fact, the younger black writers of the 1920s sympathized with Mencken when he chastized the Renaissance for not looking at the variety of reflections in the mirror of art. Mencken sensed that the Renaissance sometimes got bogged down in depicting one reality of Negro life, and he told its writers so on several occasions. Thus, when the Renaissance's younger members later decided to have a falling out with the established leaders of the movement, it was around this issue of realism that the battle lines formed. For, like it or not, realism was Mencken's gift to the Harlem Renaissance, and both the Young Wits and the Old Guard claimed to be fighting in its cause. And there is a certain ironical appropriateness that both young and old had looked to

Mencken for their aesthetic ethic. For Mencken too was at times guilty of critical short-sightedness, and this is especially clear if we look at his antipathy toward "modernism." So in tune with the emerging literature of the new century, Mencken seemed strangely out of touch with the artistic innovations of the 1920s, the decade that made him famous. Whatever its definition, if a definition is indeed possible, the one thing that modernism is not is mimetic. Mencken's realism, for better or worse, was tied to mimesis. On the surface, it seemed to encompass all avenues of art, but in truth it was as closed to some kinds of aesthetic reality as was the most hidebound genteel tradition.

Throughout the 1920s, Mencken remained committed to realism, and, for the most part, the writers of the Harlem Renaissance followed his lead. That people distorted his position, making it an excuse for their own kind of gentility, is not suprising, because Mencken himself occasionally talked as they did: Stereotypes must be avoided at all costs. Although they accepted Mencken as a model, they often chose not to pursue realism to the full range of possibilities that he encouraged. Of course, some might argue that the Renaissance should not have followed Mencken at all; that when black writers begin to bow down to white authorities, they are already in trouble. Yet can the Renaissance's intellectuals be blamed for following white models, if white models were all they had? This generation of Negro intellectuals was the first one to exist *as a generation*, in spite of the gradually diverging opinions between young and old. Because they were still unsure of themselves and needed guidance, they did not always see what was really happening in the black community. And if as a rule they did not become modernists, they did not because they responded to white intellectuals who showed an interest in them. Pound, Eliot, Hemingway, and the other expatriates were trying to escape America, and, in a sense, that meant escaping the Negro as well. Mencken became a model because he was a solid fixture on the American scene, and because he took the trouble to give them advice. Although later black writers such as Richard Wright, Ralph Ellison, and James Baldwin — to say nothing of more recent novelists such as Toni Morrison, Ishmael Reed, Alice Walker, and Ernest Gaines — came to reject the realist position, they are still indebted to what Mencken began. Seeing life from the inside, expressing a concern for craft, observing detail with the care of a scientist — all this Mencken made possible, because although he may not have been the first one to say these things to the Negro writer, he was the first to say them and have them taken seriously.

CHAPTER TWO

Mencken and
"The Colored Brother"

In 1927, while waiting to go to work, a black youth loitered in a bank lobby in Memphis. Perfunctorily, he picked up a nearby newspaper, and as he glanced through it, he suddenly fixed his attention upon a very strange article. Here in front of his bewildered eyes was a vicious attack on a man who was *not* a Negro, and yet the vehemence of the language was the kind that was usually reserved for Negroes. Why did the South hate this man so much, the youth wondered. His curiosity pricked, he borrowed a friend's library card and forged a note: "Will you please let this nigger boy," it said to the librarian in charge, "have some books by H. L. Mencken." No one who has ever read Richard Wright's *Black Boy* can forget the scene that ensued. Handed *A Book of Prefaces* and a volume of *Prejudices* (probably the *Second Series*, the one that contains Mencken's notorious satire on the South, "The Sahara of the Bozart"), the nineteen-year-old Wright returned to his lonely boardinghouse room and read far into the night. It was an experience he would never forget, and it left its mark upon him. He was stirred by Mencken's "clear, clean, sweeping sentences," his Gargantuan rage, his Olympian ridicule of "everything American." To Wright, Mencken was a warrior, "fighting with words . . . using them as one would use a club." The whole experience "frightened" him at first: "What amazed me was not what he said, but how on earth anybody had the courage to say it."[1]

This last sentence pinpoints one reason for Mencken's popularity among the black intellectuals of the 1920s. He seemed to know what they knew, that beneath the smug surface of American life was a core of rottenness. Like the child in the famous fairy tale, Mencken saw Uncle Sam without any clothes on, and he did not hesitate to laugh. His satire of southern culture (at a time when the South still reveled in its romantic

myths), his identification with the literature of realism and rebellion —
these facets of Mencken's public and literary personality had a specific
influence on the black intellectuals, but what they liked about Mencken
generally was his personal courage. His great appeal was that he never let
the shibboleths of American society compromise his honesty. Countee
Cullen called him "the intrepid Mr. Mencken" in the *Pittsburgh Courier*
the same year Wright was reading his works in Memphis,[2] but by 1927
the epithet had become almost a cliché. As early as 1918, and in another
black newspaper (the *New York Age*), James Weldon Johnson had developed this theme at greater length:

> Those who look for cleverness in Mencken are missing the best part of
> him; the best part of Mencken is truth. He gets at truth because he is de-
> void of the sentimental and mawkish morality which seems to be the curse
> of everyone who writes in the English language. In other words, he is free
> and is therefore not afraid to write the truth. Many a writer is sincere
> enough, but bound by so many conventions that he cannot write the
> truth. Mencken pays no regard to traditions and conventions as such; he
> has absolutely no respect for them merely on account of their age.[3]

Two years later, writing for the same black newspaper, Johnson repeated
his praise:

> Readers of "The Age" are familiar with our opinion of Mr. H. L. Mencken
> as a writer. We have more than once said in these columns that he is the
> brightest and cleverest of all contemporary American writers. But Mr.
> Mencken is a great deal more than bright and clever. He is sincere and
> honest. And he is sincere and honest because he is not afraid of anything:
> not even of the truth.[4]

In the same article, he noted Mencken's unique relationship to the Negro:
"Several times Mr. Mencken has written on the race question, and although he has no special interest in the Negro's rights and wrongs, he
always writes on the Negro's side, because he sees that on that side lies
the truth."

Mencken's truth telling became a byword among the Harlem intellectuals. When in a newspaper article (17 July 1927 — *New York World*)
Mencken gave out grades to black artists for their recent work and only
one, James Weldon Johnson, received a high mark, George Schuyler
observed in the *Pittsburgh Courier* that Mencken was only "telling what
God loves."[5] Similarly, in the same black newspaper a year earlier,
Walter White pointed to Mencken as the leader of those modern white
literati who had (using Mencken's own language) refused "to be ensnared
by the buncombe that forms the overwhelming mental diet of the Ameri-

cano," and he lauded Mencken in particular as having "done more than any single American to save his fellow Americans from stupidity and puritanism." He then urged his readers to buy the *American Mercury:* "If you want to be intelligent, you cannot afford not to read it each month."[6] Even when J. A. Rogers praised an article by George Schuyler as the only "honest" piece of writing on the Negro, by a Negro, that year (1928), he could not resist the following aside: "And this is not so much a tribute to Mr. Schuyler's genius and keen wit as it is to the *Mercury*."[7] In the same vein, when Countee Cullen sent his poem "Shroud of Color" to Mencken's magazine, he accompanied it with the following note: "I suppose it is absolutely foolhardy for me to submit such a long piece of verse to *The American Mercury*, but I don't know of any other magazine to which I could submit it without being afraid that it would be rejected for the obvious, but innocuous, reason that it is a poem about a Negro and by a Negro. Eric Walrond whose short stories of Negro life you have liked and one of which you published in *The Smart Set* urged me to send this poem to you."[8]

Lest all this praise be interpreted as mere flattery of a white editor, consider Claude McKay's observations about Mencken in a private letter to Arthur Schomburg in 1925. McKay was a maverick who never minced words about anybody, and often his rude candor lost him friends. If anyone can be trusted to give an unbiased opinion about Mencken, it is McKay. At the time he wrote Schomburg, he was trying to get a first novel ("Color Scheme") published and was having a hard time of it. He asked Schomburg to get some advice about the manuscript and recommended Mencken because "his standard of judgment would be entirely literary."[9] In another letter to Schomburg about "Color Scheme," he said of Mencken that "if . . . he can do anything he *will*. He is absolutely free of wire pulling."[10]

Mencken's honesty also extended to his remarks about Negroes. At least this is what W.E.B. DuBois told his readers in the *Crisis* when some of them questioned Mencken's criticism of the Harlem Renaissance in a recent newspaper article.[11] Although we may question his facts, said DuBois, "there can be no question of H. L. Mencken's attitude toward Negroes. It is calmly and judiciously fair. He neither loves them or hates them. He has a predilection for men."[12] But Kelly Miller gave the most insightful analysis of Mencken's attitude toward the Negro, and his article on Baltimore's sage appeared in two leading black newspapers, the *Baltimore Afro-American* (8 October 1927) and the *Amsterdam News* (12 October 1927). Referring to the same article as had DuBois, Miller called his piece "Mencken Mentions Us": "From the very beginning of his literary career," Miller said, "Mr. Mencken has given much attention to the Negro question." This attention in itself is not unusual; what is unusual is his objectivity: "He neither loves nor hates the Negro. He has no propaganda for or against him. He does not regard him as all good as the Moody and Sankey brand of religionists were once wont to do, nor yet as all bad, according to the exploded school of Tillman and Vardaman." Such detachment, Miller continued, makes Mencken a trustworthy interpreter of Negro life and art. He "undertakes to describe the Negro; not to reform him. Like Shakespeare, he does not make the original, but holds the mirror up to nature."[13]

In actuality, Mencken often tried to reform the Negro, and he was not above making a few judgments concerning his welfare or condition. Nevertheless, Miller is substantially right in his estimation of Mencken. Mencken did believe that an awful lot of "pish-posh" (to use one of his favorite words) had been uttered about the Negro and that the real evidence had yet to be collected, much less assessed.

Having the fastidious habits of a list maker (or a lexicographer), Mencken tried to marshal as much evidence as he could. For example, his *Mercury* editorial "A Coon Age" was an attempt to educate his fellow Americans by overwhelming them with the facts; and although he may have upset Jervis Anderson with his lack of civility, the article was enthusiastically received by black Americans living in the 1920s. The *Pittsburgh Courier* published an editorial called "Mencken Again" (the title indicates that the black newspaper kept tabs on him), which informed its readers that Mencken was to be honored for writing such an informative piece of journalism: "Here he points out what every well-informed Negro knows: that almost everything that is internationally recognized as American is derived from the dark brother. The list includes music, cooking, consumption of gin, language, the cabaret rage, dancing and religious practices. With great gusto Mr. Mencken portrays the manner in which the lowly Negro has forced his culture upon the none-too-reluctant Caucasians, and makes some highly interesting and entertaining comments thereon." The *Courier* went on to call Mencken's article "remarkable" because "it appears in the foremost white magazine in America." It concluded with the statement that Mencken is "performing a great service for us in banishing bigotry, prejudice and ignorance so effectively. America would unquestionably be a much more liveable place for the Aframerican if there were a lot more intelligent people like Mencken."[14]

The *Courier* was impressed with Mencken's knowledge of Negro culture, and it had every right to be. Mencken's knowledge was considerable, even formidable. When Mencken stated in *The American Language* that the reason he knew so much about Negro life was that he had spent "a lifetime . . . in contact with Negroes of all classes," no one snickered in Harlem.[15] Over the years Mencken had acquired a reputation

of being thorough and exact, even scholarly. More than one black intellectual was "struck," in George Schuyler's words to him, "by your
familiarity with doings in the black belt."[16] This familiarity, of course,
extended to language. Mencken was interested in Negro slang, Negro
"designations," Negro proper names, and Negro English—all of which he
discussed in great detail in *The American Language* and its two supplements.[17] As one might expect, he delighted in these three books in debunking myths about the Negro. He thought, for instance, that "sportive"
American writers had romanticized the Negro's penchant for unusual
proper names (for instance, "the Scarlet Creeper" in *Nigger Heaven*). "All
the students who have investigated Aframerican onomastics in a scientific
spirit," he said, "have found such monstrosities to be few and far between." Similarly, he deplored the falsification of Negro dialect in the
novels of white Americans: The "representation of Negro speech in literature has always been imperfect, and often absurd."[18] In addition to
language, Mencken's encyclopedic mind even took a delight in such
minor arts as Negro cooking. (He once contributed information to Walter
White's intended book on the subject.) And although his own taste in
Negro music was limited, he wanted to know about all kinds, even if he
did not especially care for some of them. (He tried unsuccessfully to get
James Weldon Johnson to write a piece on jazz for the *Mercury*,[19] and he
painfully learned the slang that surrounded it for *The American Language*.) He also prided himself on his knowledge of Negro folkways, once
surprising George Schuyler with the esoteric lore that the bite of the
"blue-gummed Negro" is venomous (Schuyler was unfamiliar with this
myth).[20] And he read Negro periodicals; on one occasion, he spent an hour
looking for the *Crisis*, finding it at last in a small Negro grocery store in
"Baltimore Harlem."[21] He even claimed superior knowledge of Negro
"religious practices," but in this case his wisdom was less than he imagined.

Mencken saw himself as a kind of amateur anthropologist, and he
gathered his information about the Negro from wherever he could, from
friend and foe alike. His objectivity explains the diversity of articles by
and about blacks in the *Mercury* and even his own linguistic practice in
his article "Designations for Colored Folk," in which he took a strictly
scholarly stance in describing the opprobrious names applied to Negroes
over the centuries. Mencken believed that the truth should be told no
matter how unpleasant, and thus in his *New Dictionary of Quotations* he
included more famous sayings unflattering to blacks than those that were
flattering, because he felt obligated to print whatever passed for folk
wisdom.[22] That the racial sneers outnumbered the racial encomiums meant
only that the quality of folk wisdom was none too high, a fact that would
hardly have surprised Mencken. Although he was immensely interested
in folkways, he rarely romanticized them.

For someone who has been accused of having a mind like a steel trap, Mencken often had a wide range of sympathies and perceptions. He wanted to understand both sides of the Negro question, even as he wished to dispel the nonsense spoken in its behalf. Although he disapproved of racial and religious prejudice in theory, he could see how it originated in fact:

> What is commonly described as racial or religious prejudice is sometimes only a reasonable prudence. At the bottom of it there is nothing more wicked than a desire to prevent dominance by a strange and more or less hostile minority. This was true, certainly, of the old animosity to the Irish Catholics, and it is true again of much American anti-Semitism. In the South it is even true, at least to some extent, of the violent feeling against the Negro.[23]

The consequences of such prejudice were absurd to him, however:

> Personally, I hate to have to think of any man as of a definite race, creed or color; so few men are really worth knowing that it seems a shameful waste to let an anthropoid prejudice stand in the way of free association with one who is.[24]

Still, he admitted to a very human response to someone who is "different":

> But I confess frankly that when a given man begins to speak English to me with a strange accent, or to demand holidays on days that I work, or to refuse to eat food that I eat—I confess that such acts make me feel vaguely uneasy in his presence.

Finally, he saw no solution to the problem of prejudice in America, for if ethnic groups continued to preserve their separate identities—and he encouraged them to do so—then this tension between people would always exist.

Recently, John McCormick has accused Mencken of not attacking "racist politics" in the 1920s and of not coming "to terms with the fact that by 1924 the Ku Klux Klan had a membership of about 4,500,000."[25] McCormick's accusation is a typical example of "liberal" literal-mindedness. The truth is, Mencken often attacked the Klan in the 1920s (and long afterwards), and yet he did not always express his contempt in an orthodox liberal manner. Perhaps the most explicit statement Mencken ever made about the Klan appeared in a *Baltimore Evening Sun* article in 1922; this article also reveals his attitude toward racist politics in the 1920s:

Personally, I dissent sharply from most of the specific enterprises of the Klan. In the combat between the emerging Negroes of the South and the ruling white trash, I sympathize greatly with the Negroes, and have done what little I could to help them. As between the Jews and general run of Americans, I am violently in favor of the Jews, if only because I have found them more civilized and more honest. As between the Americanos of pure Anglo-Saxon blood and those of other bloods, I am for those of other bloods, if only because they are apt to be more amiable and more charming. And as between Catholics and Protestants, I incline, as a Christian, toward the Catholics, especially when the Protestants, as in the case of the Ku Klux, happen to be Methodists and Baptists, whose theology seems to me to be dubious and whose ethics I deplore.[26]

Yet, in true Menckenian fashion, he cannot let the matter rest here. He cannot resist a satirical aside upon those liberals who say that the Klan is un-American. Why, Mencken says with a broad grin, it is as American as apple pie, "for practically everybody else in America, at one time or other, has sought to do what it is trying to do or approved the acts of others so engaged." He then lists the redbaiting of 1919 and a recent court order to break up a birth control meeting as examples of practices by so-called responsible citizens. Whatever abominations the Klan has committed, Mencken concludes, most red-blooded Americans have engaged in comparable acts with equal enthusiasm.

Mencken is a hard man to pin down because, like Van Vechten's Durwood, he is constantly seeing "facets" in the diamond: The Klan is not a simple aberration in America but rather a manifestation of its spiritual mainstream. He is also elusive because he is primarily a pragmatist; he takes each issue as it comes. Even his support of the Costigan-Wagner antilynching bill of the 1920s was not unqualified. He agreed with it in principle (and wrote several articles for the *Baltimore Evening Sun* defending it),[27] but he worried about its constitutionality and, more importantly, its practicality. He privately told Walter White, then executive secretary of the NAACP and major firebrand behind the bill, that he objected to it "not so much on legal grounds as on practical grounds."[28] He thought the southern states would rebel against federal intervention: "What I fear is that it would be impossible to induce any Southern jury, even in a federal court, to convict under it." Yet in this instance, so strong was his belief in the justice of the principle, he testified for the bill before a national committee.[29]

Thus Mencken could be counted on to be unpredictable, but his unpredictability usually had an empirical basis. One reason Mencken denounced attempts by the *Pittsburgh Courier* to suppress the Amos 'n Andy radio shows was that he believed that not everything in them was a lie. "Such stuff as the Amos and Andy dialogues," he told George Schuyler

in 1931, "seems to me personally to be dreadfully stupid, but I think it is
absurd to call it libelous. *I have known many such Negroes*"[30] (my
italics). Even the Octavus Roy Cohen stories, he wrote to the *Crisis*,
"always keep some sort of contact with the truth."[31] He was afraid, too,
that once Negroes got into the business of censorship, their defects would
not disappear in the public's eyes but would rather reappear in a nastier
light. In *Minority Report*, he noted that "the Negro comic character may
have engendered a certain amount of amiable disdain among whites, but
he certainly did not produce dislike. We do not hate people we laugh at
and with. His chief effect upon white thinking, in fact, was to spread the
idea that Negroes as a class are very amiable folk, with a great deal of
pawky shrewdness."[32] However, he warned that "when the last Amos 'n
Andy programme is suppressed the Negro, ceasing to be a charming
clown, will become a menacing stranger, and his lot will be a good deal
less comfortable than it used to be." Mencken seems to be making a very
subtle point here. Although white people get a distorted picture of the
Negro in these caricatures, they are responding to qualities that are
universally prized (shrewdness, amiability). Thus they end by liking their
enemy despite their "disdain." Once there are no longer any portraits to
exhibit these qualities, the white folk will fall back upon their own dark
imaginations, and the Negro will then become an unreality, "a menacing
stranger."

There may be a corollary to Mencken's observation. Truth is an
elusive matter, and no one race has access to it—not even to the truth
about itself. Even a carnival mirror, although it projects a misshapen
image of the beholder, reflects an element of truth if one looks at it long
enough. Once one refuses to look, however, or banishes the mirror altogether, one may become smug and intolerant. When the *Crisis* sent
Mencken a questionnaire about Negro art in which one question clearly
implied that *only* Negroes could accurately depict Negroes, Mencken
objected: "Is it argued that a white man, looking at Negroes, must always
see them as Negroes see themselves? Then what is argued is nonsense."[33]
The "nonsense" Mencken was referring to was the assumption that one
angle of vision could reveal all the facets of the diamond. Mencken's view
was repeated by Wallace Thurman at the peak of the Renaissance when
he defended the white novelist's right to write about blacks: "No race of
people is exactly what it believes itself to be."[34] By the end of the decade,
however, Thurman and the rest of the young black intellectuals would be
quarreling with their elders because they felt that the Old Guard was not
using Mencken's undistorted mirror to the full extent of its reflective
powers. Only in one sense would their argument echo Mencken's position
that the truth about a race was not the exclusive province of that race
alone; they would also argue, as indeed would Mencken, that the

Renaissance itself often did not have the courage or the honesty to tell the truth about black people. Mencken believed that the Negro writer had opportunities that no white writer would ever have, and that when the Great Negro Novel was written, a Negro would be the author; yet he balked at the idea that the truth about a race was the exclusive province of that race.

Mencken believed in an "aristocracy of the spirit," as George H. Douglas has nicely phrased it,[35] and he thought that the democratic urge to push people into a common cauldron was a mistake: "I like to see people stick to their own. The dogma of the melting pot has never quite convinced me: it is preached by too many palpable frauds. My belief is that it would be a calamity to the Jews, as to any other self-respecting and clearly differentiated race, to be amalgamated with the mass of Anglo-Saxon Americans. Their tenacious differentness is a valuable thing to American civilization, and on their own side it keeps the more resolute and manly qualities alive among them, and so promotes their happiness."[36] And, continued Mencken, "my preference among . . . minority peoples is for those who face the music without protesting too much." In this article, at least, Mencken believed that the Negro had passed the test. Injustice had forged him in iron, and although some of his leaders protested "too much," for the most part he had learned how to survive with dignity.

Mencken thought that the Negro's isolation in America would probably never end. Whereas the Jews, Poles, Irish, and other ethnic groups might one day merge with the general populace, the Negro would always bear the mark of his color. The solution to this problem, said Mencken, was not to try to solve it: "Great races are never satisfied with equality. What they always try to demonstrate is superiority."[37] He observed that "some of the shrewder among the younger Negroes" have urged that "the intelligent thing for Negroes to do is not to try to edge nearer to whites, but to admit and glory in their Negroism." Mencken thought this to be the right course: "It will probably bring them far nearer to equal rights and dignities, in the long run, than the effort of other leaders to obtain for them the complete equality that they can never really get. Besides, it is more self-respecting than the other scheme, for it involves neither charity nor patronage."[38] Mencken also noted that there is another advantage in not getting everything you want, that "lost rights, like unrequited love, have their high psychical uses." If the Negro had received complete equality in 1865, "he might have sunk into the complacency of a stupid and half-forgotten peasantry: It is oppression that has brought out his best qualities, and bred his most intelligent leaders."

What are the Negro's best qualities? Again, Mencken returns to his favorite themes: a toughminded realism, a sense of humor, and a talent for self-criticism strangely absent among other minorities, such as the Jews, Irish, Poles, and Italians.[39] In *Minority Report*, he illustrated these generalizations with several concrete examples. The Negro, he said, "is an adept at hoodwinking the whites, and seems to get a great deal of fun out of the process. A large part of Negro talk consists of poking fun at white people. Save among the professional race-savers, there is even enough humor in the race to make it laugh at his own difficulties."[40] And this humor of the Negro, Mencken added, "is largely founded on cynicism." Rarely is he "deceived by the white folks who profess to love him." Furthermore,

> his view of the race-leaders who prey upon him—for example, the clergy —is full of doubts and dubieties. I often wonder how many pious blacka- moors really believe that they will turn into white angels post-mortem — probably no more than a few imbecile old women. The Negro spirituals, taking one with another, are anything but confident in tone, and after singing the most hopeful of them the congregation often turns to
>
> > I went down the rock to hide my face;
> > the rock cried out, "No hiding place,
> > No hiding place down here."[41]

Clearly Mencken felt a great temptation to view Negroes as "superior," for he certainly projected many of his own values upon them.

One value he especially prized was competence. In *Minority Report*, Mencken called it "the most steadily attractive of all human qualities. . . . One invariably admires a man who is good at his trade, whatever it must be—who understands its technic thoroughly, and surmounts its diffi- culties with ease, and gets substantial rewards for his labors, and is envied by his rivals."[42] One of Mencken's favorite competent men was the Pullman porter. In 1926, he wrote an article about him for the *Balti- more Evening Sun* in which he eulogized him for doing "his work quietly and with dignity." He then praised the Negro for having created "the art of Pullman portering" and for having "enriched it with a noble tradi- tion"—two themes, it is worth noting, that are the basis of James McPher- son's wonderful contemporary short story "A Solo Song: For Doc." Mencken was so interested in this natural aristocrat that he asked George Schuyler to find a Negro porter who would be willing to write an article for the *Mercury* about his craft. Mencken wanted to know, for instance, how this man manipulated people in order to get tips from them: "I don't want, of course, an article expressing the usual moral aversion to the practice. What I would like to get is a realistic treatise on the practical business of receiving tips. I assume that there are ways and means of encouraging the public to be liberal, and that they are put into execution by all intelligent porters."[43] Eventually Mencken discovered a porter who was willing to reveal his secrets, a Mr. N. H. Hall, and Mencken published an article by him in the *Mercury*. The portrait that emerges of Hall is that of a gentleman dealing with other gentlemen. Hall deplored vulgar behavior on his train (baseball players were the worst), and he admired people whose liberality was matched by their good breeding. A man of the world, he did not make conventional moral judgments. In his eyes, Arnold Rothstein was very much a gentleman, and although "Mr. Dempsey" wanted to be "called plain Jack," he too was "a gentleman always."[44] Hall ended his account of his eighteen years of service on this solemn note: "If it is true that any white boy has the opportunity of becoming President of the United States, it is equally true that any colored boy may become the Autocrat of the Pullman car." No doubt Mencken appreciated the touch of the mock-heroic here; in fact, in light of what we know about his editorial practices for the *Mercury*, he may have added it. It might be, however, that Mencken may have expected us to take Hall's conclusion as a mere statement of fact. For Mencken, the distance separating the two ambitions of porter and president was not that great, and we can surely surmise that he would have preferred the company of Hall to, let us say, Harding.

Mencken was fascinated by the subject of forgotten men in American history, and usually competence was the quality he most admired in these unsung heroes. Left Wing Gordon was the unknown composer of Negro spirituals; John Henry was the unchallenged master of the ten-pound sledge hammer; and Black Ulysses built America's cities, only to disappear without a trace into the wilderness he continued to level. In his memoirs (the *Days* books), Mencken recalled two black heroes from his young manhood in Baltimore:

> It always amazes me how easily men of the highest talents and eminence can be forgotten in this careless world—for example, the late Abraham Lincoln Herford, manager of the incomparable Joe Gans, lightweight champion of the world. Even Joe himself, though he was probably the greatest boxer who ever lived and unquestionably one of the gamest, is mentioned only rarely by the sporting writers, and in his native Baltimore there is no memorial to him save a modest stone in an Aframerican graveyard, far off the usual lines of tourist travel.[45]

Another legendary black Baltimorean was Old Jim, the carriage washer. He was less famous than either the manager or the prizefighter but was no less formidable a figure to Mencken the boy. As Mencken remembers him, he was "a fellow of vast size and unparalleled amiability. He was coal-black and built like a battleship, and when he got into his hip-high rubber boots and put on his long rubber apron he looked like an emperor in Hell."[46]

Of course, Mencken was never one to dwell on the heroic in people. His treatment of all three men is reminiscent of the tall tale—his *modus operandi* throughout the *Days* books—and his tone always seems to border on the mock-heroic even when he is dealing with such a weighty theme as "how are the mighty fallen." His account of the epical squandering of Old Jim's "bereavement" money is one of the funniest episodes in *Happy Days*, as is his description of Old Wesley's erudition and his enormous talent for ratiocination. Even Al Herford and Joe Gans come in for some quiet kidding: "Al taught him [Joe] a lot, not only about the business of boxing, but also about the carriage and conduct of a professional man, and Joe became widely known as the most gentlemanly pugilist then on earth. His manners were those of a lieutenant of the guards in old Vienna, and many managers sent their white boys to him to observe and learn."[47] Yet despite the spoofing, Mencken has a genuine admiration for the black heroes of his youth and—what is even more surprising, considering Mencken's reputed insensitivity—a real understanding of their relationship to him. Even the most comical situations will sometimes draw out a response from Mencken which we least expect. Old Wesley's brother was a preacher, and though Wesley himself was an unbeliever, he was quite proud of his brother's oratorical abilities. As he listened to his brother on the periphery of the enraptured crowd, he would intermittently paddle the behinds of little black boys who dared to snicker at his brother's high-blown phrases. Says Mencken: "We white boys, knowing that the prevailing *mores* forbade him to paddle *us*, were bound in honor to keep quiet, and this we always did."[48] "Bound in honor" is a nice touch, for it suggests Mencken's awareness that no matter how comical Old Wesley's brother seemed to him (then and now), both the preacher and Old Wesley lived in a separate world, which Mencken was honor-bound to respect.

Occasionally, Mencken tried to see this world through the Negro's eyes. In *Happy Days*, he describes a mean Irish cop named Murphy who delighted in banging delinquent Negroes over the head with his nightstick. The situation has the earmarks of a Mack Sennett comedy, until the subject turns to the University of Maryland hospital, to which some of the battered black people are taken. All the Negroes in his neighborhood have an aversion to the hospital, for "every Aframerican knew that it swarmed with medical students who never had enough cadavers to supply their hellish orgies, and were not above replenishing their stock by sticking a knife into a patient's back, or holding his nose and forcing a drink out of the black bottle down his throat."[49] Although the low comedy never quite disappears, Mencken suddenly shifts perspectives. He is willing to entertain the possibility that this myth may be true simply because the blacks so strongly believe in it. For if someone actually was "dragged" to this hospital and had subsequently returned to the land of the living, "he was one who had come unscathed from a charnel-house, and there were certainly reasonable grounds for surmising that he had escaped only by entering into some more or less diabolical pact with the doctors. *No one wanted him about. He made everyone uncomfortable*"[50] (my italics). In the last two sentences, Mencken quite simply makes a metaphysical leap to the other side of the Hollins Street alley. Given the beliefs of their world, he can understand why the returned victims would make everyone feel "uncomfortable."

❊

But Mencken was not always so charitable in his sentiments, and if I am going to give a thorough presentation of his attitudes toward the Negro, I should begin with the worst Mencken said—or, in this case, supposedly said, for the source of these remarks is not exactly a model of veracity. Charles Angoff, whom William Nolte has called "the Prince of Liars,"[51] was a member of the *Mercury* staff during the years Mencken reigned supreme, and he did a portrait of Mencken from memory the year Mencken died. Angoff thought of himself as a Boswell to an unworthy Dr. Johnson, and in order to be colorful (as well as to pay back a few grudges), he spiced his literary stew with plenty of heavy seasoning. One time he recalled his former boss making scurrilous remarks about black authors in particular and the Negro race in general: "And another thing, professor, no smoke . . . has ever written anything really first-rate. Countee Cullen, Langston Hughes, this Johnson [James Weldon], even George S. Schuyler, they're all second-raters. The coons just haven't got it in their blood, no matter what Carl Van Vechten and all the other coon lovers say. Educate them all you want, but any teacher or professor will tell you that smokes can go only so far, then they all look at you blank. The Southerners have the right idea about them."[52]

A few points reveal Angoff's hand in the pot. First, it is doubtful that Mencken would have referred to James Weldon Johnson as "this Johnson," for Mencken and Johnson had been good friends since 1916. Second, the poem Angoff and Mencken had been discussing before Mencken uttered his crudity was Johnson's "Go Down, Death." Mencken had said in print that it was a first-rate poem, "genuinely eloquent and moving."[53]

(Mencken had also urged Knopf to publish Johnson's "reminiscences," adding that Johnson had "had a very remarkable career and writes very well.")[54] Third, for at least thirteen years before this conversation was "recorded" in Angoff's memory, Mencken had been telling southerners that they did *not* "have the right idea about" Negroes. Finally, if Mencken truly believed that "smokes can go only so far," why was he so angry when a black student, Donald Gaines Murray, was denied permission to enter the University of Maryland law school? (Mencken's argument was that Murray had been properly prepared and was mentally equipped to do the job.)[55]

Two other names that Angoff mentioned—George Schuyler and Countee Cullen— also indicate his unreliability as a guide to Mencken's racial attitudes. Right before he quit the *Mercury*, Mencken told Schuyler in a letter that "no other contributor has covered a wider area or done better work,"[56] and in 1947, he wrote a letter to the *Pittsburgh Courier* (where Schuyler worked as a journalist) calling Schuyler "the best columnist, of any race, now in practise in the United States."[57] In fact, Mencken was so impressed with Schuyler's critical portrait of Franklin D. Roosevelt after the president's death in 1945 that he reprinted it in the *Baltimore Evening Sun* with the following note: "Nothing approaching his article in intellectual acuteness and moral courage has appeared in any white journal of comparable circulation. I refrain from deducing from this the racial superiority of the colored people. But I am sorely tempted."[58]

As for Cullen, although Mencken had a low opinion of poetry generally, he did publish Cullen's poem "The Shroud of Color" in the *Mercury*.[59] He also encouraged him—as he did every other Harlem Renaissance writer—to write prose,[60] for only prose, he believed, was worthy of the mature artist. Furthermore, Mencken was infuriated when, in 1926, Cullen was refused permission to read his poems at the Hotel Emerson in Baltimore. Mencken wrote Cullen to find out all the details of the outrageous affair; he felt that the *Baltimore Evening Sun* had covered the story "inadequately," and he wanted to publish "all of the facts."[61]

Yet Angoff cannot be dismissed altogether. His "remembered" Mencken bears a resemblance, no matter how faint, to the real thing. For instance, in *The Philosophy of Friedrich Nietzsche* (1908), Mencken did make a statement remarkably similar to Angoff's "smokes can only go so far." In discussing Nietzsche's theory of the innate mental inferiority of the masses, Mencken offered "the history of the hopelessly futile and fatuous effort to improve the negroes of the Southern United States by education" as a "proof":

It is apparent, on brief reflection, that the negro, no matter how much he is educated, must remain, as a race, in a condition of subservience; that he must remain the inferior of the stronger and more intelligent white man so long as he retains racial differentiation. Therefore, the effort to educate him has awakened in his mind ambitions and aspirations which, in the very nature of things, must go unrealized, and so, while gaining nothing whatever materially, he has lost all his old contentment, peace of mind and happiness. Indeed, it is a commonplace of observation in the United States that the educated and refined negro is invariably a hopeless, melancholy, embittered and despairing man.[62]

I wish to pass over Mencken's error in logic, that is, that his empiric proof is really only another generalization, one of those "self-evident truths" that our Founding Fathers were so fond of. (As I shall show, Mencken's tendency to travel the high a priori road was part of his character.) I also wish to point out only briefly that the unhappiness of the "educated and refined negro" might be due to his living in an unjust society—a fact that Mencken would later observe with great satiric effect. I would also note only in passing that this is a young Mencken speaking, one who had yet to live through the humiliations that he and other German-Americans would experience at home during World War I. I wish to pass over these subjects because they are less interesting at this point than another subject: Mencken's own conflicting attitudes toward the Negro. In a sense, his ambivalence is a reflection of divisions in himself which he never could bring to a reconciliation: the rationalist and the empiricist, the elitist and the commoner.

That Mencken had a simpleminded hatred of the common man is still an accepted opinion, even among people who should know better. In *The Crisis of the Negro Intellectual*, Harold Cruse rejects the possibility of Mencken's connection to the Harlem Renaissance on the grounds that no one with Mencken's prejudice toward the "people" could have possibly taken an interest in this literary movement.[63] Yet in reality Mencken often credited the common man with a great deal of common sense. For instance, he once argued that the members of state legislatures should not be elected, but should be chosen willy-nilly from the populace, the way juries are chosen. Compared to elected officials, he said, "a House of malt-and-hop dealers, garage mechanics and trolley conductors . . . would deal with [a] question with quite as much knowledge, and with a great deal more honesty." Furthermore, he once argued that people who write books on sex ought to have the common sense of "a railroad conductor or an ice-man"—a point that is as relevant today as it was in 1926.[64]

Not only does the average man have common sense, but he also is capable of common "decency," an important word in Mencken's vocabulary: "By this common decency I mean the habit, in the individual, of viewing with tolerance and charity the acts and ideas of other individuals—the habit which makes a man a reliable friend, a generous opponent, and a good citizen."[65] A belief in "liberty," Mencken argued, was contingent upon a belief that "decency" was indeed "common," that on the whole the common man had good intentions. For, said Mencken, "whatever its outward forms," liberty "is a simple thing": "Translated into political terms, it is the doctrine that the normal citizen of a civilized state is actually normal—that the decency which belongs naturally to *Homo sapiens*, as an animal above the brutes, is really in him. It holds that this normal citizen may be trusted, one day with another, to do the decent thing. It relies upon his natural impulses, and assumes them to be reasonably sound."[66]

Yet what happens to the "normal citizen" in an uncivilized nation, such as these United States? In a democracy, where any man can claim to be the equal of any other, "envy" becomes the "philosophy of the state."[67] Hence the rule of tolerance is replaced by the rule of malice, and the high priest of this new authority is the puritan. His first proposition is the equality of all men, but soon the primacy of the individual gives way to the will of the majority and the belief that "the opinion of the majority . . . represents the highest imaginable wisdom." Such a culture naturally leads to witch hunts, and the witch hunted is anyone who is divergent. The culture that has finally established the "virtue of the majority . . . now devotes itself to establishing the sinfulness of the minority."[68] And the normal citizen, whom Mencken had previously admired, now becomes a mindless fool or an unscrupulous knave. He fears anything he cannot understand, and he hates anyone who is better than he is: "His eagerness to bring all his fellow-citizens, and especially all those who are superior to him, into accord with his own dull and docile way of thinking, and to force it upon them when they resist, leads him inevitably into acts of unfairness, oppression and dishonour which, if all men were alike guilty of them, would quickly break down that mutual trust and confidence upon which the very structure of civilized society rests."[69] Thus, "decency" is the cornerstone of the entire edifice of civilization, for without decency, there is only barbarism—the death of all human values.

It is in light of this attitude that one must compare the following passage praising Negroes to the one denigrating them in *The Philosophy of Friedrich Nietzsche*. In an article that Mencken wrote for the Negro journal *Opportunity*, he said,

> That Negroes, in more than one way, are superior to most American whites is something that I have long believed. I pass over their gift for music (which is largely imaginary) and their greater dignity (which Dr. Eleanor R. Wembridge has described more eloquently than I could do it), and point to their better behavior as members of our common society. Are

they, on the lower levels, somewhat turbulent and inclined to petty crime? Perhaps. But that crime is seldom anti-social. It gets a lot of advertising when it is, but that is not often. Professional criminals are rare among Negroes, and, what is more important, professional reformers are still rarer. The horrible appetite of the low-caste Anglo-Saxon to police and harass his fellow-men is practically non-existent among them. No one ever hears of Negro wowsers inventing new categories of crime, and proposing to jail thousands of their own people for committing them. Negro Prohibitionists are almost as rare as Catholic Prohibitionists. No Negro has ever got a name by pretending to be more virtuous than the rest of us. In brief, the race is marked by extraordinary decency.[70]

Seen from this angle, Negroes are Mencken's normal citizens—the decent human beings who make liberty possible in a republic. Furthermore, since they happen to live in an uncivilized world (made up of puritans and "low-caste Anglo-Saxons"), they have Mencken's sympathy and respect because they symbolize a sane minority living in a society that sometimes borders on madness. (Compare Mencken's own *Minority Report*.)

However, seen from another angle, Negroes could easily be lumped by Mencken with the lumpen proletariat whose collective hectoring threatens common decency. Such a position invariably leads Mencken to make a statement like this: "The great problem ahead of the United States is that of reducing the high differential birthrate of the inferior orders, for example, the hillbillies of Appalachia, the gimme farmers of the Middle West, the lintheads of the South, and the Negroes."[71] These "inferior orders" are the folk, and Mencken was never able to resolve his conflicting attitudes toward it. For example, in one context of democracy (majority rule), the common man lacks decency, but in another context of democracy (liberty), he has it. Mencken tried to solve this problem by saying that under democracy as it is actually practiced, the decent man becomes a minority—the "Forgotten Man," as he was to call him, "the normal, well-behaved, decent citizen."[72] Yet this does not solve the problem, for how can the Forgotten Man be normal and yet a minority?

Mencken was once asked by a hopeful biographer, "Whom do you particularly dislike?" His unpublished answer reveals the basis of his ambivalence toward the common man: "I have no active dislike of anyone. Here my cynicism protects me. I never expect much of human beings, and so what they do never shocks or outrages me. My belief is that the level of decency in the world is pretty high, but that the level of intelligence is horribly low. The most offensive things that human beings do are usually inspired by stupidity rather than by malice."[73] Mencken's low opinion of mankind is less interesting than his belief that the world holds more fools than knaves. Unlike Swift, to whom he is often compared, Mencken did not share an Augustinian view of man's fallen nature: "The good which I would do, I do not; the evil I would avoid, I do." For Swift and Augustine, even if the level of intelligence were high, the level of human decency would always be low. Envy and malice are so rooted in the human heart that the light of reason can only acknowledge but never expunge them. Mencken, on the other hand, sets up an opposition between "decency" and "intelligence," suggesting that if there were more intelligent people in America, the natural tendency for people to be decent to one another would not so easily be overwhelmed.

Yet despite Mencken's confident assertion that the "level of intelligence" of human beings "is horribly low," he sometimes modified this idea when it came to the folk. As W.H.A. Williams has noted, Mencken never confronted a question that was implicit in his criticism of American culture: How could the same America that produced a corrupt civilization also create a vital, energetic language?[74] The natural answer would be that the folk create this lively language, but Mencken's elitism made him stop short of giving full credit to the folk. When new words enter our language, said Mencken, specific individuals are responsible for this rejuvenation, not the folk.[75] Pursuing the subject of Negro slang, he told George Schuyler that it always originates with individual wits: "The idea that common people invent it is sheer lunacy. They never invent anything, not even the imbecilities that entertain them so charmingly."[76] Yet he sometimes qualified this statement: "All slang, of course, is invented by individuals, not by groups," he wrote to James T. Farrell, "but nevertheless it must accord with the speechways of the group or it is bound to fail."[77] From the folk's "speechways" to the folk's linguistic common sense was not such a far leap, and Mencken occasionally took it. In his introduction to Cooper's *American Democrat*, he praised the folk's intelligence when it came to the pronunciation of words: "Here, as in other philological cases, the instinct of the folk has triumphed over the imbecility of pedagogues, and democracy, perhaps, has earned some praise."[78]

Yet, to borrow a phrase from Mencken's favorite American novel, *Huckleberry Finn*, he would never go whole hog. He would never relinquish his position that superior people, not the folk, make for a superior language. It takes only a moment's reflection to see that this theory leads him into a contradiction. In his indictments of American civilization, he argued that democracy makes it impossible for superior people to have a voice. There is no responsible aristocracy in America, only an avaricious plutocracy, an impotent intelligentsia, and a brainless mob.[79] But if the superior people cannot be heard by the brainless mob, how then can their language be recognized and accepted? That their language *is* recognized and accepted by the common man would seem to indicate an intelligence commensurate with that of the superior people. The next step, of course, is to conclude that the common man has shared in the creation of a superior language.

Mencken took a similar position regarding Negro folk songs. In his review of James Weldon Johnson's *Book of American Negro Spirituals*, Mencken argued that "there is no such thing as a folk song. Folk songs are written like all other songs by individuals. All the folk have to do with them is to choose the ones that are to survive." What is sad is that the names of these unknown bards are lost forever:

> Ah, that we could discover the authors of some of them. What genius
> went to waste among the pre-confederate fundamentalists. But did it go
> to waste? Perhaps not. Only its possessors were lost. The black unknown
> who wrote *Swing Low, Sweet Chariot, Deep River,* and *Roll, Jordan, Roll*
> —for I suspect that one bard wrote all three—left a heritage to his country
> that few white men have ever surpassed. He was one of the greatest poets
> we have ever produced, and he came so near to being our greatest musi-
> cian that I hesitate to look for a match for him.[80]

Again the problem: How can a people innately inferior produce geniuses; and, since in fact they did produce geniuses, can we differentiate these geniuses from the folk world from which they came? In truth, Mencken was of two minds about the Negro folk. On the one hand, he wanted to know about Negro folkways, but on the other hand, he generalized about them in the same ways he generalized about the weaknesses of the average American citizen.

There are, of course, two Menckens: one a rationalist, and one an empiricist. He once said that if he had had a choice, he would have preferred to live in the eighteenth century. Although it is hard to imagine Mencken in any other setting than early twentieth-century America, there is a side to him that belongs to the French Enlightenment—as James T. Farrell has observed.[81] This is the Mencken who wishes to conceptualize experience as soon as possible. However, when Mencken the skeptic or Mencken the scientific observer holds forth, we get a Mencken who is willing to suspend belief until all the evidence is in. This is the Mencken who read Charles Darwin, Thomas Huxley, and the other heirs of eighteenth-century British empiricism. Often the two Menckens don't mesh—for example, when the student of Darwin becomes a social Darwinist. In this instance, he prejudges observation from the abstract principle of "natural selection." Thus, Mencken's eighteenth-century antipathy to the "mob," as well as his belief in Nietzsche's *Übermensch* and Darwin's "fittest," is hardly consistent with his wish to judge individuals as they really are.

Mencken the rationalist is a man who usually speaks on a very high level of abstraction: Democracy is corrupt, Slavs are melancholy (he used this one on Joseph Conrad, much to Conrad's distress), farmers are avaricious, and the mob is "anthropoid." As a rationalist, Mencken often has the reformer's zeal to correct the follies of mankind (a nice irony this, since Mencken spent much of his time attacking zealots who held "messianic delusions"). Hence Mencken chastized the Negro several times for the backwardness of his religious beliefs. Placing himself in the anticlerical tradition of the French Enlightenment, Mencken lamented that the whole South seemed to be under the spell of Methodist and Baptist shamans. Their primitive religious practices reduced people to sniveling idiots, so that any and all "theological" notions were treated with respect: "If the men of past ages had cherished that delusion we'd still be sweating under the Inquisition—nay we'd be consulting oracles and trembling before sorcerers. In other words, the whole human race would still be on the level of the Haitian voodoo-worshippers and the Georgia Baptists."[82]

Mencken was especially angry with the Negro because his homage to "ecclesiastical racketeers"[83] was at odds with his decency, dignity, and innate common sense. In "The Burden of Credulity," he accused the Negro of being kept in "a bondage to credulity and fear that is ten times as degrading as any political bondage could ever be." Such Christianity as is practiced among lower-class blacks is not "worthy of a self-respecting people": "It is extraordinarily stupid, ignorant, barbaric, and preposterous. Almost I am tempted to add that it is downright simian." Black people inherited this religion from poor white trash, and

> it has been so further debased by moron Negro theologians that, on its
> nether levels, it is now a disgrace to the human race. These theologians
> constitute a body of bold and insatiable parasites, and getting rid of them
> is a problem that will daunt all save the bravest of the future leaders of
> black America. They fill their victims with ideas fit only for the jungle,
> and for that office they take a toll that is cruel and debilitating. What it
> amounts to annually I don't know, but it undoubtedly makes up the
> heaviest expenditure of the Negro people. All they get for it is continued
> subjugation to the superstitions of the slave quarters.[84]

Mencken once said of "the colored pastor on the lower levels" that he "retains something of the character of the savage medicine-man. He is completely ignorant, and he is often more than a bit dishonest. He has no hand in the progress his race is making. He is violently against it, and he is the enemy of every leader responsible for it. When he harangues his customer, the chief butts of his invectives are the colored *intelligentsia*, clerical and lay. He is a Fundamentalist."[85] That the Negro folksongs might be products of a "Fundamentalist" environment (and not exceptions to it), that the same folkways that produced the Negro's art also produced his religion, that the clergy "on the lower levels" might have a positive effect on the intellectual and moral life of black people—these possibilities escaped Mencken. Instead, he saw the religion of the Negro common man as a main reason for his arrested development as a human being. Again, that this religion might have sustained the common man in a time of need — a time, perhaps, when a more "rational" religion would have been as useful as a new tuxedo to a starving man — this Mencken did not want to consider. Yet for all his blindness in this one respect, a fault that Mencken cannot be accused of is cowardice. He expressed his opinions in Negro periodicals, and what is even more startling, the editors of these magazines asked for them.

Mencken kept hoping that blacks would see the light at the end of the theological tunnel. He continued to exhort the race "to reorganize its religious ideas, to get rid of its lingering childishness and, above all, to deliver itself from the exploitation of frauds and mountebanks."[86] He wrote one piece in which he noticed signs of rebellion against "the hog-wallow theology" that had entrapped blacks,[87] and he encouraged George Schuyler to write an article for the *Mercury* in which these signs had become an accomplished fact.[88] In "Black America Begins To Doubt" — a title that Mencken gave Schuyler for his article — Schuyler's main thesis was that the black church was losing its hold on black people as they came of age intellectually.[89] Both Mencken and Schuyler saw themselves as modern Voltaires who were trying to sweep away the mental rubbish that cluttered the Negro's brain so that he might take one long leap from the Dark Ages into the twentieth century.

It is not surprising that from Schuyler's first *Mercury* article in 1927 to Mencken's stroke in 1948, the two men were good friends, for they were very much alike. They were both rationalists (believing that the clear light of reason made civilization possible); they were both fiercely independent (especially in their dealings with their own); and they were both deeply ambivalent about the value of Negro folkways. Mencken admired Schuyler's frankness, and Schuyler repaid the compliment by imitating Mencken's vigorous, colloquial style. (He was called the "black Mencken" in the 1920s.) When in 1930 Mencken wrote a letter of recommendation for Schuyler to the Harmon Foundation, he found himself using language that he would have approved of on his own gravestone: "The Negroes are used to a more romantic approach to their problems. Schuyler has told them the truth. . . . I think he has done far more to set up honest self-criticism among the Negroes than any other writer, or, indeed, than all other Negro writers taken together."[90]

A good example of Mencken's and Schuyler's rationalism can be seen in the controversy over the capitalization of "Negro." In *The American Language: Supplement I*, Mencken noted that the campaign against "negro" in the black press took on all the earmarks of a religious crusade. Only Schuyler, said Mencken, was brave enough to resist the onslaught. He quoted Schuyler as follows: "It really doesn't matter a tinker's damn whether *Negro* is spelled with a small or large N, so far as the Negro's economic, political and cultural status is concerned."[91] (Schuyler actually thought that capitalization was worse, since it called attention to the Negro's special status.) Having inherited a view of language from the Enlightenment, both men believed that words alone could not change reality, that the symbol has no necessary connection to the thing for which it stands. Such a view may make an appeal to common sense, but people have other needs than common sense—the need, for instance, of the semblance of dignity—even though nothing is in fact changed. With King Lear, there are those who would say, "Reason not the need."

Another example of the rational outlook that the two men shared is an article called "Black Art," which Schuyler published in the *Mercury*.[92] It presented a portrait of Schuyler's grandmother, for the title does not refer to what the Harlem Renaissance was trying to create, but rather to "black magic," or "conjure." Schuyler's grandmother claimed to be a conjurer, and as a child Schuyler took her occult knowledge quite seriously. At times, Schuyler's grandmother reminds the reader of Charles Chesnutt's Aunt Sue in *The Conjure Woman*, but by the end of the article, the difference between Schuyler's sensibility and Chesnutt's is clear. Although Chesnutt treats the subject of conjure with a certain skeptical humor, he can see the poetical value in the subject of magic. In *The Conjure Woman*, the reader feels that the world the slaves made is always more complicated and less rational than the perception of the northern narrator who frames the stories. Schuyler's attitude, however, is ultimately that of Mencken, when they are both in their Voltairean frame of mind. What Schuyler the child takes for mystery is in reality an elaborate hoax. For example, after hearing from his grandmother that a person who wanted to be an expert fiddler had to make a pact with the devil, young Schuyler runs to a swamp in the dead of night hoping to make a deal that will take him to Carnegie Hall. Unfortunately, the devil never makes his appearance, and the boy returns home half dead from the cold. The next day, when Schuyler confesses to his grandmother what he has done, she hugs him tenderly, laughs uproariously, and calls him a "damned little fool." The grandmother's last words are Schuyler's, almost as if he were saying that folklore and folk superstitions are wonderful things to amuse children with, but if we are to be a mature people, we should by no means take them for guides to living in the real world.

Although I have dwelled upon Mencken's contradictory attitudes, a thread of consistency in his ideas cannot be ignored, and to isolate any one remark about the Negro without taking into account the total context of his thought is to be unjust to him. The importance of contexts is especially crucial when one considers his use of scurrilous terms such as "coon" and "niggero." Furthermore, despite his often astringent criticism of the Negro race, his interest in it never flagged. And finally, perhaps most importantly, whenever Mencken left his Olympian mountaintop and stooped to particulars, all contradictions ceased. Like Jonathan Swift, all his love was "towards individuals" (to quote Swift's famous letter to Pope). With Swift, Mencken sometimes hated and detested that peculiar animal called the American (or the Negro), but he heartily loved "John, Peter, Thomas, and so forth."

Mencken's attitude toward the farmer is a good example of his bifurcated perspective. In "The Husbandman" (*Prejudices, Fourth Series*), he mercilessly satirized the farmer as a generic type, and yet this satiric portrait had no bearing upon his advice to young novelists. He complained that the individual farmer was hidden behind stereotypes: "We either slobber over him or laugh at him." Someone needs to do "the American *La Terre*," he insisted: "Who will get the American farmer and his wife in a solid and respectable book?" Mencken's defense of the real farmer is illuminating: This individual, said Mencken, is a "child of God *like the rest of us*, and full of trials and tribulations"[93] (my italics). In a similar situation, he told Dreiser that his greatest strength as a novelist was his "capacity for seeing the world from a sort of proletarian standpoint";[94] and yet when he categorized proletarians as a type, he lost the compassion he had for them as individuals: "The proletarian is by definition an incompetent and ignominious fellow."[95]

Mencken the empiricist judged people on their own merits, but Mencken the rationalist was quick to make general judgments. Hence, he could complain, "It will be time enough to invite Pullman porters, colored preachers, and witch doctors to dinner when white Turkish bath rubbers, orthodox rabbis, and chiropractors are invited."[96] Here Mencken is the defender of civilization against the "lower orders" (black and white) who threaten to level it; yet, as I have shown, his admiration for individual Pullman porters was very real. Whether he thought actual Negro preachers and witch doctors suitable companions at the dinner table is perhaps a moot point, but he never let Kelly Miller's Christianity stand in the way of their friendship, and he continually invited a former dishwasher, George Schuyler, to test the reputation of his wine cellar.[97] Mencken's assumed haughtiness was only theory-deep; he never stood on ceremony with a friend he seriously liked and admired, and he advised the American novelist to treat his characters with both irony *and* pity.[98]

A typical Menckenian dualism is revealed in an article about Negroes moving into white neighborhoods, which he wrote for the *Baltimore*

Evening Sun in 1925. Mencken's major theme is the greed of unconscionable men who wish to transform Baltimore into a boom town, the result of which is that lowlifers of all colors have infested the city like rats: "The worst of these newcomers, I believe, are the brethren of the darker race. Thousands of them, come up from the South during the boom, are but little removed from gorillas. Their scale of living is that of the beasts of the field. . . . They swarm in all our back alleys, driving out the more respectable people of their own race. The latter find life among them impossible; they are filthy, turbulent, and without even the most elemental decencies."

Mencken, however, warns his fellow white Baltimoreans not to judge a man by his color. Many of the individuals who move into our neighborhoods, he states, deserve better treatment from us than they have been receiving. They are good citizens, and their motives are very much like ours: "They desire, first of all, to live in cleaner, roomier and more healthful surroundings than they have enjoyed in the past and to bring up their children in greater comfort and decency. They desire, secondly, to get away from the low riffraff of their own race. Both motives are sound, natural and laudable. Both make for good citizenship—in Madison Avenue quite as well as Guilford."[99] Although the citizen versus the savage was a battle that Mencken saw acted out in a larger arena than Baltimore, here the conflict involves not pagan versus puritan, but rather unregenerate nature versus *civitas*. The colored "riffraff" have descended the evolutionary ladder (they "swarm" like fruit flies), whereas the black citizens retain their humanity and their individuality.

The word "gorillas" is part of the Swiftian nomenclature (a way of categorizing the beasts of the field), and it is worth noting that Mencken would use the term to refer to troglodytes of a Caucasian stripe as well as to those of a darker hue. During World War II, Mencken complained to George Schuyler that "two hordes of gorillas" (white and black) had invaded Baltimore and had beset "the decent colored people" of the city.[100] On one occasion, Mencken went so far as to say (to Schuyler again) that the Southern "cracker" occupied the lowest rung of the evolutionary ladder: "I find it completely impossible to believe anything good about him. He seems to me to be hardly human, and if it were proposed seriously to proceed against him with machine guns I'd certainly not object. There has never been a more miserable white man on this earth, nor black man, nor yellow man."[101] The extremity of this statement can be explained by the occasion itself: One says things in letters that one would never say in print. (Besides, Schuyler and Mencken had been tossing this subject back and forth for weeks, and their passions had reached the boiling point.) Yet subjecting the poor cracker to machine guns says something about Mencken when he was smitten with the desire to categorize people. He often forgot about the individual when he was concerned about the health of the polis.

If Mencken was a defender of individual rights and freedoms, he could also fly to the camp of Edmund Burke when he felt society to be threatened. In fact, his prejudices were often the same as Burke's: He defended the polis against those who would tear it down, because the polis was a life giver; its well-being determined the well-being of each citizen, and when it was sick (as was American civilization most of the time), so was each citizen. What prevented Mencken from openly condoning the extermination of the crackers was the other philosophical pull upon him: the belief in human decency (tolerance) and the rights of each individual to travel his own separate road.

Mencken's use of language deserves a note. He once commented that critics had often overlooked the chief virtue of his style: "It is that I write with almost scientific precision."[102] This precision, it might be added, was often that of the ironist. For instance, in his *Smart Set* article "Si Mutare Potest Aethiops Pellum Suam" (Can the Ethiop change his skin?), Mencken begins with a sprinkling of words guaranteed to offend blacks and to please illiberal whites: "niggero," "coon," and "darkey." His language, in fact, indicates that he has already answered the question he has asked in his title—a title that alludes not only to a common proverb but also to Thomas Dixon's popular racist novel *The Leopard's Spots* (1902). And just to make sure that we all understand that he is on the side of the southerner, he asks the question again: "What, ladies and gentleman, in hell or out of it, are we to do with the Ethiop?"[103] He further substantiates his moral position on this issue by insisting that he hates "everyone born North of the Mason and Dixon line" and that he "would rather be chained by the leg in the common jail of Yazoo City, Miss., fed only upon hoecake and coca-cola, than smothered in violets by all the gals of Boston." Yet like Swift in "A Modest Proposal," he has trapped the reader into believing that the author holds the same attitude as that of his persona. The reader does not take long to discover that this attitude is not the one that Mencken actually holds. Mencken's real theme is that the southerners to a man have "botched" the Negro problem. The wretched "coon" is actually their superior, "simply because the niggero has been making fast and secure progress, not in mere education, but in competence, in self-confidence, in wealth—because he has begun to find out that he can make his way, Southerners or no Southerners—because, in all that is essential and lasting, he has shown better progress than the Southern whites." Not only has the leopard changed his spots, but he is now outrunning his pursuers, who are bogged down in the aftermath of the Civil War.

W.E.B. DuBois saw what Mencken was doing. He called "Si Mutare . . ." a "delicious" piece of journalism: "To prove himself a Southern 'Gentleman' he [Mencken] intersperses his article prodigally with 'nigger,' 'darkey,' and 'coon.' But he had undoubtedly seen a vision."[104] The vision, of course, was the one that Mencken would later describe in "A Coon Age": that the "niggero" had enslaved his enslaver. Even the title of this piece, Jervis Anderson to the contrary, is a journalist's trick rather than an expression of Mencken's vulgarity. Isn't its title more likely to catch the eye of the reader than would, let us say, "The Age of the Colored Person"? The imaginary reader may not like the title, but he *will* read the editorial. There is, too, the obvious matter of Mencken's love of the American language: its energy, its color, its boldness, its salty humor. That he was insensitive in some respects may mean that he was more sensitive than most of us in others. Words like "smoke," "dinge," "spade," "zigaboo," and so forth caught other eyes and ears than Mencken's. More than one black writer of the 1920s (Zora Neale Hurston and Rudolph Fisher come to mind) were fascinated by the punch to these words.[105]

Mencken made, in fact, some rather subtle distinctions in his use of designations for Negroes. In contrast to the "Si Mutare . . ." essay, whenever he talked seriously about the Negro's virtues and vices, Mencken would address him as "the colored brother" or "the darker brother." In a sense, this kind of verbal address belongs to an older mode of discourse. As Joseph Wood Krutch notes in his biography of Samuel Johnson, the prefatory "sir" that Dr. Johnson would use to address his opponent mitigated the insults that sometimes followed. The "sir" was a signal understood by gentlemen that all conversation, no matter how testy it became, was to a degree impersonal, for they were civilized men behaving in a civilized manner.[106] Beasts, after all, did not talk to one another. Mencken, I think, employed the same device. In "The Burden of Credulity" (in which he attacked the Negro's religion) and in "Hiring a Hall" (in which he pointed to the failings of the Harlem Renaissance),[107] he begins with a generous appreciation of "the colored brother's" merits, and only after that prelude does he lay on with a birchen rod.

A final word about Mencken's interest in the Negro: Long after he had lost his general popularity (as did the Negro writers), his curiosity about black life remained sharp. He followed Schuyler's column in the *Pittsburgh Courier* ("it gives me many a pleasant lift")[108] and pestered him with questions about Negro slang and the Negro people. In 1943, he wanted to know the cause of the race riots in Harlem: "Is it a fact . . . that an anti-Semitic element appeared in the late struggle for the Atlantic Charter in Harlem?" When Schuyler sent him a long list of Negro grievances against Jewish landlords, Mencken was sympathetic. He noted that the Jews owned most of the Negro housing in Baltimore and that "the landlords . . . never make any repairs unless the police or the health department orders them. The result is that even respectable people are forced to live in surroundings that are extremely unpleasant."[109] Certainly, the myth of Mencken's blindness to economic issues should be revised. Because he hated the New Deal and because he often denigrated the common man, it has been assumed that he stood on the right side of the political fence. In truth, he sided with the Negro in most matters (as James Weldon Johnson had so acutely observed) because the Negro was an underdog in American society. Although Mencken did not always express his allegiance in terms that were flattering to Negroes, to call him a racist (as Charles Angoff has done)[110] is not only wrong but irrelevant. Mencken in fact did believe that races were different from one another. Yet what mattered in the long run was not what Mencken said about Negroes but what he did for them, and what he did for them was more than any other white man of his generation had done—and that includes Van Vechten.

CHAPTER THREE

The Age of Satire:
The Teacher and His Pupils

If I ridicule the Follies and Corruptions of a *Court*, a *Ministry*, or a *Senate*, are they not amply paid by *Pensions*, *Titles*, and *Power;* while I expect and desire no other Reward, than that of laughing with a few Friends in a Corner?

—Jonathan Swift

In 1917, Mencken woke up and discovered himself to be a Negro. The transformation was figurative, of course, but it was very real and very sudden—as sudden as the overnight metamorphosis in Kafka's famous short novel. Having skirmished with the New Humanists (as they called themselves) since 1908, Mencken found to his dismay that the Great War had given them a new weapon: patriotism. Up to 1917, he had laughed at their notion of "culture," had ridiculed their equation of art with morality, and had even questioned the accuracy of their scholarship. Unlike the contestants in the Great War, who were bogged down in their trenches, Mencken had carried the fight to the foe, and the foe did not know how to deal with his satirical tactics. One of these Humanists, Stuart Sherman, found patriotism a great refuge, and under its guise he revealed himself to be somewhat of a scoundrel. In 1917, he wrote several articles about Mencken as America went to war, and these all implied that Mencken's attack on American "kultur" was connected with his German ancestry. Given the hostile atmosphere, Mencken could not retaliate. He soon found himself writing under a pseudonym in the *Smart Set* and barred from all magazines and newspapers except the *New York Evening Mail* and the *Seven Arts*. But that was not the worst of it. The government thought him a spy and harrassed him. Friends he had counted on suddenly grew frightened and deserted him.[1]

Mencken never forgot his wartime pariah-hood. Even thirteen years after the armistice, he could speak of himself "as a member of a race lately in worse odor among 100% Americans than either Jews or Negroes."[2] Certainly the war sharpened his tongue when he was once again free to speak. If he had satirized American civilization with a certain detached amusement before 1917, he now had a gleam in his eye and fire in his breath. "The results [of the war] are now before us," he said in 1922; and what were they? They were "government by usurpation and tyranny, a complete collapse of national decency . . . the bitter and senseless persecutions of minorities, Know-Nothingism, Ku Kluxism, terrorism and espionage."[3] He complained that the old American virtues had disappeared: "free discussion, general tolerance, and a fair fight"; and he noted that the new American was simply "an ignominious goosestepper." Moreover, if during the war our conduct at home was bad, our conduct abroad was worse: We "fought when it was safe, not in the manner of soldiers but in the manner of witch-burners and lynchers." In a *Smart Set* article ironically titled "The Land of the Free" (May 1921), he listed the "complete record of tyrannies that went on during the war," and concluded that "in no other country . . . on either side, was there anything ever approaching the complete abandonment of sense and justice that went on in the United States."[4]

Mencken's language in the immediate postwar period fairly bristled with fighting metaphors. Always a gadfly, after 1917 he showed a new pugnacity, a new unwillingness to ask quarter from a society that was so suspicious of, and hostile to, new ideas, and so ungenerous and cowardly in its opposition to them. Even *A Book of Prefaces*—the publication of which in 1917 Stuart Sherman had used as the occasion to attack Mencken—tended to define American culture in military terms. In "Puritanism As a Literary Force," perhaps the most famous essay in his book, he described the domination of ethical ideas in American culture as just that, a "force." Puritanism, Mencken argued, feels called upon to do battle with anything that it doesn't understand, and thus it wages "a ceaseless warfare upon beauty in its every form, from painting to religious ritual, from drama to dance."[5] For Mencken, "Philistinism is no more than another name for Puritanism," for both hate beauty with a passion usually credited to psychopaths—"the first because it holds beauty to be a mean and stupid thing, and the second because it holds beauty to be distracting and corrupting."

In reaction to such mindless malignity, Mencken claimed that he fought with equal fierceness. In 1922, he talked about his literary criticism as though it had always been a kind of guerrilla campaign against a large but vulnerable colonial power. He said that for most of his adult life, his critical energies had been

devoted to attacking and trying to break down the formal ideas, most of
them wholly devoid of logical content, which formerly oppressed the art
of letters in the United States very severely and still hangs about its flanks.
. . . I am constantly accused, and sometimes quite honestly, of tearing
down without building up, of murdering a theory without offering in its
place a new and better theory. But it must be plain enough that the ob-
jection, however earnestly made, is quite without merit. My business, considering the state of society in which I find myself, has been principally to
clear the ground of mouldering rubbish, to chase away old ghosts, to help
set the artist free.[6]

Three years before Mencken wrote this passage, a young black
Jamaican poet named Claude McKay expressed the anger and frustration of a whole generation of black Americans in a poem called "If We
Must Die." In it, McKay employed the same metaphors of warfare as did
Mencken, but they were used in a political context, not a literary one.
Having returned from the Great War and found that America was still
the same—that the world may have been made safe for democracy but
not for them—the black soldiers, some having received the French croix
de guerre, keenly felt the sting of President Wilson's big lie. They and
their generation rallied to McKay's poem as though it were a new banner:

If we must die, let it not be like hogs
Hunted and penned in an inglorious spot,
While round us bark the mad and hungry dogs,
Making mock of our accursed lot.
If we must die, O let us nobly die,
So that our precious blood may not be shed
In vain; then even the monsters we defy
Shall be constrained to honor us though dead!
Oh kinsmen! we must meet the common foe!
Though far outnumbered let us show us brave,
And for their thousand blows deal one deathblow!
What though before us lies the open grave?
Like men we'll face the murderous, cowardly pack,
Pressed to the wall, dying, but fighting back!

When these young men (and women) began to look for ways of fighting
back, it is not surprising that they read Mencken, a man who not only
shared their anger but who told them, and showed them, that they could
control it in order to conquer the world in a new way.
    The Negro intellectuals and Mencken did not take long to find one
another. In 1917, Mencken had read an open letter written by Kelly
Miller, a professor at Howard University, to President Wilson, and he

was so impressed with its eloquence that he devoted a whole column to it in the *New York Evening Mail*. Mencken called it "the ablest document the war has yet produced in the United States" and an "unusual work of art in words."[7] What was so unusual about this letter, said Mencken, was the simplicity and sanity of Miller's argument at a time when Americans generally were swept away by wartime bombast. Miller did not resort to weeping and wailing for the wrongs done to his race. Rather, he simply petitioned the president for justice. "You ask us to be patriots," paraphrased Mencken, "to die for our country, to protect it against aggression. Well, first show us that it is our country. First protect us. First, prove to us that we will get the same return from patriotism that other patriots get."

Mencken apologized for this "crude" outline of Miller's thesis; the actual style, he said, was much more "courtly." It then occurred to him—as it would many times after 1917—that such a document by an intelligent black man put the South to shame. No southerner, Mencken continued, could have written this document: "Whatever his graces otherwise," he "is almost destitute of the faculty of sober reflection. He is a sentimentalist, a romanticist, a weeper and an arm-waver, and as full of superstition as the Zulu at his gates." This was a distinction that Mencken was to repeat many times. The "superior" southern Anglo-Saxon was in reality a barbarian and a bully, whereas men like Walter White and James Weldon Johnson were "polite, intelligent, calm, well-informed, dignified, self-respecting."[8] In short, these were civilized men of the world.

Like Mencken, the Negro intellectuals and the Negro press around 1917 seemed preoccupied with the subject of civilization, especially since those favoring America's entry into the war loudly proclaimed that civilization was the issue at stake. At first, almost everyone (except the *Messenger* crowd) had agreed with DuBois that the Negro people should "close ranks" to support the war effort. The story of their disillusionment has been well told by Nathan Huggins and David Levering Lewis,[9] but what is interesting for our purposes is the rhetoric of that disillusionment. Even during the war, we find a questioning of American civilization by the black newspapers, although they still basically supported the cause. On 2 March 1918, the editor of the *Chicago Defender* presented his readers with the etymology of an important word: "Webster's Unabridged Dictionary defines civilization as 'the state of being refined in manners from the grossness of savage life, and improved in arts and learning.' Who knows but there may be such a thing as a refined mob, composed of 'colonels,' 'Southern aristocracy' and the ever present 'best citizens'? Who doubts, after seeing their work, that they have improved on the art of torture practiced in savage life and made it more fiendish?"[10] Why do the lynchings continue, the black newspapers asked, if we are all supposed to be pulling together? If southerners are as barbarous as the enemy, why are we fighting for them?

After the war, the opposition between civilization and savagery became more pronounced in the black press. In one *Chicago Defender* cartoon, a "Blue-law Reformer" (dressed as Uncle Sam) is lecturing "J. Q. Public" on the need for abstinence. "Here's a list of the horrible, uncivilized things you must *not* do," he says, and what follows is a petty version of the Ten Commandments—"don't smoke, don't drink, etc."[11] However, the reformer is quick to compensate the citizen for his small losses. There is a list of things he may do, and these include "lynching" and "mob-law," and of course the citizen is left smiling because he is willing to behave himself in a "civilized" manner if he can play the beast under cover. In another *Defender* cartoon, a "heathen" visits America and is introduced to "civilization" by a typical American citizen. After he discovers, however, that peonage and lynching are the staples of the New World, we see him in the last frame heading for the jungle where "there.isn't any civilization."[12]

These cartoons are simplified versions of an irony that was occasionally subtle and quite Swiftian. In a *Defender* editorial, the American people are praised for their generosity to the unfortunate ones all over the world.[13] As the congratulations continue, however, the author quietly notes that there is a "virgin field" for missionaries to plow close to home—in fact, right in our own backyard. There is a class of men in America, concludes the author, "far more barbarous and uncivilized than those to whom they have administered in the past." The praise then is ironic: Doing good is simply a means by which the American can remain blind to his own barbaric behavior.

In light of this satiric attitude in the black newspapers (which admittedly had been present before the war as well), it is not surprising that James Weldon Johnson, then a journalist for the *New York Age*, sought out Mencken around 1916. Soon the two men began to exchange letters, their mutual interest in black music forming the basis of a friendship that would last until Johnson's death in 1938. (In 1942, Johnson's widow, Grace Johnson, thanked Mencken for his generous "estimate of 'Go Down Death' on publication . . . as absolute as your present conclusion which I cherish.")[14] Mencken found that he could learn a great deal about black music from Johnson, and he was not shy about confessing his ignorance. Johnson had told him about some recent songs written by his brother, Rosamond, and Mencken replied that although he knew Rosamond's early work, he had not followed his later career. "I . . . shall go into the matter at length," he told Johnson.[15]

In the later teens and early 1920s, the two men benefited from their friendship, Mencken helping Johnson to revise his preface to *The Book of*

Negro Poetry (he wanted Johnson to put more emphasis on the younger poets),[16] and Johnson helping Mencken to stay informed of the activities, thoughts, and feelings of the Negro intelligentsia. Around 1917 and 1918, both men started to mention each other in their essays—Mencken indirectly, Johnson directly. On 20 July 1918, Johnson devoted a whole column to Mencken in the *New York Age*. It began with the following words of praise:

> We have often referred to the writings of H. L. Mencken. His English is a
> mental cocktail, an intellectual electric shock. Anybody who habitually
> dozes over conventional English ought to take Mencken at least once
> or twice a week in order to keep the moss and cobwebs out of their brains.
> Mr. Mencken writes excellently on a wider range of subjects than any
> other one writer in the United States, and whatever his topic may be, he
> is always interesting. But he is at his best when he is talking about the
> theatre or literature or music or philosophy or feminism or criticism. On
> these subjects, he is an authority.
> The chief charm of Mencken is that he always has a fresh point of view
> on even the oldest subject. If the subject is one that does not admit of a
> fresh point of view, Mencken does not touch it; he considers it as already
> finished, exhausted; as a subject to be left in the embalmed state of the
> tomb of literature. It is into this very pit that Mencken always avoids that
> so many writers fall; they do not even know when a subject is exhausted. . . .
> Mencken's style is all his own; nobody in the country writes like him.
> Sometimes we know that he is laughing at his readers, and sometimes we
> suspect he is laughing at himself. We might call him a humorous cynic;
> and when he is most cynical, he is most enjoyable. He is the cleverest
> writer in America today.[17]

Johnson's purpose here was to encourage the black public to read Mencken, but he also wanted black writers to learn from him.

Two years later, Johnson was more specific about what they might learn. On 21 February 1920, he noted that

> Mr. Mencken's favorite method of showing people the truth is to attack
> falsehood with ridicule. He shatters the walls of foolish pride and prejudice
> and hypocrisy merely by laughing at them; and he is more effective
> against them than most writers are who hurl heavily loaded shells of pro-
> test and imprecation.
> What could be more disconcerting and overwhelming to a man posing
> as everybody's superior than to find that everybody was laughing at his
> pretensions? Protest would only swell up his self importance.
> There is a lesson in Mr. Mencken's method for Negro writers. Take the
> subject of lynching, for example; when the average Negro writer tackles
> the subject he loudly and solemnly protests in the name of justice and

righteousness. By this method he may reach every one, except the lyncher. As far as this method reaches the lyncher at all, it makes him take himself more seriously. Instead of allowing the lyncher to feel that he is the one to whom appeals for justice should be addressed, he should be made to feel that he is just what he is—a low-browed, under-civilized, degenerate criminal.[18]

Thus, satire should replace preaching. To humiliate your enemy is the best way of getting even. Johnson was to return to this theme again and again, and he always noted Mencken as the major source of inspiration for this strategy. On 14 October 1922, Johnson devoted a section of his newspaper column to "Satire As a Weapon." In it he said that

> there are a number of phases of the race question which are so absurd that they cannot be effectively treated except in a satirical manner. What is the use of arguing with, or even denouncing an ignorant, bigoted, Negro-burning, low white of Texas, who believes more firmly than he does in his religion that he is innately superior, not only to all colored men but even to all such foreign whites as Frenchmen and Dagoes, etc. The only thing to do is to make him feel that you laugh at his pretensions to superiority and that so far as you individually are concerned, he is a low-browed, un-cultivated, un-Christian savage, in fact, a cruel joke on civilization.
>
> Such phases of the race question offer a great field for some colored writer who could employ the methods used by H. L. Mencken in attacking various foibles of civilization in general and of the American people in particular.[19]

Here again is the antithesis of civilization versus savagery. The truly cultivated man does not stoop to the level of his enemy; a lofty disdain is the only appropriate attitude to take toward a barbarian. Similarly, art should rise above politics; the aesthetic distance created by the artist and his personal attitude toward his enemy should be one.

Johnson correctly assessed the tremendous appeal that Mencken and his method would have for black writers. Prose works such as J. A. Rogers's *From "Superman" to Man* (1917), Walter White's *Flight* (1926), Claude McKay's *Banjo* (1929), Countee Cullen's *One Way to Heaven* (1932), Rudolph Fisher's *Walls of Jericho* (1928), George Schuyler's *Black No More* (1931)—all more or less employed satire against the master race, although sometimes the satire turned inward, as in Wallace Thurman's *The Blacker the Berry* (1929) and *Infants of Spring* (1932), or became double-edged, as in Schuyler's *Black No More*. The poetry of the period also occasionally turned playful (for example, Johnson's "St. Peter on the Judgment Day" and Cullen's "For a Lady I Know"), but the obvious evidence of Mencken's influence lay in the often brilliant satirical sketches, skits, and essays of E. Franklin Frazier, Wallace Thurman, Theophilus Lewis, and George Schuyler.

⁂

When James Weldon Johnson told his readers to read Mencken and learn from him, he had in mind not only Mencken's satiric methods but his satiric themes. As early as 1913, Mencken had produced a series of portraits of "The American" for the *Smart Set*.[20] Borrowing a device used by Swift in Book Two of *Gulliver's Travels*, Mencken chose a virtue that his countrymen prided themselves upon, and then proceeded to show that real American morality was exactly the opposite of that mythical, imagined one. Did Americans claim to be a "brave" people? They were in fact frightened of their own shadows, and their politicians knew it. Did they claim to be "fair"? They had in fact the morals of a pack of jackals pursuing a wounded deer. Did the country claim to be the leader among democracies? It was in fact "the last civilized country to abolish slavery."[21] Did they pride themselves on their love of the beautiful? Why, even the lowliest Navajo weaver had more real appreciation of art. Did they boast of their "freedom"? No other country was more "doglike" in its obedience to mob opinion; no other country was more intolerant of dissident views, eccentric behavior, or difference of any kind.

Mencken would not even allow the American to claim the dubious honor of being the world's most egregious materialist. He has no real respect for "things"; he prefers factory junk to real craftsmanship: "No man is more swindled by useless middlemen and criers of gewgaws."[22] Yet it *is* possible to sum up the American in a brief phrase: "Say that he is the master sentimentalist, and you come close to giving him his authentic label." Here the flattering portrait of the shrewd Yankee is erased with a single brush stroke. The *real* American thinks with his liver, not his brains; his whole life is one long emotional binge,

> with his sudden sobs and rages, his brummagem Puritanism, his childish braggadocio, his chronic waste of motion, his elemental humor, his great dislike of arts and artists, his fondness for the grotesque and melodramatic, his pious faith in quacks and panaceas, his curious ignorance of foreigners, his bad sportsmanship, his primitive feeding, his eternal self-medication, his weakness for tin pot display and strutting, his jealous distrust of all genuine distinction, his abounding optimism, his agile pursuit of the dollar.[23]

The tragic tenor of this list of faults is mitigated, as it is in *Gulliver's Travels*, by the list itself. We are overwhelmed by the seemingly endless catalogue of folly, and our only response is, finally, laughter.

These articles, brilliant as they are, were merely preliminary runs for Mencken's tour de force, "On Being an American," which was published in *Prejudices, Third Series* (1922). In this amusing essay, the Swiftian device of satiric reversal is again foremost. Why does Mencken stand on the dock, "wrapped in the flag," waving good-by to the Young Intellectuals who have set sail for Europe?[24] Is it because he has more faith in American civilization than they do? No, he shares their complaints about its worth, but he doesn't share their bitterness. And why? Because "mirth is necessary to . . . happiness," and nowhere is that mirth more readily available than in these United States where nonsense reigns supreme. Here every abomination and folly conceivable to man passes before the eye, delights of infinite variety but all springing from the same source: the smug complacency of *boobus Americanus*, "a bird that knows no closed season."[25] Hence, "pluribus" has a new meaning in Mencken's Republic, and his "defense" of it was not exactly the kind to bring joy to humorless patriots.

It did, however, bring joy to James Weldon Johnson and other black writers who realized that *boobus Americanus* was a bird that they too might bring down. A bird of that species lived year round in the South, and Mencken on more than one occasion had set his sights on him. In fact, the Menckenian satire to which Johnson had referred his readers in the *New York Age* was a series of articles on the South, which had begun as early as 1907 and which culminated in his noisy salvo—the shot heard round the South—"The Sahara of the Bozart" (1920).

In these essays, Mencken is at his wittiest. Delightfully turning the minstrel tradition upside down in "Si Mutare Potest Aethiops Pellum Suam," Mencken prays that on the day that *Homo noir* throws off his shackles, "I shall be safe in the Alps, and not below the Potomac River, hurriedly disguised with burnt cork and trying to get out on the high gear." Although Mencken only touches upon the theme of southern intellectual sterility in this essay, he had, as Fred C. Hobson observes, discussed it often in the thirteen years before "The Sahara of the Bozart" appeared.[26] In all these pre-1920 essays (as well as several written in 1920) Mencken would ask the same question: Why are so few books written in the South? And always the answer would be the same: When the old civilization died during the Civil War, the poor whites replaced the ancient aristocracy as the dominant force in southern life. The culture they brought with them was puritanism, and the arts do not flourish in a moralistic environment.

Johnson followed these essays closely and commented upon them in the *New York Age*. He warned his readers not to take Mencken's persona seriously: "Mr. Mencken frequently refers to himself as a Southerner. Of course, he is no more a Southerner because he was born in a Southern state than this writer is a Hottentot because some of his ancestors were Africans."[27] (Understandably, Johnson played down Mencken's real ties to the South. Besides, Mencken had depicted himself in "Si Mutare . . ." as a southerner of a certain stripe: "I have the hookworm . . . and believe in infant damnation.") Johnson also, as we have seen, told his readers to pay attention to Mencken's method as a possible way of dealing with racism. Nevertheless, Johnson did not just sit back and listen. On one occasion he proceeded to lecture the Sage of Baltimore about the real reasons for the Negro's emergence in the South.

On 3 July 1918, Mencken had written a piece for the *New York Evening Mail* called "Mr. Cabell of Virginia." Once again he raised the question of cultural impotency in the South, and once again he pointed to the consequences of the Civil War as an answer. With the aristocracy defunct and the poor whites in control, the whole show below the Potomac was pure Barnum. Johnson was not satisfied with this account. In the same article in which he called Mencken "the cleverest writer in America today," he wondered if Mencken had not overlooked something. Were the poor whites "so innately inferior to the Southern aristocracy?" Johnson asked. Could they be "any more handicapped than the 'Ethiop,' who, Mr. Mencken says, 'alone shows any cultural advance'?" Johnson then proceeded to give his own explanation for the decline of intellectual life in the South:

> We do not think that the destruction of the old Southern Civilization or any innate inferiority of the poor white trash is the reason; the real reason is that the white South of today is using up every bit of its mental energy in this terrible race struggle. All of the mental efforts of the white South run through a narrow channel. . . . All of the mental power of the white South is being used up in holding the Negro back, and that is the reason why it does not produce either great literature or great statesmen or great wealth. . . .
>
> On the other hand, the Negro is not using up any of his strength in trying to hold anybody back; he is using every ounce of it to move forward himself. His face is front and toward the light; when the white man tries to force him back he, the white man, turns from the light and faces backward.

Although no one can prove that Mencken read Johnson's piece in the *New York Age*, it is more than likely that he did. He took an interest in Johnson's work around this time. (Johnson was probably the first to introduce him to the world of Negro newspapers, which Mencken read with some regularity throughout his life.) Also, the two men exchanged letters often between 1917 and 1920, and Mencken more than once seemed to be persuaded by Johnson's eloquence. Witness, for instance, Mencken's response to a letter from Johnson concerning the terrible race riots of 1919. Mencken begins by calling the "low-caste white man" a coward: "He is, by nature, a gang-fighter; a poltroon under his hide, he delights in operations which allow him to kill without risk." He ends by taking Johnson's side completely: "As you say, fighting back changes the scene. Once he is convinced that chasing Negroes is dangerous, he will stop it."[28] It is not surprising, then, that soon after Johnson's newspaper article Mencken too became preoccupied with the "mental energy" of the South. In two *Smart Set* essays called "The Confederate Pastime" and "The Confederate Mind," Mencken suggests that lynching is a psychological phenomenon—a pathological substitute for the lack of harmless amusements, which a normal, civilized culture provides as a matter of course. If, for instance, the South would play host to more brass bands and boxing matches, there would be fewer dead Negroes. As it stands now, Mencken declares, the place is a paradise for "Freudians"—and not simply for those who are "psychologists." What the South needs is a good dose of psychiatric treatment.[29]

Yet Johnson's influence upon Mencken may have been even more subtle. In the 1917 version of "The Sahara of the Bozart" (published on 13 November 1917 in the *New York Evening Mail*), Mencken had not even mentioned the Negro; all his emphasis was upon southern decadence. However, in the version published in *Prejudices, Second Series*—the one that made him a hated man in the South—Mencken gives the Negro a prominent place. Perhaps thinking of Johnson's remarks in the *New York Age*, Mencken says of the poor whites that "the emerging black" is "the cornerstone of all their public thinking." He adds that the only prose writer in recent history (besides James Branch Cabell) to write anything of note was Joel Chandler Harris, and he turned out to be "little more than an amanuensis for the local blacks." His works, continues Mencken, "were really the products, not of white Georgia, but of black Georgia. Writing afterward *as* a white man, he swiftly subsided into the fifth rank."[30]

Often in this famous essay Mencken sounds as if he has a special kind of knowledge about black America which others, especially southerners, lack. Near the end of "The Sahara of the Bozart," he refers to an article in a "stray copy of a negro paper," which had poked fun at the incongruity of an ordinance recently passed in Douglas, Georgia. It seemed that the good people of this community wished to prevent the Negro "trouser-presser" from ironing the wardrobe of white folk. Yet as the article amusingly noted, nearly all the clothing in the town was "handled" by black washerwomen, and sometimes it remained in Negro homes (Mencken quotes the newspaper as saying) "for as long as a week at a time."[31] Mencken's comment on the "absurdity" of this situation is instructive, for again it reminds us of the reasons for his tendency to identify with the Negro immediately following the Great War. He sarcastically tells his audience to keep this comedy quiet—"keep it dark" —for "a casual word, and the united press of the South will be upon your trail, denouncing you bitterly as a scoundrelly Yankee, a Bolshevik Jew, an agent of the Wilhelmstrasse." Since Mencken had been called a German spy by the same people who passed the ordinance against the "trouser-presser," it is not surprising that he would respond to the humor in a stray Negro opinion.

In another section of the same essay, Mencken mentions a "curious article by an intelligent negro" (probably Walter White), in which the author points out how easy it is for a light-skinned colored man to pass for white in the South. The reason for this, says Mencken with mock solemnity, is that not a few southerners "have distinctly negroid features." Moreover—and here the satire takes on a new dimension—the white ancestors of these Negro-fied southerners selected their sexual partners with great care: "The men of the upper classes sought their mistresses among the blacks," and thus "there was created a series of mixed strains containing the best white blood of the south, and perhaps of the whole country."[32] As for the poor whites, alas, they "went unfertilized from above." All that pride in racial purity is really only a by-product of neglect. And the despised Negro race? It has produced the mother of aristocrats.

As Louis D. Rubin observes, Mencken has reduced everyone in the South to the level of breeding animals.[33] And as Fred C. Hobson says, most of the animals bear a remarkable resemblance to Swift's Yahoos.[34] Yet there is another Swiftian touch that would have especially pleased the black intellectuals who read Mencken's essays. Says Mencken of the South, it is a land "so vast" that "nearly the whole of Europe could be lost in that stupendous region of fat farms, shoddy cities and paralyzed cerebrums: one could throw in France, Germany, Italy, and still have room for the British Isles." If we subtract the "fat farms," what Mencken has given us is not Book Four of *Gulliver's Travels* but Book Three. In the whole of this intellectual "vacuity," the emptiness of which Mencken compares to the vast "interstellar spaces," there is only James Branch Cabell, the Lord Munodi of a modern-day Balnibarbi, struggling to keep his sanity in a world given over to lunacy. But he is not quite alone. Throughout the revised "Sahara" Mencken keeps pointing to the intelligent Negro who is cracking open his cocoon and trying to fly.

Mencken is not sure how high he will fly, but he has already surpassed those who would keep him on the ground:

Like all other half-breeds he is an unhappy man, with disquieting ten-
dencies toward anti-social habits of thought, but he is intrinsically a better
animal than the pure-blooded descendants of the old poor whites, and he
not infrequently demonstrates it. It is not by accident that the negroes of
the South are making faster progress, economically and culturally, than
the masses of the whites. It is not by accident that the only visible aesthetic activity in the South is wholly in their hands. No southern composer
has ever written music so good as that of half a dozen white-black composers who might be named. Even in politics, the negro reveals a curious
superiority. Despite the fact that the race question has been the main political concern of the southern whites for two generations, to the practical
exclusion of everything else, they have contributed nothing to its discussion that has impressed the world so deeply and so favorably as three or
four books by Southern negroes.[35]

This passage is significant for several reasons. First, now Mencken's
mulatto is "unhappy" because of his environment, not because he can
never be as good as an intelligent white man. Mencken has shifted the
burden of innate inferiority to the "poor whites," a change of thinking
due, we might surmise, to his own black-washing during the Great War.
Second, the indirect references to the Johnson brothers, Harry Burleigh,
and others (composers) and to Kelly Miller and W.E.B. DuBois (political
theorists) are obvious. After 1917, Mencken took to studying what other
outsiders like himself were thinking and doing, and the results impressed
him. Finally, there is the crucial idea in this passage—one that subsequently would be taken up by some (not all) Harlem Renaissance writers
—that the "aesthetic" province is theirs by birthright. Let the white man
fumble with technology and business; the Negro will create art that will
ensure his own immortality.

As Mencken's animus toward the South grew, so did his tendency to
believe that the hope for southern literature lay in the hands of Negro
writers. In the same month (October 1920) that the revised "Sahara" was
published in *Prejudices, Second Series*, Mencken gave his prescription for
the Negro novel in his review of Ovington's *Shadow*. A month following,
he wrote a *Smart Set* piece ("Letters and the Map") in which he complained
of the lack of "realism" in southern literature, adding that the South had
never been treated in the manner that Edgar Lee Masters and Sherwood
Anderson had "done" the Middle West. The only hope that it would be
done—and done correctly—lay with "the new school of Aframerican
novelists, now struggling heavily to emerge."[36] Actually, Mencken had
indirectly hinted at the possibility of the Great Negro Novel as early as
1917, when he reviewed Johnson's *Autobiography of An Ex-Colored
Man* in "Si Mutare Potest Aethiops Pellum Suam." The novel had been
published anonymously in 1912, and Mencken had only recently learned

—from Johnson himself—that his friend was the author. He told Johnson in a letter that it was an "excellent piece of work," and his review may have been the catalyst that caused Johnson to announce his authorship.[37] However, Mencken mistook the book for a sociological treatise, and although he was favorably impressed with the information it provided, he made it clear that he would have preferred a novel. For the second work he reviewed in "Si Mutare . . ." was a novel and, though it was written by a white man, Mencken thought that it showed the Negro writer the direction he should travel.

Yet there was a certain irony in Mencken's choice of Paul Kester's *His Own Country* as a model. Kester, Mencken argued, had treated the Negro problem with impartiality and without sentimentality. He stood "above the gaudy balderdash of a Thomas Dixon as a novel by Dreiser stands above the boudoir goods of Robert W. Chambers."[38] What appealed to Mencken about Kester's hero was that he was not a stereotype; what would not appeal to the Harlem Renaissance was that he turned out to be a moral monster. A kind of black Thomas Sutpen, Julius Caesar Brent wreaks vengeance upon those who humiliated him as a youth. When he leaves Virginia, this young octoroon goes to Montreal and becomes a physician. Hearing the call of his native land, he returns, only to bring destruction upon himself, his family, and many innocent people. One can see why the Harlem Renaissance authors would not try to recreate this character; here was realism that acknowledged the existence of a grotesque, a grotesque that they feared would be interpreted as a stereotype. The advice they would take from Mencken would be that given in the Ovington review. Deal with "normalities," Mencken said, not extremes.

With this flood of articles between 1917 and 1920—dealing with both the South and the Negro novelist—it is curious that Mencken has been overlooked by critics of the Harlem Renaissance. After all, following the war Mencken was at the height of his popularity; he was read by more Americans than perhaps any other living writer. Certainly James Weldon Johnson offers proof that Negro intellectuals were not behind the times. Furthermore, as George Schuyler tells us, Theophilus Lewis was an "avid reader" of the *Smart Set*,[39] and Walter White, as we shall see, came close to believing that Mencken was a deity; when the Sage of Baltimore spoke, all was light (except of course in the South).

By 1920, Mencken had become a household word among black intellectuals. Now they not only quoted him, they sometimes sounded like him. James Weldon Johnson started saying things like "Southern bunk" and "pish-posh" when he was amused, and the following when he was angry: "One of the mysteries to us is, what is there to boast of in being a Southerner? . . . Among so-called civilized white men the

Southerner is the most backward, the most ignorant, the most uncivilized and the most barbarous in the world. His section is without scholarship, without art and without law and order; it is even without money, except what it can borrow from the North."[40] Both DuBois and Johnson saw the implications of Mencken's thesis in the "Sahara" and elsewhere as an explanation for the past poverty of Negro art. As Johnson put it in his preface to *The Book of American Negro Poetry* (1922), the reason that the American Negro has not produced a Pushkin or a Coleridge-Taylor was that he was "consuming all his intellectual energy in this grueling race struggle."[41] Although Johnson was contradicting himself (witness his *New York Age* remarks), his point was that this futile energy consumption had been forced upon the Negro by his environment (he mentions Mencken's "Sahara" as proof), and that from this moment on, the past no longer existed: The Negro now planned to devote all his energy to art.

Hence, Mencken's thesis concerning southern decadence was useful to black authors for many reasons. For one thing, it put the sock on the other foot. Instead of the Negro's having to argue that he was *not* a savage, the southerner now had to prove that he wasn't a Yahoo. According to Mencken — or rather according to his black interpreters — the Negro symbolized the last vestige of civilization in a dying culture, and, moreover, he symbolized the South's sole hope for a future regeneration. Mencken thus made it possible for the Negro intellectual to dismiss special pleading altogether. What was there to plead for, when it was clear to every reasonable human being that the superior man in the South was the one with the dark skin? In actual fact, even in the revised "Sahara," the Negro played a small part in Mencken's thesis about the South, for nowhere did he say that the Negro problem was the sole cause of the South's cultural decline. For Mencken, the South was intellectually dead because the Yahoos were in the saddle, and even if they had not ridden roughshod over the Negro, they still would have destroyed the old civilization. Nevertheless, Mencken's revisions of the "Sahara" did add a new note to the cacophony that Mencken heard below the Potomac, and if men like Johnson chose to interpret that new note as the sound of southern blues, who could blame them?

❦

When "The Sahara of the Bozart" made its appearance in 1920, the response of Negro intellectuals was intense and varied. Walter White was inspired to write *The Fire in the Flint*; Montgomery Gregory considered it a clarion call to the Negro novelist. When Jean Toomer's *Cane* was published in December 1923, Gregory used Mencken's vocabulary to describe its uniqueness: "It is a notorious fact that the United States south of the Mason and Dixon line has been, in the words of Mr. Mencken, a 'Cultural Sahara.'" Noting that "great art, like great deeds, cannot flourish in a land of bigotry and oppression," he pointed to the Negro as someone who has suffered from this blight. Hypersensitive to his wrongs, he has resisted attempts by his own artists to depict his folk-life. *Cane*, however, represented a new approach, Gregory stressed. It was a concrete example that the Negro could rise above his environment and create great art. Now, Gregory pleaded, if only the "Reader" could make the same leap above the sordid conditions that enslaved the white South—then we could have a Renaissance.[42]

For the most part, Mencken's essay provided ammunition to authors who wanted to punish the South in a straightforward, nonsatiric manner. J. Milton Sampson used a passage from "The Sahara of the Bozart" as an epigraph to "These Colored United States" in the *Messenger* (July 1923). Mary Owen, in the same magazine, called her essay "The Decadence of Southern Civilization" (February 1924); her theme was that the South has no culture because the whites spend all their energies in subduing the Negro. Yet the real impact of Mencken's essay, as Johnson had predicted, was that it led to the call for a Negro satirist. The response came almost immediately. Arnold Mulder wrote in the *Independent* (1924): "You remember how Dean Swift turned the tables on civilized man by taking Gulliver into the land of the Houyhnhnms where horses were the rational beings and where men, called Yahoos, were the subject race. And the diabolical ingenuity of Swift succeeded in making man as ridiculous, from the horse's point of view, as the name given him by those intelligent beings. Suppose a negro Swift should arise."[43]

In 1927, writing for the *Mercury*, George Schuyler said that "the intelligent Aframerican" cannot "help classing the bulk of Nordics with the inmates of an insane asylum." What we need, he continued, is a "black American Balzac" to write a new "volume of Droll Stories." For, said Schuyler, "the Negro is a sort of black Gulliver chained by white Lilliputians, a prisoner in a jail of color prejudice, a babe in a forest of bigotry, but withal a fellow philosophical and cynical enough to laugh at himself and his predicament. He has developed more than any other group, even more than the Jews, the capacity to see things as they are rather than as he would have them."[44] Schuyler's Negro, of course, had those characteristics that Mencken admired: He was civilized, clearsighted, and without illusions. In other words, he was a perfect candidate for the office of satirist.

Mencken had said essentially the same thing when he had responded to a *Crisis* questionnaire in 1926. The Negro should not complain about being caricatured by the white man, Mencken urged. Rather, he should pay him back "in his own coin": "The white man, it seems to me, is extremely ridiculous. He looks ridiculous even to me, a white man myself. To a Negro he must be a hilarious spectacle, indeed. Why isn't that spectacle better described? Let the Negro sculptors spit on their hands! What a chance!"[45] Four months later J. A. Rogers, writing for the *Amsterdam News*, would make a similar plea in "Wanted: A Satirist." Here the absurdity to be satirized was the "Nordic doctrine of superiority," the supreme delusion of a deluded culture. No other subject in America, said Rogers, has so much "comedy and even burlesque" built into it: "Some day a satirist is going to see the possibilities in the race question and produce a book that will eclipse Swift, Martial or Juvenal."[46]

Thus, when Mencken assumed the editorship of the new *American Mercury* in 1924, he was followed with considerable interest by literate black Americans. And Mencken did not let them down. By Fenwick Anderson's count, in the decade that Mencken ran the *Mercury* (1924-1933) he published fifty-four articles by or about blacks.[47] More specifically, his editorial policy in the new magazine continued to reflect his previous attitudes toward the Negro. He wanted to give Negro writers a chance to express what they thought and felt about themselves and America. Their appearance in his magazine was not to be a token performance; they would appear beside some of the most distinguished writers in the country (as benighted as it was). Mencken also wanted to cover the subject of race and racial relationships from all possible angles, and therefore he solicited articles from anthropologists and even from white southerners.

In the *Mercury*, Mencken encouraged black writers to hold forth on a multitude of subjects: politics, religion, art, folklore, black newspapers, music—even the race's "inhibitions." One attitude that appeared often —and it was one that Mencken had urged blacks to express at the outset —was the attitude of Negro superiority. In "The Dilemma of the Negro," by W.E.B. DuBois, the issue of superiority became the subject of the entire essay.[48] Although Negroes were forced to go to separate schools, said the editor of the *Crisis*, they often created educational institutions that were a cut above those attended by most whites. Yet if the level of culture among middle-class blacks was higher by far than that attained by the average white man, it had been achieved at a high cost. No matter how well educated, these Negroes were denied access to the world beyond color; the only way whites would allow them to escape their parochialism was through humiliation, and that their pride would not brook. Like DuBois, George Schuyler believed that the greatest injustice caused by segregation was cultural deprivation. In "Keeping the Negro in his Place," he said that the present dispensation "leaves the Negro all dressed up with nowhere to go."[49] And he made it quite clear that "nowhere" included the North as well as the South. Even in Harlem, cabarets segregated Negroes or denied them entrance altogether.

J. A. Rogers took an Olympian view of racial relationships in "The American Negro in Europe."[50] He systematically discussed how different countries reacted to the presence of a black man in their midst—his was a study in cultural comparisons. For instance, people of African origins were highly regarded in France, he noted; white women even "frizzled" their hair to imitate them. In England, however, the Negro's lot was "far worse than in America." Although Rogers was critical of the injustices that the Negro suffered abroad, his tone remained consistently urbane. He was Goldsmith's Citizen of the World, more amused by than contemptuous of the white man's mysterious quirks and habits.

The variety of articles by Negroes in the *Mercury* illustrates Mencken's desire to include all viewpoints—to be a kind of Diderot to the American Negro. He wanted other perspectives than those presented by the Negroes themselves. As he told Schuyler in 1929, "Lately I bought an article on the Negro question by a white Virginian. Having printed no less than twelve pieces by the dark brethren, it seemed to be high time to give the Ofays a hearing."[51] The author from Virginia defended the status quo in the South, arguing from a social Darwinist position that only the fittest should survive. He stated further that although he sympathized with the Negro's plight, he did not care to jeopardize his friendships and his ties to the broader community.[52] Mencken told Schuyler privately that he found the conclusions of the Virginian "despairing."[53]

Perhaps the most perceptive white commentator on "the Negro question" was L. M. Hussey, a chemist by profession and a personal friend of Walter White. In "Homo Africanus," he noted that the mask of humility worn by black people—from the lowly sharecropper to the most exalted academic—often hides their real contempt.[54] The Negro educator in the South, for instance, smiles at the white philanthropist because he wants his money, yet he knows too that this money serves to keep the Negro in his place. Hussey also observed that despite the simple-minded white view that a Negro is a Negro is a Negro, the members of the race live within a clearly defined class structure. Many of them know their genealogy, and some of them have found their ancestors to be southern aristocrats. These Negroes are proud—not because their blood is white, but because it is the best. Undoubtedly, both observations are insightful, the one foreshadowing Faulkner's marvelous character in *Go Down Moses* (1942), Lucas Beauchamp; and the other breaking ground for Ralph Ellison's finely drawn portrait of the Negro "educator" Dr. Bledsoe in *Invisible Man* (1952).

As interesting as these *Mercury* articles are, they are not as compelling as those that were inspired by the satiric impulse. What Mencken really wanted to offer the Negro writer was the opportunity to "spit on his hands" and write satire. We are accustomed today to look upon satire as a purely fictional art, having similar rules controlling its nature to those, let us say, which control a novel or a poem. But Edward Rosenheim is surely right when he argues that satire is difficult to pin down as a literary form because it can move so easily from references to the real world to references to Cloud-Cuckoo Land. On the one hand, it will attack historically verifiable particulars; on the other hand, it can slip into an imaginative world that is as unbelievable as the most surrealistic novel.[55] To consider the nature of satire is necessary, because the Harlem Renaissance has been accused of writing very little satire.[56] This accusation is true if we define satire as a genre that sustains its dramatic illusion from beginning to end. However, it is not true if we consider satire a hybrid form: half rhetoric, half fiction. The essays that the black writers wrote for Mencken's *Mercury* make no claim to being fictional, but that is part of the fun: The world in these "United Snakes" which they proceed to describe is completely loony, and yet it is all "real."

Another point about the Renaissance's satire is worth making. Though they wanted to ridicule their white adversary, the black writers of this period did not wish to appear boorish in their revenge. Boorishness smacked of the very propaganda that they sought to steer clear of, and satire, if pushed too far, sounded suspiciously like propaganda. So they developed the urbane voice, one that Mencken had urged them to take all along. Yet Mencken had hardly taken that voice in "The Sahara of the Bozart." When he lashed out against the South's lack of civilization, he himself did not hold back—his loud guffaws and his Brobdingnagian contempt reduced the whole notion of urbanity to a top hat in a wind storm. However, the black writers of the 1920s in this instance preferred Mencken's advice to his example; the sharp breeze of urbane satire was safer than the eye of the hurricane. Perhaps this is one reason that the Renaissance did not produce a *Gulliver's Travels* or even a "Sahara of the Bozart."

Throughout the 1920s, Mencken told black writers to assume an urbane persona, especially when writing for the *Mercury*. The postulates that made up this persona went something like this: You are a civilized man; the racist is not; do not fight with the enemy on his own ground but make him fight on yours; do not plead with him to grant you your humanity, but laugh at the loss of his; do not admit inferiority in any sense, but claim—directly or indirectly—that you are superior. It is he, after all, who is the savage, the vulgarian, the fool.

Thus, in "A Negro Looks at Race Prejudice," James Weldon Johnson can only shake his head over the subject he is to discuss. The closer he looks at it, "the more paradoxical and absurd it seems."[57] He is especially puzzled by southern behavior. Why is the black mammy the sine qua non of aristocratic distinction—especially in light of the fact that southerners claim to despise Negroes? Also, if there is so much animosity between the races, why are there so many mulattos in the South? Could it be that there is a discrepancy between myth (the taboo of miscegenation) and reality? And then, another behavioral quirk strikes Johnson as extremely funny. Whites seem to think that the darker brother spends most of his time dreaming up ways to enter the social world of the Caucasian. Johnson assures them that Negroes do not need their company to enjoy themselves.

This point, however, brings him to a more serious subject, and now Johnson shifts his tone from amusement to clinical detachment. The racist, he decides, is really a case for the "psychologist." Like the puritan who cannot stand people enjoying themselves, so too the prejudiced man tries to prevent the Negro, through segregation, from enjoying the goods of this world. Johnson concludes his essay with an anecdote that illustrates the theme of Caucasian incivility—nay, even pathology. On board a ship returning from Europe, Johnson discovers from a friend that one of the white passengers has asked that Johnson be removed from the first-class dining room. The incident leads to the following reflection: "What is it in him that makes the sight of a solitary Negro sitting in a cafe in Paris or Berlin allow him no peace of mind until he has put forth every effort to have the black man kicked out? I admit he is a fanatic, but I also insist he is a vulgarian and a bounder." In short, the racist is Mencken's puritan redux, the petty moralist who makes truly civilized behavior impossible. He is less evil than pathetic.

Johnson's rhetorical stance is that of the outsider, a traveler in a strange land who is observing the habits and mores of some rather peculiar people. This was the approach that George Schuyler took in "Our White Folks," published a year earlier in the *Mercury*. In a letter, Mencken had encouraged Schuyler to do an article on "how the whites look to an intelligent Negro." He told Schuyler that he had asked "various dark literati of my acquaintance" to attempt it, but "they couldn't get rid of politeness." Do "something realistically and fearlessly," he said, "like your excellent stuff in the *Pittsburgh Courier*."[58] When Schuyler replied that he hoped to spoof the white man in the manner Mencken suggested, Mencken responded enthusiastically: "Lay on. . . . I'd be delighted to see him dosed with the same kind of medicine that he has been giving the Ethiop for so many years. Certainly he must be a ridiculous figure seen from without."[59] Yet Mencken also warned Schuyler on another occasion that he should not express anger when he exposed his enemy: "In such writing it seems to me that the really effective weapon is irony. The moment you begin to show indignation you weaken your whole case."[60]

Thus Schuyler was to be "fearless" but cool-headed; angry but urbane; plain-dealing but smooth as glass.

In "Our White Folks," Schuyler has followed Mencken's advice. Instead of being depicted as a monster, the white man is shown to be a source of endless amusement to the Negro. Although the southerner claims to know everything there is to know about the Negro, he fails to realize that he too is under observation. His knowledge of the Negro is usually superficial, whereas the Negro knows his enemy intimately—he has to, to survive. And "knowing him so intimately, the black brother has no illusions about either his intelligence, his industry, his efficiency, his honor, or his morals."[61] At their worst, says Schuyler, upper-class whites are lazy and hypocritical; their lower class counterparts, appallingly stupid.

The "one-drop theory" especially brings "mirth" to the darker brother, says Schuyler. In a recent court ruling in Virginia, fifty white children were barred from a white school because it was feared that they had been tarnished by the tarbrush. Could one find better farce in a minstrel show? And the side show up North is no different, except that the hypocrisy is more blatant. Still, Negroes have learned to live in both worlds, and their sense of humor is their salvation. The word "amusement" runs all through Schuyler's essay, for the tone he wants is Horatian, not Juvenalian. Nevertheless, the indictment of white people is all-encompassing, including even white intellectuals. Says Schuyler: "They have a great deal of information but are not so long on common sense. . . . They lack that sense of humor and gentle cynicism which one expects to find in the really civilized person, and which are the chief characteristics of even the most lowly and miserable Aframerican."

Nineteen twenty-seven seems to have been the year for satire. In "Blessed Are the Sons of Ham," Schuyler argues that a black man's life is never dull in a world full of foolish Nordics. Just to have a meal out is an adventure, as managers and waiters fumble to find reasons why a poor Ethiop cannot be seated, and customers buzz their indignation. "I cannot help but enjoy all this," says Schuyler. "Over a hundred proud Nordics nonplussed by a lone Negro."[62] If he tries to go to a play, the hilarity increases. When the ticket agent tells Schuyler that the seats he has reserved are sold, Schuyler watches the man's face, caught in his lie: "I smile. He blushes. A look of annoyance comes over his face. That is my reward; it fills me with glee—just that expression."

In this essay, Schuyler wavers between genuine amusement and whistling in the dark, but in "Our Greatest Gift to America," also published in 1927, his ironic tone never falters. This wonderful spoof works on several levels. First, it is an obvious satire on the white man's ability to delude himself; and second, it casts a comic glance at apologists such as

DuBois who are forever pleading, on the basis of the Negro's contributions to civilization, that the Negro is a human being. Schuyler says simply that the white man needs a "nigger" to bolster his self-esteem; in short, the Negro's greatest gift is flattery. His presence in America allows the lowliest white man to think himself a superior person. Seeing a minstrel show, he can always say to himself that at least he is "not like these buffoons." Besides, he can stand upon the black mudsill of humanity and claim kinship with Rockefeller, Edison, and Carnegie because of his white skin.[63] Democracy has worked better because of the Ethiop's presence, says Schuyler with tongue in cheek: White men in America have reached toward the stars, propelling themselves upward by shoving the darker brother further into the mud. Yes, concludes Schuyler, we have "roused the hope and pride of teeming millions of ofays—this indeed is a gift of which we can well be proud."

Schuyler's satire depends upon a clever rhetorical reversal: The Negro's greatest gift is what the white man desperately needs. If he did not have the Negro's flattery, God knows how he could live with himself. In 1927, Theophilus Lewis also published a piece that depends upon an ironic reversal for its satiric effect. It is a variation on Swift's "Modest Proposal," its humor directed at both the Negro intellectuals and the South. Lewis argues that the Negro has made a mistake by not exploiting the southern myth that the black man is a natural rapist. Why not glamorize this fiction, says Lewis, and make the Negro into Don Juan, a daring lover who makes love on the run? Instead of the "burly brute" of southern lore, we would then have a "romantic rogue with a certain fascination about him." You can be sure, says Lewis, that once southerners got wind of this new interpretation, they would drop the rapist label like a rotten watermelon. Furthermore, smiles Lewis, it would spare the Negro from writing so many tedious pieces of useless propaganda.[64]

Schuyler's essays also implied that the white man's delusion depends upon an imaginary Negro; and the satire of both Lewis and Schuyler stressed that the white man in America can achieve psychic wholeness only if he has a nigger to complete him, to assure him that he is indeed what he would like to be. Take away the imaginary Negro, and down comes the scaffolding. It is clear, then, that white people are insane, and that the caste system is the cause of the insanity.

In 1927, E. Franklin Frazier explored the theme of Caucasian insanity in a brilliant satiric essay called "The Pathology of Race Prejudice." Like Schuyler, Frazier pretends to take a purely scientific attitude toward his topic. In this "treatise," he sets out to demonstrate that "the behavior motivated by race prejudice shows precisely the same characteristics as those ascribed to insanity."[65] For instance, the insane construct an elaborate system of ratiocination to "support their delusions," says Frazier;

it is not true that they are simply "irrational." So, too, southerners weave webs of logical arguments to support the "delusion" of the racial inferiority of the Negro. First they find a convincing theory to prove "that white blood is responsible for character and genius in mixed Negroes"; then they find an equally convincing theory to show "that white blood harms Negroes." But no matter what the theory, if a person is insane, he will always use it to contravene the facts of experience; he will always use it to protect his obsession. A normal mind is flexible; an insane mind is not. Thus, even in the face of overwhelming evidence, the southerner will not give up the belief that "the Negro is a ravisher." It is an *idée fixe*, Franklin observes with detachment, a "projection" from the inside outward. Because "inmates of a madhouse are not judged insane by themselves, but by those outside," a southerner's behavior never seems peculiar to another southerner but only to people outside the South.

Like others of his generation, Frazier was inspired in this piece to see the South as Mencken had seen it in his seminal satiric essays. The South was a casebook for pathologists; and lynching, a manifestation of cultural rot. Having lost its aristocracy, the South had been given over to the white trash; having lost its principle of order, the South had de-evolved into Conrad's Congo or Swift's Houyhnhnm-land without the Houyhnhnms. The whole culture, then, was topsy-turvy. The bottom was at the top, and the top either was dead or had fled to the North. For Frazier, racial prejudice is the dominant symptom of the South's insanity. His essay ends with a quotation from Nietzsche: "Insanity in individuals is something rare—but in groups, parties, nations, and epochs it is the rule." Certainly for this generation of Negro writers, Mencken had shown that it was the rule for the South.

If Frazier made fun of the insanity, Walter White considered it deadly serious. Still, the persona of the civilized outsider visiting a strange, mad world remains the same. In "I Investigate Lynchings," which White wrote for the *Mercury* in 1929, he tells hair-raising tales of outwitting the local yokelry as he tried to gather information about the horrors of Bedlam.[66] A year before, Knopf had published his *Rope and Faggot: The Biography of Judge Lynch* (1928), ostensibly an objective study of a peculiar societal phenomenon, lynching. Actually, White's document is more satirical than scientific. Quoting Mencken frequently, White psychoanalyzes the South. He finds close connections between the South's religious fanaticism, its sexual obsessions, and lynching. For White, the continued presence of lynching in the South, like heroin for a dope addict, deprives the culture of the psychic energy necessary for it to transcend its inertia.

In *Rope and Faggot*, lynching is just one form of pathology in a sick society. Again, Mencken's thesis prevails. Lynching exists in the South, argues White, because the South has no real civilization. It is a world of insane puritans, dull towns, and boorish bumpkins. In such a world, the obscene becomes an everyday occurrence. In such a world, a civilized man is as rare as a flower on a sand dune. Although White is willing to admit that some light has recently brightened a corner of the general gloom (for instance, Howard Odum's work at the University of North Carolina), he gives the final impression that the area is still a case study for a Freudian textbook.

Generally, however, blacks publishing in the *Mercury* did not dissect the South with such grimness. In "Traveling Jim Crow," for example, Schuyler sees the comic side of segregated travel. His South is mad indeed, but it is like being lost in the funhouse. Schuyler delights in documenting one absurdity after another: a one-mile stretch of railroad track in Kentucky where passengers must observe the Jim Crow laws (after riding one hundred thirteen miles without them); a light-skinned "colored" lady who passes for French in order to ride with the gentry, yet "who would starve to death in France if she had to order her own meals";[67] a southerner who won't speak to Schuyler as the train passes through the South, but who treats him as a long-lost friend once the train enters the North.

Of course Mencken did not leave all the wit to the Negro writers. One butt of his satire was the self-appointed racial authority, such as Madison Grant or Lothrop Stoddard. He delighted in puncturing their pseudoscientific theories about the long-headed Nordic, the round-headed Alpine, and the broad-headed Mediterranean (the latter, as Mencken noted, "with his vague smears of Ethiopian blood").[68] In his last year with the *Smart Set*, Mencken laughed at novelist Gertrude Atherton for her attempt to apply the wisdom of these two savants to American fiction. Atherton had complained that the novel as an art form had been inundated by authors of Alpine origin, and that this inundation had resulted in the vulgarization of our national letters. Mencken gleefully called his rebuttal "Nordic Blond Art"; in it, he sardonically seeks to investigate the truth of Atherton's claims by examining her own recently published novel, *Black Oxen*. By the end of his criticism, he comes to the conclusion that although the "inferior herd" of which Atherton complains may be vulgar, it has more life than the whole lot of "dolichocephalic Nordic blonds" who inhabit her novel. Nevertheless, since he, Mencken, is a Nordic blond "of the purest type, Teutoburger Wald or greyhound," he has taken her advice to heart and has sent "copies of her article . . . to all of the principal middle western novelists, including Dreiser."

Mencken continued his warfare against the defenders of Anglo-Saxon purity in the *Mercury*. Month after month, Franz Boas or Melville Herskovits or Raymond Pearl (his personal friend and a member of the

Johns Hopkins Medical School faculty) would blast the idea of a pure race.[69] Mencken, of course, had other reasons for printing these articles than the desire to defend the Negro. He also wanted to attack the Anglo-Saxon's unwarranted arrogance, one manifestation of which was what he called "Ku Klux" literary criticism. Throughout the *Mercury*, he kept up a constant artillery barrage against "Anglo-Saxonism," noting that the dominance of this racial type was giving way to that of the hyphenated-Americans. The method of attack was usually Shavian. What were the Anglo-Americans doing when Dreiser's ancestors "were raising grapes on the Rhine"? Mencken's answer was that they "were hanging witches in Salem." We need not add that someone like Alain Locke was quick to seize upon Mencken's distinction. If Dreiser's ancestors were civilized men when the New Englanders were barbarians, Locke would claim that his ancestors were also superior men. Long before Salem, the Africans had maintained a tradition of craftsmanship and elegance in the visual arts.[70]

Another implication of Mencken's remark concerning the Salem witch hunts was that the early puritans were the ancestors of the present-day Negrophobes. The tendency to see the world in black and white terms on a metaphysical plane can easily be transferred to seeing it so on a physical one. Recognizing this phenomenon, Negro writers in the 1920s were fond of linking the American's thoroughgoing moralism with his myopic racial prejudice. It is not surprising to find, therefore, that two of Langston Hughes's stories from *The Ways of White Folk* (1934) first appeared in the *Mercury*, and that the enemy in both stories is puritanism. The Pembertons of Mapleton, Vermont ("Poor Little Black Fellow") and Mrs. Art Studevant of Melton, Iowa ("Cora Unashamed") are not southerners and are not rabid racists. Their crimes against humanity are the results of their constricted hearts.[71]

In keeping with his desire for balance, Mencken encouraged Negro writers to satirize black life as well as white. In one article, Eugene Gordon tells tales out of school and discusses the Negro's "inhibitions."[72] Here he is speaking primarily of the modern middle-class Negro who has become so embarrassed by objects associated with his past — watermelon, pork chops, fried chicken, bright colors, razors — that he seeks to avoid them at all costs. As a consequence, he has become "a sad Freudian case." Moreover, he has as many prejudices as white men, one being a preference for light-skinned members of his own race. Foreshadowing a theme that Wallace Thurman was to develop in *The Blacker the Berry*, Gordon says that a truly black girl, no matter how talented, does not stand a chance in Negro society.

Gordon wasn't always so critical of his own kind, however; he could take a wry, amused attitude if the occasion warranted. When he discussed

Negro newspapers, for instance, he was both informative and satirical. "There was a time," he smiled, "when the ordinary colored American laughed at the suggestion that he read Negro newspapers." Now both highbrow and lowbrow read them eagerly, the lowlifers fixing their eyes on the tabloid murders and baseball scores and the sophisticates turning their attention to the theater section and editorial pages.[73]

Rudolph Fisher too could take an amused view—this time of himself. He wrote an article for Mencken discussing the cabaret scene, in which he expresses shock at discovering that the old hangouts are filled with white people. Instead of being outraged, he is amused that some of these "Ofays" dance even "better than I." Perhaps on a deeper level, he thinks, they "have tuned in on our wave-length." Could it be, he asks, that "they are at last learning to speak our language"? Although he doesn't try to answer this question, he is ready to admit that perhaps Negroes may not have judged their Caucasian brothers as fairly as they ought to.[74]

Other *Mercury* articles by Negroes, however, did not use the light touch when it came to discussing their own; and, as we shall see, the astringency of this satire sometimes indicated a break between two generations of black writers in the 1920s. George Schuyler is a case in point. Nothing by him appeared in Mencken's magazine until December 1927, and then he became the most published *Mercury* writer, black or white, in Mencken's tenure as editor. (Between 1927 and 1934, no less than nine of Schuyler's titles graced the famous dark green covers.) By 1927, both Mencken and the Young Wits had begun to question the movement's integrity, and thus in the *Mercury* Schuyler often took a hard look at Negro foibles, as if they in themselves might provide a clue to what had gone wrong with the Renaissance. For instance, Schuyler complained in "Uncle Sam's Black Step-Child" that the progeny of American Negroes in Liberia had learned the wrong lessons from America's past.[75] Though black themselves, they not only exploited the native population, but they also practiced a system of slavery remarkably similar to the American kind. (Schuyler would later give dramatic expression to both subjects in his novel *Slaves Today* [1931].) And in another article—actually, a series of sketches of Negro soldiers—Schuyler pointed out that many woes were of the Negro's own making.[76] He satirized the delusions of a Sergeant Jackson who had been taken in by the patriotic jingoism of the white press during World War I. Given a wartime promotion, the naive sergeant proudly wore his captain's uniform back home, only to be humiliated by a passel of Southern whites. Instead of focusing upon white cruelty, Schuyler took the opposite tack: A smart man would have known when not to ask for trouble. In another sketch, Schuyler ridiculed a penny-pincher named Hodge who in the end got fleeced in one of his own get-rich-quick schemes.

❧

Schuyler was to become the most acid-tongued critic of black life—not only in the *Mercury* but elsewhere. To appreciate the sheer versatility of his wit, as well as its development, one should begin with his apprentice years with the erratic *Messenger*, a magazine whose politics changed as often as its owners. As early as 1923, Schuyler wrote a satiric column called "Shafts and Darts," and in these delightful pages he managed to insult everyone, black and white. For a while, his friend Theophilus Lewis shared the column, the two declaring their "dominant motive" to be malice. No one was to be spared their lashes, they smugly claimed—not even "the President of the Immortals."[77] Yet the tone throughout was light and breezy, with Mencken hovering somewhere in the background as the patron saint of all those who would smile at contemporary follies. And like Mencken, Schuyler pretended to be indifferent to moral reform, pretended merely to delight in the endless parade. In reality—again like much of Mencken's satire—the demolition work was to serve as a preface to new construction.

Schuyler's lampoons of white people followed Mencken's advice to the letter; high comedy held center stage at all times. In one piece called "The Caucasian Problem," Schuyler discusses, with mock-gravity, various solutions to the white menace. It is true, he says, shaking his head in sad disbelief, that the "offenses" of this "minority group" are quite "serious."[78] Indeed, its members have almost ruined civilization with their pushy, monomaniacal theories about hard work, thrift, and success; but then they are ignorant people, Schuyler explains, and know no better. "Given the opportunity," he assures his readers, "we know that a white boy or girl can absorb as much knowledge as a colored boy or girl." It is all a question of education, really, and he for one is against such extreme measures as "segregation" or "extermination."

In another article, Schuyler warns his readers that they should not automatically assume that the Negro is "superior to the Caucasian."[79] The white immigrants, he patiently explains, were mere savages when they came to America, and "it takes time to civilize such poor stock." These unfortunate people just did not have the advantages Negroes had in Africa. While Negro ancestors were weaned on a great civilization, theirs were running about the woods, half-naked and smelly. However, their progeny do show healthy signs of adaptation, and if they can just rid themselves of such lamentable bad habits as "gullibility" and "superstition," there might yet be hope for the poor unfortunates.

On another occasion, Schuyler pretended to agree with the white polemicists. His ostensible position is that the African cultures of the past produced nothing to equal the accomplishments of the modern Caucasian civilizations. Nevertheless, Schuyler's Western smugness is assaulted by a gadflyish friend. What about African art, his skeptical companion asks: "Look at the magnificent sculpture, excellent pottery, clever ironwork and wonderful weaving." Schuyler dismisses the comparison, showing himself to be just as American as George Babbitt. "How absurd!" he exclaims: "The idea of comparing handicrafts with machine-made goods. What of the white man's movies, comic strips, billboards and Sunday supplements? Only a dozen people may see some excellent mask in a jungle village, but a million Nordics see Mutt and Jeff everyday."[80] Here, of course, is Mencken's "third-rate" culture in all its glittering emptiness. And it is worth noting that Schuyler in this instance is *not* claiming to be merely a "lampblacked Anglo-Saxon," as he did in "The Negro Art Hokum."[81] In that controversial piece, he was talking about the Negro from an anthropological perspective, underlining the same point that James Baldwin was to make in *Nobody Knows My Name* (that one is created by one's culture—made in America—whether one likes it or not). Here he is criticizing the world that made him by comparing it to a place, a civilization, that still has some sense of aesthetic values.

When Schuyler attacked his own kind in the *Messenger*, the satire also focused upon the loss of values. He told his audience in 1925 that in spite of complaints, he was going to "continue to hold up the mirror to Aframerican life without camouflage."[82] We are not as good as we think ourselves to be, Schuyler insisted: There are real "skeletons" in "*our* racial closet." And at different times, Schuyler thought all sorts of Negro behavior, at all levels, to be ludicrous. His favorite targets were hair straighteners, bleaching creams, or any of the paraphernalia that promised a new human being but produced, instead, the same old corruptible Adam. Coming from someone who called Negroes merely "lampblacked Anglo-Saxons," this constant reminder of black pride seems a bit surprising, but what may appear to be a contradiction is actually a perceptive insight. Negroes may have been the products of a certain culture—as indeed were whites—but being an American did not mean that one had to sacrifice his personal integrity. In trying to look like someone else, a person gave up his own identity, just as in joining a mob, he relinquished individuality. Conformity meant that a person no longer believed in himself, that he was no longer a moral agent. In the *Messenger*, Schuyler tells an amusing tale about a young black girl who works as a maid for a lecherous middle-aged white man. The girl is ashamed of her dark skin and takes arsenic tablets to lighten it. At the same time, she has a very high regard for her chastity, so that when her employer predictably tells her that he wishes to set her up in a plush apartment, she replies, "No, Mr. Morrison. I'm one colored girl that can't be bought." The irony, of course, lies in the fact that she has already been bought. She has prosti-

tuted herself to a system that says "white is right," and her haughty
refusal of Mr. Morrison's offer is a moral gesture by someone already
compromised.[83]

Schuyler waged an endless war against such trivial items as hair
straighteners because he saw them as symbols of capitulation, of the loss
of the moral self. (He comically remarked on one occasion, "As a group
we have year by year been getting lighter and lighter, both as to com-
plexion, morals and brains.")[84] The inability to make moral distinctions
was a constant theme in his attacks upon black society's "best people." In
one *Messenger* story, "Seldom Seen," a gambler courts a high-toned
young lady but is rejected by her parents because his "profession" is not
dignified enough. However, a fast deal with a bootlegger brings him new
wealth, and he buys a partnership in a "tonsorial" parlor (actually a front
for his illicit booze). As a consequence, because he now owns "half-
interest in the biggest Negro business in Baton Rouge,"[85] he undergoes a
sea change in the girl's eyes and her family's. Cash has cleared up his
reputation (the beer bottles hiding behind the barber chairs are conveniently overlooked), and he is given permission to marry the girl.

In other tales, color replaces cash as the prime corrupter of ethical
values. The value placed on a light skin in "At the Darktown Charity
Ball" emphasizes the irony of the play's title.[86] The "best people" have no
charity, and the darker brother is a pariah at his own dance. In a farce
called "The Yellow Peril," a prostitute admits that she is only another
white woman downtown, but "up here I am worshipped by all the
successful businessmen, professional fellows and society swells, because I
am a high yaller."[87] Here Schuyler's satire is directed less at the girl than
at the "swells" who are duped by her. She herself is a symbol of their
grand illusion that they are important because they have her on their
arms.

In Schuyler's satire, the "best people" are both foolish and vicious.
They have an unreal picture of themselves, and Schuyler does not hesitate
to puncture the balloon. "This black bourgeoisie consists of doctors,
lawyers, dentists, undertakers, school teachers, kink removers, editors,
barbers, and the proprietors of some small businesses. Many of these
people have considerable means, but in the main, they are really black
coated workers—white collar slaves—catering to the needs, desires and
whims of the Negro population. The Negroes of the Empire State are
precariously hanging onto the fringes of the economic life of the com-
munities in which they live."[88] That is, this social class is no leisured
aristocracy. Also, it is an odd assortment of miscellaneous types, most of
whom are on the make, but who are in fact being made themselves by the
system under which they live. Nevertheless, they do think of themselves
as the old aristocracy, especially the "doctors, dentists, undertakers,

clergymen, and, of course, the ubiquitous school teachers."[89] Schuyler's comedy grows sharp when he notes that money—the one thing the "best people" all worship—has brought the old aristocrats some strange bedfellows. In "At the Darktown Charity Ball," doctors and dentists rub shoulders with bootleggers and "number barons," criminal elements that now make up the new aristocracy.[90] Although Old Money presently snubs the new aspirants to social recognition, Schuyler suggests that the latter's flourishing green, like a patented spot remover, will soon rid their reputations of all blemishes. After all, the "best people" once looked down upon the lowly undertakers, until "the influenza epidemic [of 1919] made their social position unassailable."

The lust for money among the "best people," to the exclusion of all other values, leads Schuyler to discourse upon his favorite theme: the "Higher Mendicancy." The new "mendicants" are "gentlemen of color who became experts in the art of extracting coin to save the race."[91] They are professional beggars who use moral issues like lynching and segregation to prey upon the sympathies of whites and make money for themselves. Although it is tempting to charge Schuyler with a certain insensitivity in attacking people like W.E.B. DuBois and Walter White, we must keep in mind that he was after much larger game than just these individuals. Schuyler's satiric point was the same as Mencken's: the tendency in American life for every idealistic venture to develop into a scam, and for every scam to hide behind an idealistic facade. For Schuyler, Negro artists have learned the "game" from the professional "mendicants":

If old Kinckle and "Rusty" of mendicant fame,[92]
Grabbed off wads of cash in the panhandle game;
Cannot we alleged writers and singers and such,
Playing on "racial differences," cash in as much?[93]

Although this jingle seems to express a hostility to Negro art, Schuyler was attacking the "hokum" side of the Renaissance, not the Renaissance itself—as we shall see in chapter 4.

That the best-intentioned plan may go astray is Schuyler's theme in his first novel, *Black No More* (1931). Dr. Crookman has developed a formula to turn Negroes into white men, but no matter how altruistic his intentions at the beginning, he is soon corrupted by his invention. Inevitably, one form of graft (selling color for money) leads to another. Max Disher (now a white man known as Mat Fisher) uses his newly cleansed exterior to con his way into the Knights of Nordica (heir to the defunct Ku Klux Klan), to marry its leader's daughter, and to become one of the most powerful figures in the South. He is, of course, Schuyler's "nigger in the woodpile." Since Max knows so much about the white man's fears, he has achieved his place of authority by preying on them. The results of his methods illustrate Mencken's thesis that intelligent discussion on any issue in America is impossible, because sooner or later all controversy degenerates into emotionalism, into the holding forth of the "bugaboo." In one situation, Max is called in by a group of factory owners to stop a possible strike in their plant. He does so by pretending to be a labor organizer who is desperately worried that among the workers may be some newly whitewashed Negroes. All discussion of rights and wages ceases; racial purity becomes the battle cry of the moment. At the end of the purge in their own ranks, the workers return to their jobs, as poor and as ignorant as the day they challenged their bosses. Objects of laughter and not pity, they have duped themselves. When the flag with the word "nigger" was waved, they charged blindly after it.

Schuyler's satire stretches even further, however. It seems that the new process of color conversion has caused havoc among those Negroes who have been making money from the racial conflict in America.[94] Madame Sisseretta Blandish, who has risen to a prominent place in the black community because of her hair straighteners, whitening creams, and arsenic tablets, now goes bankrupt. So too the leaders of the National Social Equality League (the NAACP) are in a panic because there is no longer any Negro to save, and thus no longer any money coming in from white philanthropists. Here is a situation worthy of Bernard Mandeville's "Grumbling Hive: Or, Knaves Turn'd Honest." Suppose, the eighteenth-century satirist imagines, that all the members of a society become completely virtuous overnight, would we then have a utopia? Well, yes and no. The moral order would be restored, but the society would be poor. Suppose, said Schuyler, that the Negro could lose overnight the stigma that condemns him to pariah-hood, would all Negroes be happy? Not quite. Max Disher has found happiness because he has developed a new scam, but Dr. Shakespeare Agamemnon Beard (DuBois) and Walter Williams (White) are miserable because they have lost theirs.

One reason Schuyler's book has been neglected by modern readers (or has simply been misunderstood)[95] is that he is recreating an older kind of satire: the world of knaves and fools, which so delighted classical antiquity and the English Renaissance. Max Disher is the clever servant who turns the tables on his masters. Moreover, the novel's ending repeats an important theme in Swift. In his famous "Argument Against Abolishing Christianity," Swift reminds us that man's flaws cannot be removed simply by legislating against them. So too we discover in *Black No More* that the removal of skin coloration has not solved the racial problem in America. Those who took Crookman's cure are now being discriminated against; since they are paler than real Caucasians, it has become fashionable to cultivate a sun tan in order to prove that one belongs to the original, exclusive group.

In *Black No More*, the perversity of human nature continually reasserts itself, and for Schuyler this perversity is best described in terms of the endless folly of human nature. The novel's theme implies that self-interest will always be a more powerful drive than either race loyalty or moral integrity. However, Schuyler never quite gives up hope. Near the novel's conclusion, when almost the whole world is white, Max Disher discovers the existence of one woman who has refused to go along with the mob, who has refused to conform to the general norm of literal and metaphysical paleness. "How come she didn't get white, too?" Max asks his friend Bunny. The latter responds, with "a slight hint of pride in his voice," "She's a race patriot. She's funny that way" (p. 195). For Schuyler (as for Mencken), one sane man tests the rule that all men are mad; one generous man tests the rule that all men are corrupt. There is only a hint of light in this American *Dunciad*, but a hint is enough.

Given Schuyler's overall theme, it is not surprising that he asked Mencken to write an introduction to *Black No More*:

> You are in my opinion the best person to write such an introduction because I think you most thoroughly appreciate my point of view. What I have tried to do in this novel is to laugh the color question out of school by showing up its ridiculousness and absurdity. Practically all writers who have sought to deal with this question have been too damn serious either in one direction or the other depending on the so-called race to which they belonged. I have tried to deal with it as a civilized man; to portray the spectacle as a combination madhouse, burlesque show and Coney Island.[96]

The "point of view" that Schuyler expected Mencken to understand was one that Mencken himself had often assumed. In America, Schuyler seems to be saying, the racial "spectacle" is irrational, but a "civilized" man can make sense of it. He can detach himself from the lunacy to see certain universal principles at work. In addition, although the spectacle threatens to overwhelm us with its immediate and inescapable presence, the artist can distance us from it through laughter. Finally, since the spectacle is simply another manifestation of human folly, there is no hope for altering it. Pious writers of both races have wasted barrels of ink in trying to find utopia. Their appeals have always been to the fine sentiments of mankind, never to its intelligence. *Black No More*, Schuyler implies, will appeal to those who belong to Mencken's spiritual aristocracy—to those who take pride in the sharpness of their wits, not in the fullness of their emotions.

Yet Schuyler's attitude does not express the whole truth about the
Renaissance's satire. Its members wanted to do more than laugh "with a
few friends in a corner"—to quote the epigraph that I have chosen for
this chapter. They seriously expected that satire would be efficacious.
That is, they assumed that whereas the racist would not be moved by
direct appeal or rebuke, he would feel the sting of satire. This view was
wishful thinking, as was the belief that Negroes would be respected as a
people once they could prove to the world that they were artistic. It did
not take the Renaissance's writers long to discover the fallacy of both
ideas, yet they could never quite escape the ideals of civilization that lay
behind them. Even in *Black No More* Schuyler hoped that civilized men
would stand together against folly; if they could not remove it, at least
they could laugh at it—in concert.

Thus it is not surprising that W.E.B. DuBois could admire *Black No
More*, even though he had been personally attacked in the novel.
"Schuyler's satire," said DuBois, "is frank, straight-forward, and universal."[97] By this he meant that the enemy was clearly defined, be he
black or white, and so were the values that the satirist held. Yet DuBois
was harshly critical of Schuyler's second novel, *Slaves Today*, and his
criticism pointed to what DuBois believed was happening to many of the
decade's younger writers. The trouble with *Slaves Today*, said DuBois,
was that Schuyler substituted his brief impressions of Liberia for solid
research on the subject.[98] The implication was that Schuyler had become
facile where once he had been profound, and, as we shall see, Mencken
was to share the blame for what was considered the new flippancy of the
younger generation.

Yet before I treat this theme in more detail in chapter 5, I shall
look at the dream that both old and young held before it fell apart. It was
a dream as ancient as Western civilization itself, but it had been given
new life by the special circumstances of the 1920s. For if the Renaissance
means anything, the intellectuals argued, it means that artist and audience
live in a unified community—a community in which artist and audience
share a common experience and a common understanding. If white people
refuse to hear the black artist, that is one thing; but surely he may count
on the good will of the people whose lives he is expressing. That this
dream turned out to be without substance is a large part of the history of
the Harlem Renaissance, a history that began with grand ideals and
ended in bitter arguments and fragmented perspectives.

CHAPTER FOUR

The Dream of the Secular City: Mencken, Locke, and the "Little American Renaissance"

Without great audiences, we cannot have great poets.

—Walt Whitman

If there was one literary figure in the America of the 1920s who symbolized the divisions between country and city, it was Mencken. Though often gruff and uncivilized in person, he always spoke for civilized values—a sense of fair play, a refined aesthetic response, a heightened intelligence—and he saw the city as the provider of these values. Mencken sometimes gave the impression that *all* rural areas were simply the South writ large. Occasionally he sounded as if he could take the place of Dorimant on the Restoration stage, to whom it is said, "I know all beyond Hyde Park's a desert to you." This of course applies to the public Mencken, the Mencken given to large generalizations; the private Mencken could be much more charitable to country pleasures.[1] Yet it is the public Mencken who caught the eye of the Harlem Renaissance's intellectuals, and they often shared his sentiments about the country, especially if the country meant the South. In Mencken's sometimes polarized world, the country was peopled by the boorish "Husbandman" whose greed threatened the economic fabric of the Republic and whose morality forced Prohibition upon its cities. The word "Prohibition" meant more to Mencken than just a short supply of spirituous liquors; it suggested the very antithesis of good temper, amiability, grace, and "moral innocence." It suggested a world of nay-saying, pinchy-assed Puritans. As we have seen, the Renaissance's intellectuals more than once made the connection between puritanism and racism, and Mencken tended to locate both in the country. A very real reason that Mencken appealed to the black intellectuals of the 1920s was that he personified an idea of the city for them—the city as a community of sophisticated men and women.

Why at this time was the opposition between country and city so acute? Light is shed on this question by a simple statistic that startled Americans in the initial year of the decade. In 1920, the census takers had noted for the first time in the nation's history that there were more people living in the cities than in the country. To be sure, the percentage of city over rural dwellers was small—about 51 to 49 percent—and the survey itself was not precise (the census takers had named as cities small towns of twenty-five hundred people).[2] Nevertheless, the facts revealed by the census were indicative of what had been happening to America since the end of the Civil War. It was rapidly becoming an urban civilization, though not without—as the political battles of the 1920s showed—some strong resistance to this new turn of events. As we know, black people shared in the general migrations to the cities, and the process had been accelerated by the worsening conditions in the South. "Before 1910," states Burl Noggle, "some 90 per cent of all blacks in the United States lived in the South," but during World War I, "a half-million" southern Negroes fled to the urban North.[3] A statistic such as this explains Alain Locke's emphasis upon the city in *The New Negro* (1925), the anthology of arts and letters which served as the manifesto of the Harlem Renaissance, but it does not explain his idealization of Harlem as a cultural Mecca.

It is possible to consider Mencken's view of Baltimore as a clue to Locke's conceptualization of Harlem, though both attitudes can be traced back to a pattern of ideas about culture which belong to the pre-World War I years of the "little American renaissance." Mencken was very much a part of that period's optimism about America's literary future, but he also came to question its first premise, the idea of the unified community, a premise that Alain Locke and other Renaissance intellectuals wanted to believe was a distinct possibility for Harlem. In fact, when the dream of the secular city failed for the Renaissance, Mencken was often the first person the intellectuals turned to for an explanation. Nonetheless, Mencken did believe that the city was America's last, best hope. Yet it was not the gaudy "carnival" of New York that he admired, but Baltimore—a city small enough to accommodate elegance and urbanity as well as a proper reverence for neighborhood and the household gods. In short, Mencken wanted the best of both worlds, for his ideal city was a kind of fifth-century Athens, in which one could be both cosmopolitan and a citizen. Although he worked in New York, he continued to live in Baltimore all his life. His complaint against Gotham was that few people owned their own homes, so that the mass of New Yorkers were reduced to the level of rootless vagabonds.[4] His ideal, as was Alain Locke's, was a city that is also a community, and the artist-audience debate among black intellectuals that took place in the 1920s was tied to this ideal of the city as the locus for the perfect community.

Thus, Locke engineered a view of Harlem in his anthology, *The New Negro*, that tried to achieve just the right balance between the citizen and the sophisticate, between community and culture. For instance, in James Weldon Johnson's *New Negro* essay, "Harlem: The Culture Capital," Johnson argued that Harlem is like an "Italian colony," but it is not a "quarter." The Harlemite is a villager in that he belongs to a well-defined community, and he is also a world traveler in that he can participate, if he so desires, in the rich life of the city beyond his immediate neighborhood.[5] In *The New Negro*, Locke himself marveled at the diversity of black people in Harlem—West Indian, African, city Negro, country Negro—at the same time saying that "their greatest experience has been the finding of one another" (p. 6).

In his introductions to the separate sections of *The New Negro*, Locke constructed a model of the perfect community, one that he believed to be based upon empirical evidence. He argued in his anthology that the present migrations of Negroes to Harlem have resulted in a cultural metamorphosis. The old rural Negro was naive, mentally insular, and afraid of his own shadow. Before the urban experience, the only bond between black people was "that of a common condition rather than a common consciousness; a problem in common rather than a life in common" (p. 7). However, in this new city-state in the North, Negroes are finding that their shared experience as a people comes not from an outer-directedness (we versus they) but from an inner-directedness (I am like him because I live with him in this community). By living together in Harlem, Locke said, Negroes are coming to maturity as a people—they are undergoing a "spiritual Coming of Age" (p. 16). In the past, they saw through a glass darkly, but now they see each other face to face.

The advantage of this communal situation for the Negro artist is obvious: If the great Greek dramatists were nurtured by Athens and, in turn, wrote great plays to sustain its spirit, the Negro artist might recreate this perfect symbiotic relationship between artist and audience in Harlem. Even now, Locke noted, the younger generation is experiencing this "life in common." Throwing off the "trammels of Puritanism," it refuses to depict black people as victims, the community of black people as the oppressed (p. 50). Young people are investigating their Negro heritage and the life around them in the hopes of creating realistic portraiture rather than propaganda. Soon the black audience will recognize its face in the mirror of art, Locke believed, no longer seeing the gross distortions of the past, and it will support and applaud the black artist: "So, in a day when art has run to classes, cliques and coteries, and life lacks more and more a vital common background, the Negro artist, out of the depths of his group and personal experience, has to his hand almost the conditions of a classical art" (p. 47).

For Locke, the "personal" and "group" experiences will be one. Whereas before Negro writers "spoke to others and tried to interpret, they now speak to their own and try to express." Locke's sentence—neatly holding antithetical elements in balance—reflects his belief in the value of the unified community for black artists. In the past, they spoke from the outside to the outside; they described themselves as case studies to people who knew them not. Now, however, they express themselves from within, yet the "expression" is always larger than "self," since it comes from an individual who has been formed by the living community. Thus, no matter how individual the voice, the artist's work will always reflect the community's values and consciousness. Locke's basic premise is that Negro artists "now speak to their own," because their own are ready to listen.

The crucial element in Locke's paradigm is the black audience. As he was to admit many years later, the literary movement had symbolized the triumph of realism and the defeat of special pleading, but more importantly the young writers of the 1920s had "turned inward to the Negro audience in frankly avowed self-expression."[6] Yet even before 1940, he would also admit that the first generation of New Negro writers (1917-1934) had been "handicapped by having no internal racial support for their art, and as the movement became a fad the taint of exhibitionism and demagogery inevitably crept in."[7] What had happened to the black audience? Like the rabbit in the magician's hat, it seemed to appear and disappear in the same instant. Whatever happened to it, the dream of there being one to support the Harlem Renaissance was shared by every black intellectual of that generation—including George Schuyler, who had insisted that the whole literary uproar was pure "hokum." People as different as W.E.B. DuBois and Wallace Thurman, or Kelly Miller and Theophilus Lewis—men who had trouble agreeing on a consistent attitude toward the Ku Klux Klan—did agree on this one thing: the need for a Negro audience. Old Guard and Young Turks alike complained of the Negro's unwillingness to support his own, and the point most often repeated was Whitman's: "Without great audiences, we cannot have great poets."

In truth, Locke's ideal black audience in *The New Negro* was a myth, just as was his city-state (Harlem). But it was a useful myth, one that had been put together with great care. And it had not been his alone: The nostalgia for the organic society was a seminal idea in the literary and cultural revolt that had been going on since the turn of the century—the revolt against the genteel tradition. Both Mencken and Locke played their parts in this revolt—Mencken fighting in the trenches and Locke mopping up after the real battle had occurred.

The real battle, of course, had been fought by a generation of white writers which had preceded the Harlem Renaissance by only a few years. Known as the "little American renaissance," this group of writers and critics had included such distinguished names as Van Wyck Brooks, Waldo Frank, and Randolph Bourne, and their influence may be seen in the works of Lewis Mumford and Paul Rosenfeld. All these men were concerned with the subject of a proper audience for the American writer. They felt that if the American public could provide a sympathetic atmosphere for the artist, then a rebirth of the arts was possible. Mencken had been on the periphery of this group, but he never actually joined it. Nonetheless, he not only contributed his views to their analyses of American culture, he also wanted to believe in their ideals. At times, he was seen by the members of the "little American renaissance" as the grand old warrior in the fight against puritanism; and yet his cynicism and flippancy were often deplored. In truth, Mencken was as ready as the next man for the renaissance to arrive; and, like the others, he too was preoccupied with the theme of community and the artist's relationship to it. That he was less optimistic than the members of the "little American renaissance" was due to his natural skepticism; a small voice kept telling him that Americans were never going to escape the heritage of their past. He also doubted whether the artist's audience would be—or could be—as extensive as the more enthusiastic of the younger men believed. Acting as the gadfly of the "little American renaissance," Mencken ironically came to play the same role vis-à-vis the Harlem Renaissance.

Appropriately, it had been Locke's former mentor at Harvard, George Santayana, who had defined the spiritual divisions in American society which came to preoccupy the members of the "little American renaissance." Santayana argued that the weekday ways of Americans had nothing in common with their professed ideals—ideals that had been bequeathed to them by society's Brahmins.[8] These ideals formed the basis of the American's conception of "culture," for they were garnered from Great Literature, and they existed in the rarified atmosphere of Thought. Moreover, these same ideals stood guard over our Morals, refined our crude Sensibilities, and provided the criteria by which all literature was to be judged. Unfortunately, said Santayana, such "opinions," while noble in themselves, bore no relationship to life as Americans actually lived it.

These opinions, which were expressed from the Ivory Tower (the pulpit and the academy), came to be associated with both the genteel tradition and puritanism.[9] To the rebels of the "little American renaissance," the first tradition suggested an effete, emasculated literature, and the second, a literature fit only for Mencken's shoe-drummers and shopgirls. Thus, for those critics around 1911 who wished to champion a new American literature, puritanism and the genteel tradition were joined in an obscene embrace. To flagellate puritanism, then, became a way of dealing with genteel conservative critics—Paul Elmer More, Irving Babbitt, Stuart Sherman—who represented the literary establishment and who made it difficult for a writer such as Dreiser to gain an audience or even to get published.

While the critics of puritanism gathered like a crowd at a public hanging, the intellectuals who most interested Locke—Van Wyck Brooks, Randolph Bourne, Lewis Mumford, and, to a lesser extent, Waldo Frank—attacked puritanism with the hopes of overhauling the very foundations of American civilization. To these men, puritanism consisted of a set of attitudes which had persisted throughout our history and which had prevented Americans from experiencing a sense of national community. Bourne called the dominant puritan trait "the will to power."[10] It was the cancer of the disconnected self, who in arrogating everything to itself—whether salvation or money—destroyed the possibility of community. For Brooks, Bourne, Frank, and Mumford, the battleground was located in the antinomy of puritan versus polis. The puritan was moralistic, egocentric, and life-denying; the polis was pagan, social, and life-affirming.

It was Brooks who expressed for his generation this gap between the floating Faustian spirit and the viable community that could have supported him:

> The vague ideal of every soul that has a thought in every age is for that communion of citizens in some body, some city or state, some Utopia, if you will, which the Greeks meant in their word πολιτεία [commonwealth]. Those artificial communities—Brook Farms and East Auroras—are so pathetically suggestive of the situation we all are in. "We get together" (what an American phrase that is!) because we *aren't* together, because each of us is a voice crying in the wilderness, individuals, one and all, to the end of the chapter, cast inward upon our own insufficient selves.[11]

And in *America's Coming-of-Age*, Brooks further developed Santayana's idea of puritan dividedness. Puritanism, Brooks argued, has led to a strange bifurcation in the American character between the lowbrow, acquisitive businessman who can not rise above business and the highbrow intellectual who retreats to the Palace of Art in order to escape being overwhelmed by amorphous American life. Here, in short, is the tragic lot of the American artist: Unable to plant himself in the rich soil of a community, he speaks in windy abstractions to a nonexistent "ideal" audience.

Nevertheless, it was left to two disciples of Brooks, Randolph Bourne and Lewis Mumford, to find an urban home for the organic community.[12] Bourne had been impressed with the cultural unity of the European village, and he argued that this situation could be repeated within the American city. Taken as a whole, he said, America is an anticulture, represented by the colorless, tasteless "'movies,' the popular song, the ubiquitous automobile."[13] In this sense, nothing is distinctive about the American people; the melting pot has only melted out all their unique, individual identities. Fortunately, continued Bourne, this anticulture has a weak hold on Americans—they still remain a "federation of nationalities." Borrowing a phrase from Josiah Royce (another former teacher of Locke at Harvard), Bourne believed that "the Beloved Community" could exist within the walls of the city.[14] Given its diffuse population in a single geographical space, the city could foster separate "villages" of ethnic groups, and these would be healthily "provincial" in the Roycean sense of the word (belonging to a province whose collective self gave ballast to the individual ego). At the same time, these groups would be, by necessity, "unprovincial," for in living next to individuals who are as distinctive as they, they are forced to be tolerant and broadminded.

Bourne died of influenza at thirty-two, in the same year that the Great War ended, but his dreams for an American city-state were passed on to Lewis Mumford. In his first book, *The Story of Utopias* (1922), Mumford set out not simply to describe the history of imaginary societies, but rather to present a rigorous criticism of our own social failures. The irony of Mumford's study is that these unreal cities (for cities are the utopias he had in mind) are more real than our own botched cities. For although they are fictions of the imagination, they are in touch with the needs of the human spirit. Plato, said Mumford, could not have conceived of a city-state whose population was so large and so spread out that all sense of community was lost.[15] After all, the purpose of a city is to foster the interrelationship of human activity, the communication of ideas, the continuity of human experience. Once the city loses its telos—its capacity to bind people together in a living organic whole—it is no longer a city. It becomes something else: a place for manufacturing goods, a place for selling real estate, a place for "a rabble of individuals 'on the make.'"[16]

The medieval cathedral town is Mumford's ideal, but its destruction came with industrialization. The country house and coketown symbolize the bifurcation of the modern city, the schizophrenia, as it were, which corrupts it.[17] In the country house (the suburbs, in contemporary terms), goods are preferred to the good life; and in coketown, goods are produced for the consumers living in the country house. In this setting, art is simply a "product" like any other product; it no longer symbolizes the spiritual wellsprings of the community. In classical antiquity and the Middle Ages, Mumford argued, this divorce of art from the actual life of the polis was unknown. In fifth-century Athens, a person did not step outside his ordinary round of activities when he went to see a play; the play was as much a part of his existence as was the shoemaker's shop. By making art into a product, we have essentially reduced it to being "picturesque"— something to be "seen," without a relationship to any other experience. (One can easily discover here the basis of Locke's complaint against the treatment of Negro life as picturesque. Not only is it unrealistic, but also, by restricting the Negro character to being "colorful," the artist is abstracting him from his communal life; he is in fact creating a product for the "exotic tastes of a pampered and decadent public.")[18]

Mumford also had another point to make about art in its proper social context. In an ideal society, art is not "a personal cathartic for the artist"; it is "a means by which people who have had a strange diversity of experiences have their activities emotionally canalized into patterns and molds which they are able to share pretty completely with each other." The purpose of art is "to impregnate the community in which it exists with its ideas and images," and in turn the artist is nourished by the "patterns and molds" which he finds in the continuing community. Not only is the relationship between artist and audience reciprocal, but the common man is not excluded from the idea of an audience. "The notion," said Mumford, "that the common man despises art is absurd. The common man worships art and lives by it; and when good art is not available he takes the second best or the tenth best or the hundredth best." In a spiritually healthy society he gets the best; in a sick society he feeds on sick art: escapist literature, propagandist literature, "Pollyanna in the face of Euripides . . . 'just folks' in the face of Swift . . . niceness in the face of Rabelais."[19]

Throughout the 1920s, Mumford continued to hammer away at his favorite theme: art as a reflection of the health or sickness of a society.[20] It is worth noting, however, that this had been Mencken's theme throughout the pre- and post-World War I years, and that Mencken too had seen the city as a counterforce to the pervasive puritan hegemony. In fact, in 1917 he had contributed to the glow of optimism surrounding the "little American renaissance," for he ended his essay "Puritanism As a Literary Force" with this remarkable statement: "Maybe a new day is not quite so far off as it seems to be, and with it we may get our Hardy, our Conrad, our Swinburne, our Thoma, our Moore, our Meredith, and our Synge."[21] Although Mencken lampooned puritanism throughout this essay with his usual fierce indignation, he also fixed the reader's eye on those bursts of urban creativity which might pose as models for a revitalized American society. The English Renaissance in London, the French Enlightenment in Paris, Dionysus in Athens—these suggest an alternative to puritan sterility. And there is always the question of those feisty ethnic groups who have formed the mudsill of American civilization. Mencken described their quiet but heroic accomplishments in his usual, mock-deprecating way: "The only domestic art this huge and opulent empire knows is in the hands of the Mexican greasers; its only native music it owes to the despised negro."[22] This strange combination of ethnic creativity, Dionysian energy, and urban sophistication was to find its home in Locke's Harlem.

What Locke set out to do in *The New Negro* was to teach white Americans that the Negro had learned the truth of Oswald Spengler's remark that "all great cultures are city-born." This had been a significant theme in Robert Park's coauthored book on the city (*The City*), which was published in the same year as Locke's anthology. Locke would have known of the work of this noted sociologist through Charles S. Johnson, a former student of Park's at the University of Chicago and the man who had handpicked Locke for the role of Renaissance spokesman.[23] In *The City*, Park had argued that whereas the Anglo-Saxon became a romantic adventurer in the city, the immigrant sought to establish a community within the larger urban scene. Anglo-Americans, insisted Park, had much to learn from the "solidarity" of the Jews, the Negroes, and the Japanese.[24]

Solidarity, of course, is the theme of *The New Negro*, and the changes that Locke made in the original source for his anthology indicate the emphasis that he sought to achieve. Basing *The New Negro* upon his Special Negro Number for the *Survey Graphic* magazine (March 1925), Locke revised old material and added new. The *Survey* issue had attempted to depict Negro Harlem in all its various hues; it was seen as a dome of many-colored glass. *The New Negro*, in contrast, generally refrained from staining the white radiance of eternity—the Harlem it showed tended to shy away from either harsh realities or negative interpretations.[25] For instance, Locke excised an article from the *Survey* issue which had exposed the stark economic conditions of Harlem. In "Ambushed in the City: The Grim Side of Harlem," Winthrop D. Lane had listed all the ills that met the rural Negro as he got off the train: ruthless landlords, quack doctors, fake druggists, numbers runners, fortune tellers, bootleggers, gamblers, and other con men of various colors and persuasions. The article that replaced Lane's was Paul Kellogg's "Negro Pioneers," which applied Frederick Jackson Turner's thesis about the frontier to Harlem—this environment created new men, leveled class differences, called for "the spirit of team play" (p. 274).

Two other articles that Locke deleted from the *Survey* issue were Kelly Miller's "Harvest of Race Prejudice" and Eunice Hunton's "Breaking Through." Both articles saw the idea of a segregated community, such as

Harlem was, in a bad light. As Hunton said, Harlem was "self-sufficient, complete in itself," but this very fact made it a ghetto and created ghetto minds: "bound."[26] This was hardly the point Locke wanted to italicize in his new book. He sought to stress the living community as a force for the liberation of art, ideas, and consciousness. He steered clear of a Harlem where Blake's "mind-forged manacles" imprisoned the Negro within a world of warped perspectives and debilitating anger.

The most significant change that Locke made in his new book was to replace an article entitled "The Church and the Negro Spirit" with one (written by himself) called "The Legacy of the Ancestral Arts." The city of art was to be the Negro's new church—not the city of God. This secular city would bring him the salvation that the old dispensation had promised only in another world. And it would be salvation, for though Locke was supposedly talking about a real place, the idea of a city did have religious overtones for him, as is illustrated by his substitution of one DuBois article for another. DuBois's *Survey* article ("The Black Man Brings His Gifts") was just that—a survey of past contributions, whereas his *New Negro* article ("The Negro Mind Reaches Out") looked toward the future. Locke placed this essay at the end of *The New Negro*, in a clever rhetorical ploy. The image Locke wanted in the reader's mind as he closed the book was the portrait of Liberia—"a little thing set upon a Hill" (p. 414). This country was the New Negro's "City upon the Hill," the beacon light in Africa which called attention to the black man's new status in the world.

Thus Locke began and ended *The New Negro* with the idea of a city. He began with Harlem as a potential Athens (or a potential Dublin, Prague, or Paris) within the American scene,[27] and he ended with Liberia as an embryo that would grow into a new millenium for black people within the world. As a mythmaker, Locke seemed to be going against the American grain, for he was turning the pastoral myth upon its head: Harlem was a return to paradise, not a flight from it, and the chief characteristic of *his* American Adam was not innocence but urbanity.[28] And Turner's frontier—the place that magically turned Europeans into Americans—became a city in which doctors, lawyers, and ministers, by following their clientele from the South, were now capable of identifying with the masses. These new bonds meant that an audience was out there waiting for the Negro artist to express its "common consciousness." Locke never precisely identified this audience in *The New Negro*, but he assumed it was there, and he further assumed that the masses made up a good part of its membership.

What did not find a home in *The New Negro* was Mencken's general skepticism concerning the common man as a potential audience for a potential cultural renaissance. In order to appreciate the differences between Locke and Mencken on this matter, as well as to understand the source of a similar ambivalence that beset them, we must look more closely at Mencken's opinions concerning the idea of an audience for the American artist. If Mencken was not a full-fledged member of the "little American renaissance," he certainly accepted its basic premise. He agreed that the need for an audience was undeniable. "The notion that artists flourish upon adversity and misunderstanding, that they are able to function to the utmost in an atmosphere of indifference or hostility—this notion is nine-tenths nonsense. . . . Who was it who said that, in order that there may be great poets, there must be great audiences too? I believe it was old Walt. He knew."[29]

The problem with American culture, as Mencken saw it, is that the tyranny of the majority makes the existence of "great audiences" impossible. When the average man acts in concert with his brothers (and is given full power as in a democracy), he intimidates others so that they behave as he does. Thus mass man, paranoid and incapable of intellectual curiosity, attaches "bugaboos" to any object under discussion, and these stick like gum to a shoe. No idea is treated disinterestedly in America; it is either jingoed to the skies or hooted down, and those who hoot the loudest are often the very people who should serve as a responsible, spiritual aristocracy. From fear of being un-American, from fear of not showing the correct moral rectitude, they abandon their intelligence for emotionalism.

There is also another reason that America has failed to produce a spiritual aristocracy, an audience that would protect and support the American artist. Americans may be too good at what they do best. Because they are such expert hewers of wood and drawers of water, they are never tempted to give up this "industry" to do anything else. Consequently, America's rich "are too diligently devoted to maintaining the intellectual *status quo*" to serve as movers and shakers. "A great literature," states Mencken, "is thus chiefly the product of doubting and inquiring minds in revolt against the immovable certainties," so what chance does the artist have in a world of Bottom the Weaver?[30] The answer is, not much: "The artist in America stands in completer isolation than anywhere else on earth."[31] And the blame for this sad situation lies "chiefly . . . in the failure of the new aristocracy of money to function as an aristocracy of taste."[32]

Mencken's attack on America's philistinism could be misleading, because he did believe that money provides the necessary foundation for true aesthetic appreciation. The "connoisseur," he argued, is the "finest flower of civilization"—he makes possible the birth of beautiful things —yet his growth "presupposes economic security." This soil "is as essential to civilization as enlightenment."[33] Without money, there can be no intelligent sympathy, no "eager curiosity," no "educated skepticism," no "hospitality to ideas"—all those qualities that belong to the spiritual aristocrat,[34] the man who is free of chill penury. What has happened in America (and here Mencken was in agreement with the analyses presented by members of the "little American renaissance") is that money and material progress have become ends in themselves. Put quite simply, philistine self-satisfaction goes hand in hand with puritan self-righteousness. Energetic in their pursuit of money, Americans are intellectually slothful; they can not imagine ways of living other than their own, and lives they do not understand they call evil. Thus, when philistinism feels threatened, puritanism becomes a "force," carrying a banner for what it considers the Moral Order. In this situation, puritanism then calls itself the New Humanism. When philistinism feels at ease in Zion, puritanism simply becomes The Way of looking at the world. In either case, said Mencken, "the artist, facing an audience which seems incapable of differentiating between aesthetic and ethical values, tends to become a preacher of sonorous nothings, and the actual moralist-propagandist finds his way into art well greased."[35]

For Mencken, no class in American society escapes the curse of puritanism: The plutocrats count their money instead of buying books; the intelligentsia settle for "correctness" instead of vision; and the common man is simply indifferent to art. Is the last-named incapable of appreciating it, or is he corrupted by the antiintellectual nature of the society in which he lives? Mencken never quite answered this question. On the one hand, he took a firm stand against the common people as a possible audience. When William Allen White wanted to elevate the culture of Kansas by making arts "more a part of our daily lives," Mencken responded, "The truth is that the common people have no more capacity for comprehending the fine arts than they have of comprehending astrophysics."[36] Here he implied that even without the leveling effects of democracy, they would choose a barroom ditty over Beethoven. On the other hand, what about the railroad conductors and ice-men whom Mencken said knew a hawk from a handsaw? If they could "comprehend" sham, could they not also "comprehend" Beethoven? And further yet, was there ever a time when a barroom ditty might be an example of the "fine arts"? When he talked about the unknown bards of the Negro spirituals, he implied that such men might rival Beethoven. Did only "superior" men sing these songs, or were they sung by the masses? And if the masses did sing and listen to them, would that fact not argue for some kind of sophisticated aesthetic response—not the response, perhaps, needed to appreciate Beethoven but a response that might be just as sophisticated, only of a different kind? That Mencken never seriously considered this possibility, that he remained tied to his concept of High

Art despite his passionate interest in "folkways," is one of the mysteries of his personality. And it is also one of the paradoxes that plagued the Harlem Renaissance. Its leaders were determined to have a literary movement supported by the common people, and yet they could not quite believe in that group's intelligence or artistic tastes.

Raymond Williams has pointed out the serpent that lay waiting in Locke's urban paradise. Although in his excellent book, *Culture and Society, 1780-1950*, he is discussing English social thought and not American, several of his generalizations provide an incisive critique of *The New Negro* — and, for that matter, of "the little American renaissance." Those who argue for an organic society, says Williams, face a special problem. They wish to posit a society based upon interrelatedness, not individualism, and they argue for human values, not material ones. They set qualities such as "refinement," "loyalty," and "art" against the "cash nexus," the *only* bond in a society run by a laissez-faire philosophy. In short, they set "culture" against "anarchy," against a world that fails to make meaningful discriminations. Yet in the very act of asserting that there are bonds more precious than cash, that there are values more important than material goods, lies a dangerous tendency to define culture as something separate from, and superior to, common people.[37] The organic society then slips into a feudal arrangement in which, as Locke said in *The New Negro*, "the cultured few" interpret the folk-spirit to the yet inarticulate masses (p. 53).

The linchpin of Locke's entire aesthetic philosophy was the hope that the masses would become articulate. The Renaissance was to embrace everyone. Locke's complaint against modern society was that its life has no center, and hence its art reflects its fragmentary condition, its state of ill health. "It is the art of the people that needs to be cultivated," he told Negro writers, "not the art of the coteries."[38] Yet "cultivation" for Locke was a term of ambiguous reference, and he was not always sure how he wanted to use it. On the one hand, he tilled the common soil in the hopes that the common people would be "cultivated," that is, made responsive to their own artists. On the other hand, he talked of cultivation as something reserved for a special class of people. In this case, the mutual responsibilities of artist and audience (Locke's Athenian democracy) collapsed into the single responsibility of an aristocracy to the "best that is thought and said."

In his essay "The Ethics of Culture" (which originally had been a speech addressed to the elite of the Negro race, the students at Howard University), Locke contrasted the cultured individual with the "crowd" ruled by "the tyranny of the average and mediocre." The person who is self-reliant, Locke argued, can develop a refined sensibility and a discerning judgment. Such a man becomes the backbone of a civilization or a race; if enough like him exist, he is capable of turning a country into a culture. Quoting Cicero, Locke took the aristocratic point of view; the elite of any country or race have an obligation to become cultured "for the welfare of the Republic."[39] Moreover, "when all the other aristocracies have fallen, the aristocracy of talent and intellect will stand."

Locke warned the Howard students that they might be working in certain areas of the country which could truly be called the "Saharas of culture": "You betray your education, however, and forgo the influence which as educated persons you should always exert in any community if you subside to the mediocre level of the vulgar crowd." In this essay, Locke assumed that the attitudes of the masses are more or less permanent, and that the man of culture must separate himself from them: "In the pursuit of culture one must detach himself from the crowd." Yet we see here two influences at war upon Locke. He wanted to believe with Royce that the "mob-spirit" in man was only temporary—the consequence of not having a genuine community to give him definition.[40] Yet, like Mencken, Locke simply could not rid himself of the idea that the masses are unintelligent.

Another generation of Negro writers would argue that the masses failed to support the Harlem Renaissance not because they were stupid but because they were poor. Furthermore, even though they were poor, they did love art—not the High Art of the Renaissance but the art of everyday life: music, dancing, the oral tradition. Curiously, Locke had demanded that this folk art be recognized, that it be treated in literature, but in this he remained ensnared by a version of the genteel tradition from which even Mencken had not freed himself. The written word was superior to the oral word, and literature was still to be spelled with a capital *L.* Poetry, by definition, was superior to either the blues or jazz, so Locke used it, and not music, as a means by which to measure "the present cultural position of the Negro in American life." It, and not music, was "the serious art which can best represent to the world the Negro of the present generation."[41] Both he and Mencken rebelled against middle-class gentility but ended up substituting an aristocratic gentility that would not take the art of the masses seriously.

Mencken took the superiority of literature one step further. He recognized hierarchies of excellence within literature itself. Poetry was inferior to prose because it was a purveyor of emotion, not ideas; the very nature of its form made it fit for lyricism but not for philosophy or realism. And yet Mencken loved music, perhaps the most emotional of all the arts. Given his low view of an emotional appeal in art, how could he argue that Beethoven was more "rational" than jazz? Still, he did just that because, like Locke, he was committed to High Art as he narrowly defined it, and so he overlooked the significance of jazz artists like Duke

Ellington, Fletcher Henderson, and Jelly Roll Morton who had large white followings, and he appeared to miss entirely the purer black artists such as Bessie Smith, Ma Rainey, Blind Lemon Jefferson, and Charley Patton. This last omission is especially ironic since, as we know, as poor as the black masses were, they did support an art that reflected their real culture. The phenomenon known as "Race Records" is a case in point. In the 1920s, recordings of black blues were sold out of suitcases and off the backs of trucks in impoverished rural areas, and in funky music stores (or in any kind of store) in the urban ghettoes. And though the sharecroppers, housemaids, and garbagemen who bought them were hardly "connoisseurs" in Mencken's sense of the word, they did have the connoisseur's nonmaterialistic appreciation of art. After all, they were often so poor that they had difficulty financing their next meal, and yet they bought records (and financed a musical industry) that fed their souls. We know, for instance, that by the mid-1920s Race Record companies were selling "five or six million records annually" (to a Negro population of about double that number), that "blues records were not cheap" (seventy-five cents to one dollar each for the expensive ones), and that even high prices "did not deter sales of over 20,000 for the more popular Bessie Smith issues."[42] Here indeed was an audience willing to sacrifice a good deal for art.

Yet neither Mencken nor Locke recognized this kind of cultural response to art, because they were plugged into a certain view of culture. And in this light, it could be argued that the intellectuals of the Harlem Rensiassance simply repeated the same circular pattern that had limited the members of the "little American renaissance." *Seven Arts* magazine (1916-1917), as Warner Berthoff notes in his stimulating book *The Ferment of Realism*, had announced in its first issue that the time was ripe for a rebirth of the arts in America, and in such an epoch "the arts [would] cease to be private matters." American artists would now participate in a new fellowship to express the "national self-consciousness" of a people, perhaps even to create it. Yet Berthoff points out that even as this ideal relationship between artist and audience was being set forth, *Seven Arts* also asked the artist who contributed to its pages that he be true to his own artistic vision, to "self-expression without regard to current magazine standards."[43] In this instance, "self-expression" is set in opposition to "magazine standards," which are seen as a debasement of culture. However, if those standards are the same as those of the polis itself, how can an artist be responsible both to himself and to a world he feels alienated from? And even if those standards are not the same, asking the artist to be true both to himself and to the polis inevitably brings up the question of conflicting loyalties. Berthoff argues that the paradox of the artist's responsibility to himself and to the "consciousness" of a people was never resolved by the American intellectuals in the decade before the 1920s[44]—nor, it might be added, has it been resolved since.

Both Locke and Mencken had talked about the need of the artist to express himself—"avowed self-expression" was Locke's phrase—and yet they assumed that his expression could change things in the outside world. Mencken liked to believe that the audience for the American artist would be "aristocratic," but he left the door open to that august company for men such as N. H. Hall, the Pullman porter whom he published in the *Mercury*. And if the truth be told, he never quite gave up on the middle class—either the sodden plutocrats or the hustling "booboisie." In one *Smart Set* review after another (and the title of the magazine indicates his audience), Mencken attempted to raise the consciousness of readers whom he supposedly had given up on. And this didactic effort on Mencken's part (which continued in the *Mercury* as well) perhaps explains the difference between Mencken and most other white intellectuals in the postwar period. What they had realized was the total impossibility of elevating the consciousness of a nation whose middle class controlled not only the magazines but all cultural life in America. After the war, they fled to Europe, and although they sometimes wrote about America, they had no hope of expressing its soul. Intellectuals such as Mumford and Rosenfeld who remained behind still believed in the old dream of "great audiences" supporting "great poets," but the Harlem Renaissance actually tried to make the dream a reality. As Christopher Lasch and Marcus Klein have shown, the postwar white American writer had rebelled totally against a middle class that he felt was beyond saving.[45]

This was not really true for Mencken, however, and it was even less true for the Harlem intellectuals. For if one distinction can be made between the white intellectual of the 1920s and his black counterpart, it is this: The rebellion of the black American writer against his middle class was riddled with ambivalence. He may have done his share of complaining about the values of the middle class, but he hoped for, and expected, its loyalty. No spokesman for the postwar "little American renaissance" ever made the appeals to the white middle class that the black intellectuals made to theirs—nor did he express the corresponding disappointment and anger when that loyalty failed to materialize. Throughout the 1920s, the black middle class was cajoled, threatened, and satirized. One need only look at the title of an article written by Locke in 1925 to see the difference between black and white expectations. What white writer in 1925 would have entitled his attack on the middle class, "To Certain of *Our* Phillistines"?[46] (Italics mine.) Throughout his essay, Locke's anger is a clue to his real attitude—he wants to humble his audience so that it will recognize the true value of the Renaissance and support it. (It is no wonder that Locke's essay never had the effect he intended, for, as Larzer

Ziff observes, how does one educate the middle class without alienating it?)[47] Locke ended his essay with an analogy between the Negro artist as David and the black middle class as Goliath, and these two, we might say, remained engaged in mortal combat throughout the 1920s. No self-respecting white intellectual would have even thought of warfare with the middle class by this time — it was simply a lost cause.

Perhaps an explanation for this ambivalence concerning the black middle class can be found in the belief in the word "art." Throughout the 1920s, it was taken for granted that "art" was a talisman. Even the disgruntled DuBois was not an exception to this rule. Although he claimed that "all art was propaganda," his conception of propaganda was the same as his conception of art: truth about black life. Once that truth was told, then the Negro people would buy books about themselves. The counterpart of "art" was an audience whose taste was, to use DuBois's word, "catholic." Somehow the turn to art was to occur in a hermetically sealed world where the brute facts of economics were just a bit beside the point. It took the black writers of the 1930s to point out the errors of the Renaissance's ways. How can one talk about such matters as "culture" and "urbanity" and "taste," implied Richard Wright in 1937, when people are starving?[48] When it should have concerned itself with the environment in which Negroes lived, the Renaissance had been preoccupied with art. No Negroes bought its books, because none could afford them. And this situation was almost as true for the black middle class, argued E. Franklin Frazier in 1950, as it was for the masses. The "old" middle class, Frazier maintained, had inherited a cultural tradition from the nineteenth century, and though its members too had been poor, they loved beautiful things. The "new" middle class of the 1920s became infatuated with money, which nevertheless eluded its grasp. Desiring respectability as a substitute for the economic security it did not possess, the new middle class turned its back on the Renaissance, which was neither marketable nor respectable.[49]

And yet, despite its naivete, the Renaissance's preoccupations still tease us into thought. Locke wanted to believe that Brooks's organic community was present in Harlem, and, like Mumford, he wanted to believe that the common man loved art. Yet in fabricating a Harlem that never existed on sea or land, he created a New Negro who simply was not "common," and in throwing out the nastiness of city life, he managed to throw out the baby as well as the bathwater. For if Harlem had the "conditions for a classical art," was it still possible for that art to be "communal"? Not as Locke defined "classical art." An essay that reveals his definition with all its prejudicial overtones is "The Legacy of the Ancestral Arts," which he added very purposefully to *The New Negro*. In this essay, Locke clearly recognizes that African art is grounded in the lifeblood of the community; yet such was his penchant for High Art that he focuses upon the "classical background" of the African aesthetic heritage (p. 256). Discipline, technique, control, form, abstraction—these are qualities that belong to the Great Tradition in Western art as well, and these are qualities that Locke says the Afro-American artist should strive to achieve. Also, since the mastery of these qualities takes a lifetime of diligent application, Locke implies that only someone with sophisticated aesthetic taste can respond to this art. In fact, he strongly implies, and the article itself is proof, that with this kind of art we will need someone like Alain Locke to explain it to us.

Locke did not see that a people could have a communal art that might not be High Art but might in fact be the best art. The implications of Mumford's remark about the common man are relevant here. The common man loves art, said Mumford, and will take "the second best or the tenth best or the hundredth best" if good art is not available. But could not the "hundredth best" be the best if it were truly an expression of the people, like jazz or the blues? Locke's dilemma was that he wanted to recognize communal art, yet he kept trying to superimpose aesthetic values from without. Negroes should learn to appreciate literature, painting, and sculpture because they are superior art forms. Like Mencken, Locke ultimately cast his vote for an art that was elitist, and this was the flaw in his dream for a "democratic" utopia. He wanted art to be communal but not too communal, real but not too real, pagan but not too pagan.

As we have seen, Mencken opened the pages of the *Mercury* to black intellectuals so that they could discuss problems important to them, and no problem was more important in the 1920s than the subject of an audience. Since this same subject had preoccupied Mencken long after most white intellectuals had judged it a red herring, it is not surprising that he published an article by James Weldon Johnson that discussed the Negro author's "dilemma" regarding his audience. In this article, Johnson deviated from Locke's theme that the Negro now spoke primarily to his own, for Johnson noted that the black writer can not help thinking about a white reading public whether he wants to or not. In fact, Johnson defined the Negro author's dilemma as a kind of cultural schizophrenia, as a variation on DuBois's famous statement that the Negro in America sees the world with divided vision—as a Negro and as an American. Johnson said in the *Mercury* article that the Aframerican author faces a special problem which the plain American author knows nothing about—the problem of the double audience. It is more than a double audience; it is a divided audience, an audience made up of two elements with differing and often opposite and antagonistic points of view. His audience is always both white America and black America. The moment a Negro writer takes up his pen or sits down to his typewriter he is immediately called upon to solve, consciously or unconsciously, this problem of the double audience. To whom shall he address himself, to his own black group or to white America? Many a Negro writer has fallen down, as it were, between these two stools.[50]

According to Johnson, if the black writer fulfills the expectations of the white audience, he outrages his black audience; if he satisfies the black audience, he bores his white audience. The white reader wants the black character in literature to fit his conception of the black character in life: His nature is comic and his society is primitive. The black reader, however, wants a "*nice* literature," one that reflects the bourgeois aspirations of the race. "This division of audience," Johnson lamented, "takes the solid ground from under the feet of the Negro writer and leaves him suspended." In the future the best segments from these two audiences might fuse, Johnson suggested, but for the present the situation must remain uncertain.

The *Mercury* article was not Johnson's last word on the subject of audiences. He wrote an article for the *Crisis* six months later entitled "Negro Authors and White Publishers." In it he warned the black writer against making a "fetish of failure" as the result of believing the myth that white publishers accept only works that degrade the Negro. He pointed to an enormous list of recently published books reflecting the "upper" levels of black society, noting as well that they were far more numerous than those dealing with Harlem lowlife. The gist of his essay was that all levels of black life should be open to the artist and that the talented black authors have "as fair a chance today of being published as any other writers."[51] In short, Johnson urged the black writer to create art and to worry less about how he appeared to both black and white audiences.

In these essays Johnson spoke from two different platforms. In the first, he assumed that an artist created a work of art for a specific audience. "It is doubtful," he said, "if anything with meaning can be written unless the writer has some definite audience in mind." In the second, he argued from another position: The sanctity of art is the artist's only concern, and white publishers judge a man's writing on the basis of its intrinsic merit. Thus on the one hand, art is its own end, but on the other hand, it is rhetorical—its ultimate purpose is communication. Although

Johnson's two essays are not necessarily contradictory, the second reflects an unconscious answer to the dilemma stated in the first: If the black artist can not depend upon an intelligent audience, black or white, he can claim that he has an obligation to a higher authority, art. Johnson did in fact make such a claim at the end of his first essay, after he had admitted that the problem of an audience remained unsolved: "Standing on his racial foundation," he said, the Negro artist "must fashion something that rises above race, and reaches out to the universal in truth and beauty." Johnson's lofty conclusion in the face of his dilemma partially explains why the Negro artist in the 1920s sometimes became a poseur. Unable to trust either a black or a white audience, the black artist grew insecure and then self-conscious. He loudly declared that only "pure art" mattered, and he withdraw to Axel's Castle to create it.

Perhaps the most curious case of being troubled by a double audience was that of black novelist Walter White. In 1924, the year Knopf published *The Fire in the Flint*, White wrote to one correspondent, "I have told several publishers . . . that the reason colored people do not buy books is because publishers have not brought out the right sort, i.e. they have published caricatures of the Negro like the stories of Octavus Roy Cohen, Hugh Wiley, and Irvin Cobb, or base libels on the Negro like the vicious novels of Thomas Dixon."[52] However, when he talked about his own novel to Mencken, he claimed he had written it for white people. After Doran had rejected the manuscript of *The Fire in the Flint*, Mencken promptly suggested that White send it to a black publishing house, pointing out that he would meet the same "difficulties" from other white publishers "as you encountered with Doran."[53] But White replied that he wanted a white publisher, the more established and conservative the better. "Colored people know everything in my book—they live and suffer the same things every day of their lives. It is not the colored reader at whom I am shooting but the white man and woman who do not know the things you and I know."[54]

Now here is a strange paradox: White had complained to Eugene Saxton at Doran that no novelist in America's past had adequately portrayed "what an intelligent, educated Negro feels."[55] His novel, he argued, depicted the Negro in all his humanity. Surely, then, such a character as White's Dr. Kenneth Harper should appeal to black readers, yet he had said that he was "shooting at" a white audience. Why? He certainly wanted a black audience, for he told Mencken that he expected a huge sale to members of the NAACP.[56] I suspect, however, that White unconsciously knew that the black audience he had promised to white publishers was illusory. And, in fact, records in the Library of Congress indicate that it was illusory. White did try to sell the novel for Knopf through the NAACP, and the results were disastrous. For instance, the Denver branch returned seventy-six of the hundred copies it was asked to sell to its members, and since White had assumed financial responsibility, his royalty went toward paying for these copies.[57] Similar situations occurred in Sioux City, Omaha, and Des Moines,[58] and although White never gave up on the idea of securing a black audience, he quickly realized that the chief supporters of the Renaissance were white people.

Yet the problem of what the Renaissance imagined its audience to be is as interesting as the issue of why black people generally did not support it. Who made up this imaginary audience? What attitudes should it have? These were the questions James Weldon Johnson asked in his *Mercury* article, and they were asked by others throughout the decade. There is no doubt that the Renaissance's intellectuals expected their audience's tastes to be mature. In 1926, DuBois complained the "the young and slowly growing black public still wants its prophets . . . unfree." Talk of sex frightened it; religion insulated its outlook; its worst side had been shown so often "that we are denying we have or ever had a worst side." He urged "that catholicity of temper which is going to enable the artist to have his widest chance for freedom. We can afford the Truth."[59] Both Jean Toomer and Claude McKay agreed with DuBois that the black middle class had not grown spiritually. McKay told James Weldon Johnson that the Negro middle class did not like his novel *Home to Harlem* (1928) because it showed the realities of lower-class existence, which embarrassed them. He then added ominously, "We must leave the real appreciation of what we are doing to the emancipated Negro intelligentsia of the future, while we are sardonically aware now that only the intelligentsia of the 'superior race' is developed enough to afford artistic truth."[60] By the word "sardonically" McKay implied that no white man, however intelligent, can replace the black writer's rightful audience; at the same time he also repeated Mencken's complaint that his middle class had not developed into an "aristocracy of taste." Toomer too was to echo Mencken's view of the middle class, that it continued to remain mired in the puritan tradition. In a letter to Mae Wright, he noted that Negroes had never spiritually freed themselves from their enslavers: "We who have Negro blood in our veins, who are culturally and emotionally the most removed from the Puritan tradition, are its most tenacious supporters. We still believe, in fact we believe it now more so than ever, that a man's worth should be gauged by material possessions. . . . We are sceptical of the value of art."[61] In that same year, Toomer told Sherwood Anderson that he wanted to start a literary magazine "that would function organically for what I feel to be the budding of the Negro's consciousness." Yet, while he saw a "tragic need" for a magazine to provide "creative channels" for young black talent, he also suspected that black people generally would not respond to it. "In fact," he said, "they are likely to prove to be directly hostile."[62]

This theme of intellectual rot at the core of black middle-class life led Langston Hughes to attack the enemy in a Menckenian vein. For that matter, it might be said that all onslaughts upon the philistines involved Mencken's premise about America's plutocrats—that they had not developed into a spiritual aristocracy. That the Renaissance's intellectuals rarely stopped to ask if their plutocracy wasn't more show than substance is not surprising. For them, art had an intrinsic worth, so that they assumed that its brilliance should automatically attract people, whether they had money or not. If art did not attract people, then the people themselves were to blame. Langston Hughes, in his well-known essay "The Negro Artist and the Racial Mountain," could celebrate the Negro artist's triumph over two obstacles, racial prejudice (white people) and class indifference (middle-class black people), without looking too closely at the subject of an audience. "We," said Hughes—and here he referred to the other artists of his generation—"stand on the top of the mountain, free within ourselves."[63] A year later, however, writing for a black newspaper and not the *Nation*, Hughes would lash out twice against the narrow-mindedness of his own in a manner that sounded very much like Mencken's castigations of the American public. His attitude in these two newspaper essays fluctuated between his tacit belief that the artist stands in need of a select, understanding audience (which the present middle-class reader fails to provide) and his view that he could, if need be, make a virtue of Mencken's pronouncement that the American writer may have to do without an audience entirely. In any event, both essays seem to question Hughes's assured stance in "The Negro and the Racial Mountain."

In these articles, Hughes's anger is the outrage of disbelief more than anything else: How can my own people be this obtuse, this perverse? Does the middle class not realize that although *Cane* was well received throughout literate America, it remained virtually unknown in the city of Toomer's birth? Hughes found it incredible that the "best people" expected flattering portraits of themselves instead of honesty from Negro artists. And why? Because they wanted white people to think well of them. What great artists, Hughes snapped, echoing Mencken's attack on America's cultural humility, hold up their characters for a foreigner's approval? "Does George Bernard Shaw write plays to show Englishmen how good the Irish are?" And then Hughes added something that was more telling than he realized. "Does any true artist anywhere work for the sake of what a limited group of people will think rather than for the sake of what he himself loves and wishes to interpret?"[64] Some, like Mencken, would have answered "yes" to this question, if (and it was a big "if") that "limited group" had an intelligence and sympathy commensurate with the artist's own. Without realizing it, Hughes's criticism was putting him and his fellow artists in a room with only one exit. He ended the second article by implying that perhaps Negro artists would have to write for one another, since they could not depend upon anyone else in the community. We get some idea of the dilemma Hughes faced vis-à-vis his black audience if we pay attention to the implications of a statement he made in his *Nation* essay. Here the racial mountain is higher than he imagined: "Whereas the better-class Negro would tell the artist what to do, the people at least let him alone when he does appear." But to be "let alone" was hardly what Hughes and others of his generation wanted.

George Schuyler thought that there was a way of getting "the people" interested in the Renaissance, but it meant getting rid of what he called the "bulwarks of snobbery."[65] By this last phrase, he referred to the literary clubs in the black community which were usually "social affairs where much tea is guzzled and someone recites Gunga Din."[66] However, he did believe that these clubs contained the potentiality for creating a viable audience for the Negro writer, and he singled out The Saturday Evening Quill in Boston as a glowing example of what ought to exist: "There is room and need for one in every Negro community. Those who write ought to get together, read each other's work and get the value of each other's criticisms." In forming such a group, Schuyler urged, the common man should not be forgotten. "An effort should always be made to get the intelligent people in the community, irrespective of how much book knowledge they possess, to support such movements. Some will be found washing dishes, others doing laundry work, a few waiting tables or driving automobiles. It will be impossible to find very many because there are not very many intelligent people, but the majority will (or should) come from the working classes."[67]

In another article, he warned his fellow intellectuals that they must "humanize [their] knowledge and make it understandable to the washer-woman, the dishwasher, and the stevedore."[68] Avoid verbal fireworks, he advised young writers, and you will have an audience: "The bulk of readers, black and white, read to be entertained and not dazzled by the intellectual brilliance and rhetorical gymnastics of sophisticated literati." This does not mean, he continued, that you have to "ditch your themes and write garbage" to be appreciated; develop a lucid prose style to express them, and you will find that you will be read. For "it is nonsense to contend, as some of our literary folk do, that Negroes do not read. Negroes *do* read. Negroes read the daily newspapers, the Sunday Supplements and all of the magazines from *Breezy Stories* to the *American Mercury*."

Like Mencken, Schuyler was giving his elitism a democratic twist. There are not very many intelligent people in the world, but what few there are will not be found among the tea-guzzlers. Also, the onus suddenly shifts to the author, not the audience. Now it is the author who should be less elitist and more responsible to the common sense of his readers. Thus, Schuyler took Mencken's notion of the natural aristocrat and put the emphasis on the natural, not the aristocrat. Yet Schuyler, as we shall see, did not always have the courage of his convictions, and like other members of his generation, he wavered between an elitist view of art and an art that could flourish among the masses.

Schuyler's friend and partner in wit, Theophilus Lewis, also oscillated between an elitist attitude and a real belief in those lower down. He too agreed with Schuyler that the masses should take a more active part in the Renaissance, but the problem as he saw it lay in an appropriate method whereby they could be tricked into reading. First, a noble soul should take it upon himself to start a Negro publishing house. ("Next to a good fifteen-cent drink of liquor," such a venture is what "this country needs most.") Then he should employ some subtle strategy in his opening procedures. Since the masses know nothing about "art," the publishing house should begin by publishing junk—"adventure stories, uplift stories, love stories," and so on—but junk immersed in black life. This pulp would not only be profitable, it would also have a great educational value for both author and audience. "The success of the venture would turn the eyes of Negro writers inward toward the things and people they are familiar with." Once the "market for trash" had been conquered, the firm—and white firms as well—could then consider publishing books for "the intelligent minority of the race." Since by this time Negro writers would be accustomed to writing about their own kind for their own kind, they could now address themselves to producing good literature for an appreciative audience that presumably might begin to include some people from the lower classes. For Lewis, this step-by-step process was the only way out of an intolerable situation, black writers affecting "the ultra-sophistication of Oscar Wilde or James Branch Cabell" in order to please a white publisher who thought he knew what books by a black author white people would pay to read. The solution was that both writer and audience had to be educated by degrees to see the light.[69]

Schuyler and Lewis agreed that the common man had an aesthetic sense, but they took the position that it was unformed. They backed off from the possibility that it might have been formed in another direction. One can see, however, that in shifting the responsibility from audience to author they both had the uneasy feeling that perhaps High Art might not be the only kind of art. Here they were sharing Mencken's ambivalence. Not all black critics, however, felt that "standards" should be lowered.

Walter White argued that black artists must continue to strive for excellence, for prizes given to them could be pernicious if given "only because the artist is a Negro." White praised Sinclair Lewis for refusing the Pulitzer Prize, saying that "the battle for honest standards . . . has a direct bearing upon the future of Negro writers and poets and, in turn, on all of us." White assured his readers that if the artist refused to yield to mediocrity, his audience's taste would improve.[70]

The whole idea of "honest standards," of course, was the reason that most black intellectuals tended to look toward the middle class for their audience. Despite his interest in elevating the tastes of the proletariat, Schuyler had certainly placed his faith in the middle class. When Jessie Fauset's novel *There Is Confusion* was published in 1924, Schuyler was enthusiastic: "Here for the first time we are presented with a novel built around our own 'best' people who, after all is said, are the inspiration of the rising generation." He urged Negroes to buy her book, so that "there will be a widening field of opportunity for our rising group of young writers, struggling to express the yearnings, hopes, and aspirations of the race."[71] But the "best people" did not turn out to be the inspiration Schuyler had hoped for. Three years later he chastised these "best people" for complaining about *Nigger Heaven* and yet not supporting their own authors who *do* try to portray the most respectable side of Negro life: "Jessie Fauset's book *There Is Confusion*," Schuyler said, "fell almost flat from the standpoint of sales."[72]

Schuyler's disappointment in a black audience sheds a little light on why he might have written "Negro Art Hokum." If there were no internal support for the Renaissance, why not argue that there was no such thing as Negro art, only American art? If the Negro were only a "lamp-blacked Anglo-Saxon," then he merely reflected the larger sins of the Republic, which, as Mencken had shown, had proven catastrophic for the American artist. Although Schuyler could occasionally creep into Mencken's haven of skepticism, he was not — as indeed Mencken was not — always comfortable there. For someone who believed that Negro art was a misnomer, Schuyler spent a disproportionate amount of time trying to talk Negroes into supporting their writers.

If the masses were immature and the middle class superficial and cowardly, where did one turn? Theophilus Lewis's theatrical criticism in the *Messenger* tried to turn in all directions at once. Predictably, Lewis noted that a "discussion of the theatre can quite properly begin with the public." For "nowhere," he continued, "is the intimate relationship between art and life more clearly expressed than it is by the reciprocity existing between the public and the stage."[73] But the Negro public, Lewis complained, has not held up its end of the bargain. The groundlings support the Negro theater with their "quarters and half-dollars" but unmistakably impose their low taste and standards upon productions. The middle class, offended by such buffoonery, stays away and criticizes from afar. Thus, the black theater has remained "at a standstill."

Lewis's solution to this stagnation has a familiar ring. We must create a new black theater, he argued, based upon a merger of the two black audiences. But how do we get the middle class to attend the Negro theater? Lewis admitted that this would be no easy task; it would require a very subtle kind of seduction. At first, the plays for this hypothetical Negro theater would be of a very low order—melodramas, farces, mysteries—and their lack of class would probably alienate the very people we were trying to attract. Nevertheless, the key to success lies in this: A play would "addresss its appeal exclusively to colored audiences." By imposing this realism upon low-grade material, we may slowly develop an appreciation for truth; and once a black audience has been secured, no matter how common, "higher forms of drama can be judiciously inserted in the repertory as a means of educating the audience." Now the "best people" will no longer stay away.[74] And thus, we can have our Renaissance: "The way for the Negro to make his contribution to world culture is to narrow his art down to the tastes of his own little group. . . . Ask the ghost of Shakespeare if he didn't write his masterpieces for the strictly English audience of the Globe Theater."[75] Yet Lewis never quite got over his general pessimism concerning the Negro audience. As early as 1924, he was disturbed by a terrible contradiction in the Negro community: We have a collective life crying out to be dramatized, he noted, but no one seems interested. Given these ripe conditions, we should "expect to find malcontents leading revolts, amateurs making exhilarating and novel experiments; kibitzers vociferously offering advice, criticizing; a considerable minority of the laity aware that something is wrong and disgruntled by it, even if not just sure what is wrong. No such healthy discontent exists among Aframericans."[76] All the impetus for fostering a Negro theater, Lewis concluded, has come from white people, and all the good plays about Negro life have been written by white people. Where does that leave us?

The problem was, it did not leave Lewis with much. No doubt there was discontent aplenty among "Aframericans," but when it expressed itself in art, it usually took the form of music—blues and jazz—not plays. Thus, Lewis was left with Mencken's position: The American artist "stands in completer isolation than anywhere else on earth." Stuck to his theory of High Art, the tar-baby of the Harlem Renaissance, he could only lament that this situation was probably built into the scheme of things, that the artist was naturally at odds with the mores, opinions, and sensibilities of his age. On one occasion, Lewis discussed the "man of genius" in the abstract; and we may assume, I think, that his discussion represents a reaction to bested hopes. The "creations" of the true artist, Lewis argued,

> will at first appear unintelligible to men at large in proportion as they are original. Since what is unintelligible cannot be appreciated the repudiation of the artist by the crowd is both honest and sensible. The artist must wait until the more clear sighted of his contemporaries perceive the liaison between his creations and the trends of events and communicate the discovery to their fellows. This requires time and it usually happens that the original artist is not adequately appreciated until he is decaying in old age or eternity. Which is not all important, for the function of the artist is not to win applause for himself but to search the unknown for reality and interpret it in terms of beauty.[77]

On the surface, this statement about the artist's integrity suggests Joyce's remark that he wrote for the ideal reader with the ideal insomnia. In other words, the artist should damn the whole notion of an audience and get on with his work. Certainly, a later generation of black writers such as Wright and Ellison would be more sympathetic to Joyce's outlook, but only after the discovery that the idea of a black audience proved to be an *ignis fatuus*. When Lewis made this statement in 1925, however, he still wanted to believe that the potential for a black audience was a real possibility. In moments when he was tempted not to believe in this ideal, when the artist's audience seemed to disappear, then the pursuit of beauty became the artist's only raison d'être. This emphasis upon the purely aesthetic had also seemed an alternative to Mencken when he was faced with an unintelligent and unappreciative American audience. Then, almost by definition, the artist became an outcast and a loner. Nevertheless, both Mencken and Lewis hoped that an audience would emerge from the gloom, a hope that they never entirely abandoned. Tied to the mimetic tradition, they assumed that the artist and his audience were looking at the same thing, the external world as it was reflected in art. What kept people from appreciating art (other than their innate stupidity) was their inability to escape the fixities of their culture, for example, puritanism. When disillusioned, Lewis could only hope that some day the "original artist" would be appreciated by a more general audience. What he really wanted, of course, was that there would be no gap in time, that the black audience he had been seeking would suddenly appear, magically, with no questions asked.

Several years after the hoopla surrounding the Harlem Renaissance had ended, two novels by Negro authors appeared at the same time, and each focused in its own way upon the black writer's ambivalence concerning his audience. Both published in 1932, *Infants of Spring*, by Wallace

Thurman, and *One Way to Heaven*, by Countee Cullen, illustrate the extent to which the theme of artist and audience preoccupied the best minds of the Harlem Renaissance. If Alfred North Whitehead is correct—that an age is defined not so much by the answers it gives but by the questions it continues to ask—then these two novels contribute to the decade's definition by repeating at its end the concerns that began it. And these are concerns, I insist, which the "little American renaissance" had subsequently dismissed (with the exception of Mumford and Rosenfeld) but which lived on in Mencken's criticism of American society. What these two novels also illustrate is a moral confusion that perhaps explains why artist and audience could never have found each other during the 1920s, even if Harlem had been the utopian paradise that Locke had described in *The New Negro*.

In Wallace Thurman's *Infants of Spring*, Hughes's mountain is renamed "Niggeratti Manor," and it too symbolizes (though this time the irony is conscious) the dilemma of the Negro artist. Euphoria Blake, a black Mabel Dodge, has turned her house over to a group of Negro literati, believing that this center of flourishing creativity will fill "a real need in the community."[78] The artists, however, do everything but create—they throw parties, seduce women, and talk incessantly about art. What was to be their haven has turned into a trap. Flattered by white society's temporary interest in the "New Negro," they think they need only live like artists to be artists. They are infants born into a false spring; they gather in a hothouse only to wither and die.

On the surface Thurman's satire is obvious, but at points he strikes much deeper. In his novel he has documented the tragic insularity of the black writer, who is blind both to the worth of his own talent and to the world right outside his front door. Raymond, a novelist (and a portrait of Thurman himself), and his white friend Stephen have conversations on the theme of isolation and community. Stephen eventually leaves Niggeratti Manor, disgusted with the degenerate company in which he finds himself. Raymond explains to him that he cannot leave, that he has to make do with what he has. "I am forced to surround myself with case studies in order not completely to curdle and sour" (p. 194). But he *has* curdled and soured. Unable to relate to the black middle class, he finds bohemian life equally stultifying and debilitating. Determined to start afresh, he tells Stephen that he plans "to write . . . a series of books which will cause talk but won't sell. . . . Negroes won't like me because they'll swear I have no race pride, and white people won't like me because I won't recognize their stereotypes" (pp. 214-15). Real rebellion, Thurman finally suggests, lies in the artist's making contact with the audience of "a quarter million Negroes" living in Harlem (p. 222).

The question never answered in *Infants of Spring* is who will buy Raymond's books, if and when he ever writes them. Since Thurman always remained an elitist—often complaining as bitterly about the "mob" as he did about the middle class[79]—it is doubtful that he had any hopes about the "quarter million Negroes." Furthermore, any possible affirmation we may have expected from Raymond's new intentions is forestalled by the novel's conclusion. In his best *fin-de-siècle* manner, Thurman describes the comic death of one Paul Arbian, a young bohemian who has modeled himself on both Huysmans and Oscar Wilde. As a grand finale, Paul arranges to commit suicide during a party, leaving his unpublished novel where it will be discovered by the guests. But the bathtub in which he dies overflows, the flood making his manuscript unreadable. Instead of showing any kind of hope commensurate with Raymond's intentions, the ending illustrates rather Thurman's generalization "that the more intellectual and talented Negroes of my generation are among the most pathetic people in the world today" (p. 225).

This is also the uneasy feeling we get from Countee Cullen's *One Way to Heaven*. Like Thurman's, Cullen's novel deals with the theme of infant damnation. In this case, the infants are not artists but connoisseurs of art, as if both Thurman and Cullen had intended that their novels taken together should illustrate Mencken's twin themes—that the American artist stood "in completer isolation than anywhere else on earth" and that the new aristocracy of money failed "to function as an aristocracy of taste." At Constancia Brandon's elegant home, the wealthy meet twice a month to discuss books written by Negroes. The original purpose of the "Booklovers' Society," stated by Constancia herself, is *"to be a small but loyal body on which the Negro writer can depend for sympathy, understanding and support."*[80] Thus, Constancia's house is the counterpart to Niggeratti Manor. If Thurman's house of artists was to brighten the secular city with its radiance (like Ezekiel's temple in the revived Jerusalem), so too Constancia's "temple" is intended to provide a sanctuary for the black artist. Unfortunately, the people who attend Constancia's soirees are interested in other matters than self-education and civic responsibility, and books soon take a second place to food, drink, and gossip.

It is clear that Cullen admires Constancia herself. Intelligent, urbane, and witty, she fits the Menckenian ideal of a true marriage between wealth and taste. Yet she has surrounded herself with people whom she laughs not with but at. As the original purpose of her soirees fails, she begins to arrange them for her own amusement, the guests often becoming the objects of that amusement. Thus, Cullen treats Constancia as the Negro artist who takes revenge upon the very people who force him into isolation. However, although she has little in common with the guests of

similar background, she has no more in common with her maid, Mattie—
and herein lies the novel's real theme. The plot is split in half because
Negro life is split in half: Artist is separated from audience, wealth from
intelligence, rich from poor, reason from emotion. That Mattie and her
husband, Sam—a con man, a gambler, and a vagabond along the lines of
Black Ulysses—are overlooked by Constancia and her guests is a fit
comment on the bifurcated Negro community.

There is a further irony: Sam may be a more genuine artist than any
of those who attend Constancia's parties. The novel begins and ends with
a "performance" by Sam in which he displays all the histrionic talents of
a seasoned actor. In the opening scene, he feigns a religious conversion to
make money, and he also wins Mattie's heart; in the concluding scene, he
tricks Mattie again, pretending to hear the bells of the Heavenly City on
his deathbed, so that she will not waste her life grieving for him. In a
sense, this con man's escapades are more successful than Constancia's
efforts to secure an audience for the black artist. Every time Sam "per-
forms" in church, he plays to a packed house, and he actually moves
people to pity and fear. "I'm far from being certain," says a minister who
is on to his game, "that you aren't an unwitting instrument in the hands
of Heaven" (p. 31). This same minister, it might be added, tells a story
about himself which helps bring Cullen's satire into focus. Having been
invited to dinner by Mattie and Sam, the preacher recalls his maiden
sermon to his first congregation. In the old days, he says, this initiation
was intended as a kind of ordeal, for the backs of the preacher's audience
were turned to him. If, by the end of the sermon, he succeeeded in making
half of the congregation face him, he won his job. Sam asks him how he
did, and the preacher responds, "I won them all . . . but I ended up with
my coat and collar at my feet" (p. 226).

Perhaps Cullen suggests by this story that the artists who became
celebrities during the Harlem Renaissance had it too easy. Because they
were wined and dined by the white intelligentsia, they never extended
themselves to speak to their own as the preacher had to. They expected
the people to extend themselves, for wasn't High Art worth the effort? At
age twenty-five, Cullen undoubtedly thought it was, for he had been
published regularly in prestigious white journals, and he too had been
courted by the high and mighty. Yet by age thirty-two when he wrote
this novel, he must have decided that there was, after all, more than one
way to go to heaven. To put all the blame on an unappreciative black
audience was simple-minded and even a bit dishonest. Still, like Thurman,
Cullen never quite lost his elitism. To the end of his life, he wanted to be
thought of as a poet and not as a Negro poet. Even in *One Way to
Heaven*, Constancia remains the central figure, as though Cullen were
saying that if the true artist has any hope of receiving intelligent sympathy,

it will come from someone like her, someone who embodies the Menckenian "civilized point of view."

By the mid-1930s, the idea that a cross-section of society might support the artist as he treads his weary way toward Parnassus seemed to be, to paraphrase *The Great Gatsby*, buried under the cement of the Republic. Yet if the Renaissance never quite resolved its attitudes toward the common man, perhaps later black writers benefited from its inability to solve the artist-audience dilemma. Perhaps in exhausting this question, the Renaissance made it possible for Wright and Ellison and Baldwin to forget about it and write great novels. During the 1930s, the dilemma of artist and audience continued to exist but was absorbed into a political context generally foreign to the decade of the 1920s. And even though the question of artist and audience appeared to die after 1940, the idea of an appeal to Everyman seems important to American art and is likely to be periodically renewed. Witness the efforts by many black writers at all levels to reach the common reader in the 1960s, the case of Imamu Amiri Baraka (LeRoi Jones) specifically illustrating a major black writer who began his literary career as an aesthete and became one of the leading advocates of black communal art.

As we have seen, the zenith of the artist-audience cycle occurred within the 1920s, the black intellectuals lining up sometimes for an audience of the masses, sometimes for an elite audience, and sometimes for the artist alone. The dream of the Harlem Renaissance had been a secular city that was nourished by art and in which people of all classes supported their artists. The dream, of course, had belonged to an earlier generation of white intellectuals, and one underlying principle of the new America was to be Mumford's belief that the common man does not despise art. It was Mencken, however, who precisely pinpointed what both white and black intellectuals really wanted: The audience was to consist of a spiritual aristocracy, one that could include the common man. The problem for both Mencken and the black intellectuals was that they remained haunted by the suspicion that the common man would never cast off his ignoble self. Thus, no matter how democratic in spirit the Renaissance claimed to be, it really shared Mencken's skepticism about *boobus Americanus*, that he was a bird more common than Mencken's decent "normal citizen."

By the end of the decade, the Renaissance's intellectuals came to the conclusion that a native audience for their literary movement did not exist, in the sense of either financial support or aesthetic appreciation, and this realization caused some of them to rebel against the Renaissance's original conception of itself. We get an inkling of this self-questioning if we look at an interchange of letters between Walter White and Claude McKay. In 1925, an enthusiastic White had urged McKay to submit something quickly to a publisher because blacks were riding the crest of a wave, but McKay's response was more tentative: "It's all right to have the boom, but are the people buying?"[81] By 1930, Sterling Brown would complain in "Our Literary Audience" that not only were the people not buying, but as readers they lacked "mental bravery."[82] Using Walt Whitman's well-known words as an epigraph—"Without great audiences, we cannot have great poets"—he again stressed the need for an organic community, only this time his tone was elegiac and bitter: Our own people, he said, have not risen to the occasion; they have failed to be "great audiences" because they lack the courage to look at themselves in the mirror of art. Mencken was to make a similar charge in 1927, though in his view the onus fell upon Negro artists and the Renaissance's failure to produce great ones.

CHAPTER FIVE

Et Tu Mencken?
The End of the Romance

❧

Mr. Mencken: What Is He—Satirist, Humorist, Pessimist
or Just Plain Sophist?

—Editorial, *New York Age*

But there is no doubt that they read Mr. Mencken.

—Editorial, *Chicago Defender*

Although Mencken thought in 1920 that a worthy Negro novelist would soon appear on the scene, he had to admit in 1922 that there was no sign of life. Negroes, he said, continue to produce "religious and secular verse of such quality that it is taken over by the whites," but the number "who show a decent prose style is still very small, and there is no sign of it increasing."[1] The damning blow here was Mencken's explanation for this sad predicament: "Poetry is chiefly produced and esteemed by peoples that have not yet come to maturity"; by implication, those people who have come to maturity write novels.

In the very same year that Mencken made this ex cathedra pronouncement, James Weldon Johnson introduced him to Walter White, a young Negro who had only recently arrived in New York. Having left an insurance firm in Atlanta to become assistant secretary of the NAACP, White was brimming over with enthusiasm for the wonders of New York; and when he met Mencken, the city seemed truly to be paradise. White had always followed Mencken closely, but to the young man fresh from Georgia, the publication of "The Sahara of the Bozart" in 1920 seemed an event of special importance. (He was later to credit it as being

117

indirectly responsible for the Harlem Renaissance itself.)[2] For one thing, Mencken had looked at the southern darkness and had not winced at what he saw. For another, he had called White's own state the very heart of that darkness. "Virginia is the best of the South to-day, and Georgia is perhaps the worst. The one is simply senile; the other is crass, gross, vulgar and obnoxious."[3] Inspired by Mencken's theme, White set about writing a novel, and almost singlehandedly Mencken got it published.

The history of the novel's publication is fascinating for several reasons. First, it debunks a number of myths about the Harlem Renaissance; second, and more importantly for our purposes, it marks the beginning of Mencken's skepticism about a Negro literary movement that in 1924 had only begun to stretch its wings. For between 1924 and 1927, Mencken's feelings about the idea of a Negro Renaissance underwent a radical change, and his new attitudes affected the black writers themselves, causing them to split into two separate camps. This may sound as if Mencken had an undue amount of influence, but it is significant that his name and his ideas were tossed back and forth with some regularity by the contestants.

The first serious thought White gave to writing *The Fire in the Flint* came with a letter he received from Mencken only a few months after he had met the Sage of Baltimore. What did he think of T. S. Stribling's newly published novel, *Birthright*, Mencken asked. (Stribling was a white southerner and had written about a small town in Tennessee.) White gave a direct answer: Stribling knew all about Negro servants, but he didn't have the slightest clue as to what an educated Negro was like. According to White's autobiography, published twenty-six years later, Mencken then asked White whether he couldn't do "the right kind of novel."[4] The impression given by White is that Mencken's suggestion took him completely by surprise.

In fact, the unpublished correspondence between the two men shows that White probably had the novel in mind before Mencken mentioned it. In his letter to Mencken damning Stribling, he added, "I am praying for the advent of a first class colored novelist—but, no publisher would yet print his story if he told the whole truth."[5] White was a clever strategist. The one thing that would catch Mencken's eye, he correctly surmised, was an untold tale that everyone was afraid to print. Besides, the author would be a Negro, the one person who could reveal the "inner life" of the race. And to add frosting to the cake, that author would be a refugee from Georgia, the state that Mencken had designated in "The Sahara of the Bozart" as the most degenerate spot in the entire Confederacy.

Spurred on by Mencken's encouragement, White wrote *The Fire in the Flint* in twelve days during the summer of 1922, and he then submitted it to Doran and Company. The publishing firm at first accepted the manuscript, but then had doubts. "Practically speaking," wrote Doran's representative, Eugene Saxton, to White, "there is nobody in court but the attorney for the prosecution."[6] Naturally White was distressed, as his language in his reply to Saxton shows. He agreed that the southern white man had a "case but, by all that is holy, all we've had is his side." However, he admitted that his novel was far from perfect, that Saxton's criticism was just, and that he would be willing to revise the manuscript to close the "five per cent gap" that existed between the opinions of author and publisher.[7]

It is worth mentioning these details because White's account of his dealings with Doran is quite different from that revealed by his unpublished correspondence with the firm. Much later, whenever White told the story of how the novel came to be published, he pictured himself as a black David taking on a modern-day Goliath (Doran) who represented the philistine South. In his autobiography, he said that Mr. Doran himself had wanted him to make some "changes" in his Negro characters—they "uh, uh—are not what readers expect."[8] He added that southern humorist Irvin Cobb had read the manuscript and was convinced that publication would cause "race riots in the South." Rather than "submit to emasculation," he told Robert Kerlin (after Knopf had accepted the novel), "I informed them [Doran] that I would destroy the manuscript."[9] This tale, related to his friends and described in *A Man Called White*, is the one in which he came to believe more firmly as the years went by: He had withdrawn his novel from Doran because he would not be coerced into revising it.

The truth is less heroic but more interesting. White was not lying about Irvin Cobb's attempts to undermine his chances. The southern humorist had read the work and had urged Doran not to publish it. Yet it is doubtful that Cobb's advice had any real effect on Doran's final decision. As the correspondence indicated (and as any modern reader of *The Fire in the Flint* will readily admit), Doran had justifiable aesthetic reasons for rejecting White's manuscript.

Naturally White did not mention these aesthetic objections to Mencken when he wrote to tell him of the novel's rejection. He insinuated strongly that the novel had been sacrificed on the altar of southern justice. Knowing Mencken's "prejudices," he focused on Cobb's southern chauvinism and Doran's moral cowardice. "Irvin Cobb's influence on Doran," he lamented, "was too strong for me."[10] Mr. Doran, he said, did not "dare" publish the novel (he had been told by Eugene Saxton) because the publishing firm had been "fearing the effect on the South."[11] (Of course White neglected to speculate why, if Doran had been so terrified of the South, he showed any interest in the manuscript in the first place.) White further stressed that he had said "something worthwhile" in the

novel—"something which though not new in fact yet is new in publication. This is one of the first times that the viewpoint of intelligent Negroes
has been given and the only question is whether or not that voice shall be
heard."

Now the novel's fate took on a new significance for Mencken. Until
this time, he had been curious about it, but not to the point of knocking
on doors. White had convinced him that once again the South was responsible for suppressing the truth, so Mencken asked to see the manuscript, read it, and made a strong recommendation to his own publisher.
"I have already told Knopf," he wrote White, "that I think it would be
good business to publish the novel."[12] And Knopf must have agreed,
because he accepted it in December 1923.

This story is worth retelling because White's modern critics have
overlooked his expert manipulation of Mencken's attitudes toward the
South. On the contrary, they have tended to see the publishing history of
The Fire in the Flint as a parable for the difficulties that the black writer in
America had to face in the 1920s.[13] This last point is a difficult one to
assess, because by 1923 the intellectual climate had changed considerably;
firms such as Doran and Knopf, which had previously published "darkey"
stories, were now ready to welcome other modes of Negro portraiture.[14]
Much of the credit for this enlightened attitude belongs to Mencken,
although what he himself had not counted on was that he could be duped
by his own prejudices. For if the publishing history of White's novel
indicates anything, it indicates that the tough critic from Baltimore could
be a soft touch in the right circumstances.

As White's novel neared publication, both White and Mencken acted
as if they were co-conspirators against the South. Several times Mencken
wrote White urging him to send his novel to "the worst Negrophobe
papers . . . for review, and so draw their fire." He added that his "own
books have been greatly helped in the South by that means. The confederate is always an ass."[15] On another occasion, he said that "the best
plan, I think, is to egg on the Ku Kluxers. Can't you have some letters
written to the leading Southern papers when the time comes, denouncing
it as subversive and urging them to stir up the police? These imbeciles will
then do all your advertising for you." Mencken also promised to review
the novel in the *Baltimore Evening Sun* "to stir up some interest among
the Negro Intelligentsia (if any!) there."[16] White readily agreed to all of
Mencken's proposals, and had Knopf send copies of the novel to the
major newspapers in the South. He told Mencken, "I expect and hope to
be furiously assailed from that quarter."[17] In the meantime, he told Carl
Van Doren that he was preparing an article for the *Mercury* in which he
intended to prove, in the Mencken mode, that it would have been better

if "Negroes had been masters and whites the slaves in the South."[18]

With the publication of *The Fire in the Flint*, White found himself lionized by the literary establishment as though he were the promise of the future. Respectable critics such as Lawrence Stallings of the *New York World* and Harry Hansen of the *Chicago Daily News* fulsomely praised his book. Carl Van Vechten sought him out after reading the novel, the two forming a friendship that would be profitable to both parties. Even before publication, Sinclair Lewis read his page proofs "page by page and line by line," and wrote some puffery for Knopf saying that White's novel and Forster's *Passage to India* "will prove much the most important books of this autumn."[19] In 1926, after White's novel had been available for only two years, Jim Tully pulled out all the stops: "*The Fire in the Flint* is the greatest novel yet written by an American Negro."[20] Such attention soon led to important social engagements and to White's being the focus of interest at fashionable parties. White began to call such people as Heywood Broun, Carl Van Doren, and Alfred Knopf by their first names and, not surprisingly, he grew somewhat vain through his contact with these luminaries.

Although White used his influence with the white literati to foster the growth of the Harlem Renaissance, helping writers such as Countee Cullen and Rudolph Fisher to find publishers, he sometimes seemed blinded by the brilliance of his own success. Having established himself as a Knopf-published author, he became, at times, arrogant and inflexible. He would, for instance, brook no negative criticism of his novels from black critics, although he was occasionally guilty of whoring after praise from white ones. If he gladly gave advice and aid to the members of the Harlem Renaissance, he was also guilty of great personal ambition and, like Pope's Atticus, he could "bear no brother near the throne." Furthermore, he never really caught sight of the fact that a renaissance means the rebirth of ideas as well as the recognition of its artists in the literary columns of popular magazines. Too often he treated his relationship to the Harlem Renaissance as though it were an extension of his former job at an insurance company in Atlanta: The more he advertised it, the better off it would be. That the literary movement finally suffocated from too much glitter and tinsel may suggest that White hurt its chances for survival as much as the unjustly maligned Van Vechten.[21]

Mencken was not unaware of all the things that were happening to White. Although he never attacked White directly, he concentrated on the pampered Negro author as a symbol of what had dimmed the bright potential of the decade's opening years. Also, he never reviewed *The Fire in the Flint*, as he had promised White he would do, and we can only imagine that he found the novel embarrassing. He had gotten it published and then he saw it praised beyond its meager merits. Three years after the novel's publication, he did eventually talk about it at length, but his attitude was no longer one of eager expectation for the future.

With the *Mercury*, Mencken had other things on his mind than the development of Negro authors, yet whenever anything good came along, he was full of high spirits. He was especially pleased with the prospects that the publication of *The New Negro* (1925) implied. In early 1926, he reviewed Alain Locke's anthology of recent artistic accomplishments with enthusiasm, calling the book "a phenomenon of immense significance."[22]

As usual, Mencken read into the work what he wanted to see. He focused upon the boldness of this literary venture and the dignity of the men who contributed to it. For Mencken, it meant "the American Negro's final emancipation from his inferiority complex, his bold decision to go it alone." After reading this volume, said Mencken, one can no longer "think of the black brother as Sambo and his sister as Mandy." This Negro is a man of the world, "full of an easy grace and not at all flustered by good society"; and he is an urbane realist, discussing "the problems of his people soberly, shrewdly and without heat"—even, at time, poking "fun at their follies." The whole book, Mencken concluded, "is a masterpiece of self-possession."

Naturally, Mencken could not resist a side thrust at his old enemy, the South. Could anyone imagine, he asked, "a posse of *white* Southerners doing anything so dignified, so dispassionate, so striking? I don't mean, of course, Southerners who have cast off the Southern tradition: I mean Southerners who are still tenaciously of the South, and profess to speak for it whenever it comes into question." Mencken then weighed the wits of the Negro intellectuals and those of the die-hard southerners and decided that "the contrast is pathetic. The Africans are men of sense, learning and good bearing; the Caucasians are simply romantic windjammers, full of sound and fury, signifying nothing."

Nevertheless, Mencken saw some hard times ahead for this avant-garde of Negro intellectuals. Having declared their independence, he noted, they will have to go it alone. They will get no help from the "vast majority of the people of their race." These latter are "but two or three inches removed from gorillas," and it will be a long time before they become excited by "anything above pork-chops and bootleg gin." And, he added, the brave souls of *The New Negro* will receive little consolation from certain members of the black intelligentsia who are tied to the purse strings of the whites. This patronage has compromised their integrity, making it impossible for them to be free men. Mencken concluded by picturing the men and women of *The New Negro* as sailing a boat in hostile waters, "having cut the painter." They will be tempted to call it quits, "but no race, I believe, ever gets anywhere so long as it permits itself to think of turning back. It must navigate its own course, in fair weather and foul. . . . Let us, then, sit back tightly, and observe what the colored brothers do next." Little more than a year later, however, Mencken did not have the patience to take his own advice.

On 17 July 1927, in an article that he wrote for the *New York World*, Mencken set about assessing the artistic contributions of the Negro race to date.[23] By 1927, we should remind ourselves, the Negro vogue was in full swing, and Mencken himself would add to the general melee by writing "A Coon Age." In the *World* article, however, he took a completely different tack, although he began his piece in the most complimentary way. New York has been hospitable to the educated, middle-class Negro, he wrote, and the latter has deserved it: "The colored brethren, now that they go everywhere, add a great deal to its charm." These people are "amusing fellows," Mencken continued, "and not at all over-impressed with their new triumphs." But now came the rub: "The acceptance of the educated Negro removes his last ground for complaint against his fate in the Republic, and leaves him exposed to the same criteria of judgment that apply to everybody else."

Finished with the civilities, Mencken moved directly to his new critical point. Once we drop the notion of special consideration for the Negro artist, what do we find? "So far, it seems to me, his accomplishments have been very modest. Even in those fields wherein his opportunities for years have been precisely equal to the white man's, he has done very little of solid value. I point, for example, to the field of music." The best jazz and ragtime today, said Mencken, are being created by George Gershwin and Paul Whiteman, and although the spiritual is supposedly another Negro invention, "Where is the Negro composer who is writing spirituals today—I mean good ones?"

Mencken then considered the Negro poets, again distressed at what he saw. With the exception of James Weldon Johnson, they "have done very little to justify the excessive hospitality with which they have been received. Put all their work together and it is not worth much more than any one of a dozen of the epitaphs in 'The Spoon River Anthology.'" And it is the same with prose:

No Negro novelist has ever written a novel even remotely comparable to such things as *Babbitt* and *Jurgen*. No Negro writing short stories rises

above the level of the white hacks. There is here no prejudice to overcome,
and, so far as I know, there never has been.

   Even the Negro publicists make a sorry showing considering their opportunities. It is seldom, indeed, that one of them turns out an article or a
book of any genuine value. Even on the subject of their race's wrongs they
do not write as well, taking one with another, as the white scriveners
who tackle the same subject. All the really first-rate books written by
American Negroes since the Civil War could be ranged on a shelf a foot
long.

Mencken concluded on a rather surprising note, surprising because of its
tone. In 1920, not only had he been willing to wait and see, but he had
actually predicted that the Negro writer would emerge. In 1926, when he
reviewed *The New Negro*, he repeated his wait-and-see attitude with the
same optimistic emphasis as before. Now, however, a certain cautionary
skepticism appeared. The successful leap over the social barrier is all well
and good, said Mencken, but to the Negro it means little

   save a chance to show what is really in him. I am not altogether sure that
   his prospects in the fine arts are as good as his more optimistic partisans
   seem to think. He has shown that he can do respectable work, but he has
   certainly not shown that he can do genuinely distinguished work.

   It may be that he has ventured into the arts too soon—that they can
   flourish only in a house more solid and stable than the one he is just moving into. It may be that his greatest success during the next generation or
   two will be made, not in the arts, but in business. There he seems to be
   making rapid progress, and it is no longer fictitious and transitory.

   A number of points may be made concerning Mencken's about-face.
For one thing, he may have been fearful that public acclaim had turned
the head of the Negro artist and that he needed some taking down if he
were to do good work. Fred C. Hobson has noted that after "The Sahara
of the Bozart," Mencken had tried, with some success, to provoke the
South into proving him wrong, and there is no reason to think that his
motive here was any different. He was playing the gadfly at a time when
there were all too few of these. Further, although he makes the same
absolute statements as in "The Sahara of the Bozart" ("No Negro novelist,"
and so on), he seems less exasperated with the Negroes than with the
southerners—perhaps because he sees the hubris of the Negro as produced
by an outside source, white flattery. Finally, and perhaps most interest-
ingly, Mencken has put his finger on a sore spot for the entire literary
movement: money. That he was wrong about the Negro's present success
in business is less important than the issues he raised. Did money, or
patronage, help or hinder the artist? Mencken never quite followed this

question to a conclusion, as it pertained to either the black or the white artist. On the one hand, Mencken complained that the best minds in America went into business, not the arts; on the other hand, he was quick to observe that the artist needed sensitive and intelligent appreciation from a class of people who could afford to support him. The problem in America, as Mencken saw it, was that the rich were neither sensitive nor intelligent. But how could that be so if the best minds had gravitated toward the world of making money? If money created the "connoisseur," did it also rot his intelligence? Likewise, Mencken never quite decided when patronage was debilitating and when it was helpful. Concerning the Negro artist, Mencken noted that white patronage hurt his independence (for example, in the review of *The New Negro*), but he was also quick to point out that Negro arts and letters needed firm financial backing. What he did not see—but then, few did—was that Negro backing might also be fraught with problems. What he did see was that the Harlem Renaissance would have difficulty surviving without a firm economic base; and, sure enough, when the Depression came, the chief supporters of the "boom," white people, faded away like the roses of summer.

Of course, the most egregious howlers that Mencken made were his remarks about Negro music. At a time when Duke Ellington, Louis Armstrong, and Fletcher Henderson were revolutionizing jazz, Mencken was talking about Paul Whiteman. What is interesting here is not so much Mencken's misjudgment about particular men but his larger misperception, shared by others, concerning the nature of the Renaissance. Both Ellington and Henderson had come out of the same middle-class backgrounds as had Alain Locke, yet they instinctively recognized that their future lay in the smoky dives of Harlem night life. (Ellington even gave up a scholarship to the Pratt Institute to pound a piano in them.) While Locke was talking about "urbanity," Ellington was listening to the real sounds of the city as they whistled through the streets. Mencken chose Whiteman as his representative jazzman because Whiteman had refined the primitive sounds of Negro music. Similarly, Mencken and the Negro intellectuals chose literature over popular music, because literature sumbolized a "classical tradition." Despite their strong interest in Negro folk art, literature, as James Weldon Johnson noted in his *Book of American Negro Poetry* and as Locke was to emphasize in "The Negro's Contribution to American Culture" (1929), was the main criterion that determined whether a race was great.

Mencken could not leave well enough alone, and two months later he returned to the theme of the Negro artist in his column in the *New York World*. As usual, his demeanor remained unruffled, even though, as he said, his July article had met with a "roar": "I was at once bombarded

with proofs of his [the Negro's] high attainments."[24] He admitted that he
had changed his mind in one particular (he had forgotten about Dr.
Nathaniel Dett's spiritual "Listen to the Lambs"), but he stood firm on his
basic premise, to wit, that in these last few years Negro artists have made
few original contributions to the world of music, literature, and art. For
the most part,

> colored composers have done a great deal to popularize the music of their
> race, but they have done very little to develop it. It remains, in their
> hands, simple folksong. It is not Negroes but Jews who have turned it to
> more ambitious uses. In much the same way it is white novelists and
> dramatists and not Negroes, who have best utilized the Negro as a dra-
> matic figure. The imaginative authors of the race all seem to be hampered
> by a propaganda purpose. They are so intent upon depicting the Negro as
> the hero of a moral melodrama that they fail to show him as a human
> being.

As Mencken warmed to his subject, of course he chose the novel as the
art form to illustrate this most grievous failure to depict human beings.
He singled out Walter White, the author of "perhaps the most successful
Negro novel yet written," as a man with real talent who was blinded by
moral earnestness. The hero of *The Fire in the Flint*, said Mencken,
needed "to do something weak and human."

> If he broke into a hoedown now and then he would be greatly improved.
> And it would be a relief to see him sit down to a hearty meal of Virginia
> ham, chitlings, cabbage sprouts, hominy cakes and corn pone, with a
> beaker of country buttermilk to wash it down.

Mencken's own rich language was meant to stand in marked contrast to
White's racially pallid novel, and the humor of the above passage was
intended to underscore the humorlessness of *The Fire in the Flint*. But as
we shall see, White's aesthetic failings were due in part to Mencken's
influence as both a literary and social critic, an irony that Mencken
probably never recognized.

In this *World* article, Mencken saw a connection between the Negro's
artistic failures and "the self-satisfaction which now afflicts the race not
only in the aesthetic department but all along the line." (This seems like
an absurd charge, unless we keep in mind the public attention given to
the Negro intellectuals during the 1920s.) The inability to create "human"
characters, said Mencken, means that not enough candor exists among
the Negroes themselves. Once again he focused on the Negro preacher as
a symbol of the world of illusion still at the core of Negro life. Until the
Negroes themselves undertake to skewer this mountebank—along with

the "Negro Babbitt, who now begins to roar precisely like a white Rotarian"—they will never do anything befitting a civilized people. But fortunately, added Mencken, "the Negroes, despite their generally solemn and humorless mien, do not lack critics of their own race, and some of these critics, notably George S. Schuyler of the *Pittsburgh Courier*, are extremely realistic. . . . Led by the Schuyler aforesaid, a number of young colored intellectuals address themselves to flaying the follies of their people."

If Mencken's intention was to start a row in the Negro newspapers with these two *World* articles, he certainly succeeded. As the *Chicago Defender* noted after the first Mencken piece, "It is no mean feat to get this Race of ours to read and discuss topics, even if the topic happens to be the Race. But there is no doubt that they read Mr. Mencken."[25] The *Defender* thought Mencken right in pointing to the church's failures, but it was willing to suspend judgment concerning the Negro's artistic merits— it first wanted to hear from the Negro artists themselves. However, it did thank Mencken for raising a ruckus, perhaps the best thing about the piece, "in that he provoked more discussion among the leaders and followers [of the race] than has been heard in these parts since Chief Sam started back to Africa."

Others besides the *Defender* thought that Mencken was simply telling the truth. Kelly Miller in the *Baltimore Afro-American* did not comment upon Mencken's opinion but admired his honesty.[26] George Schuyler in the *Pittsburgh Courier* agreed with most of Mencken's pronouncements on Negro art: "Indeed I have said much the same thing myself."[27] In music, continued Schuyler, we "have been far surpassed by the whites," and although Professor Mencken may have been too severe upon our poets, "judged by world standards, they haven't made much of a big noise." Even judged by the standards of American poets, Schuyler said sadly, "they are second-rate." And our prose writers? "Their record is worse."

But Schuyler did not let Mencken have the last word:

On the other hand, it seems to me that Br'er Mencken's attitude is a little pontifical. He forgets, it seems to me, that American writers generally haven't contributed much timeless literature, nor have any American composers, white or black, rivalled Beethoven, Wagner or Liszt. Our American poets, too, with the possible exception of Whitman and Poe, are decidedly not of the first water. The fact is that this is a young country just emerging from the pioneering stage. Heretofore, it has been absorbed with building a civilization and has just begun to criticize and interpret it.

In a sense Schuyler was pointing Mencken's guns right back at him. Mencken had criticized American writers "generally" for their mediocrity, and so—Schuyler seemed to be saying—if he was going to single out the Negro for special disapproval, he should put him in the slow company of his countrymen, most of whom had not the Negro's disadvantages.

Yet Schuyler did agree with Mencken that Negro artists needed a solid substructure: "Wealth and leisure must come first before we can properly subsidize art." His conception of art (like Mencken's) was aristocratic.

> It must have a monied class to which to adhere for its sustenance, for great art must have a limited audience and is seldom popular. Almost all great artists whether with pen or brush have been subsidized or have had great personal wealth and thus are free from the burden of making a living. There are few examples in the history of art and literature to which one can point where, money and leisure being absent, great work has been done. Negro composers in order to get along and make a living have had to take up most of their time writing coarse popular songs about "Mah Baby" and "Mah Man," while Negro writers have been largely engaged in writing racial propaganda and trying to voice the aspirations of what Dr. DuBois called "the mired mass."

Typical of Schuyler is the link between the "coarse popular songs" and the "mired mass," and yet he had previously looked for the intelligent stevedore within this mass. Again, the crucial question of the Renaissance hangs in the balance: Can the average Joe who listens to Bessie Smith singing about her man be educated by degrees to appreciate Beethoven? Although Mencken and Schuyler gave a qualified "yes" to this question, they added the codicil that the masses as a rule usually stay mired. But then, isn't the same true of the rest of the social classes? Natural aristocrats are rare birds, for the bird most commonly found is the *boobus Americanus*, one that not only knows no closed season but knows no particular social class. Hence both Schuyler and Mencken hedged on who made up the "great audience"; they both agreed that it would be "fit company though few," but they could not quite agree upon where the few could be located. The poor might be mired down, but the rich (or the pretenders to wealth) had their own sloughs to wallow in. One thing neither Schuyler nor Mencken would admit: the possibility that the stevedore or sleep-in maid who adored Bessie Smith had just as refined a taste for music as did the "connoisseur" who melted over the Great Masters.[28]

Not everyone was quite so hospitable to Mencken's views as were Schuyler, Miller, and the editor of the *Chicago Defender*. In its reaction to the first *World* essay, the *Amsterdam News* laughed at Mencken's "half-truths": "The Negro has not been accepted socially, whether educated or not, and if Mr. Mencken doesn't know, it is not to late for him to find out for himself."[29] Since his basic premise is faulty, the editor concluded, the rest of his argument is "shaky." The newspaper credited Mencken with having "sincerity" but lamented his naivete. The *Amsterdam News* was even harsher in its treatment of Mencken's second *World* article. It was angry that Mencken was "undismayed by the protests of Negroes against his criticism last July"[30] For the benefit of those who might have missed Mencken's message, the newspaper flashed it in neon. "He calls the Negro preacher the worst enemy of the Negro and describes him as a magnificently uneducated, self-seeking ignoramus with a swamp-bred theology and a pork-chop culture. He thinks that one of the Negro ailments is self-satisfaction and prescribes a dose of George S. Schuyler and unsentimental self-analysis." The *News* laughed (and justifiably so) at the idea of Negro "self-satisfaction." ("His trouble all along has been that he had too little of it.") And it sarcastically praised Mencken for finding one worthy composer (Dr. Dett) "since July." It then lumped Mencken with all the other whites who were mesmerized by the Afro-American; stuck to the tar-baby, "once they take hold of him they cannot let go."

Other responses to Mencken ranged from anger to ambivalence. The *New York Age*, frankly puzzled by Mencken's tactics, entitled its review of his July article, "Mr. Mencken: What Is He—Satirist, Humorist, Pessimist or Just Plain Sophist?"[31] But one composer, Will Marion Cook, was outraged by Mencken's slander, and in a rare (and rather odd) coupling, he linked Van Vechten and Mencken together as twin sources of evil, both responsible for Harlem's moral degeneracy. "Stop Van Vechten-ing and Mencken-ing my race,"[32] he sharply ordered, as if the two white men were conjurers caught in the act. Poor Schuyler, as it turned out, was proven guilty by association. In the *Pittsburgh Courier* Schuyler noted that the *Philadelphia Public Journal* had called him an "infidel" when it discussed the Mencken articles. Schuyler bravely responded that if such an epithet put him in the company of such men as Mencken, Voltaire, and Shaw, then the said newspaper was free to call him one.[33]

Responses to Mencken by DuBois and Locke tended to be less emotional than those of the black newspapers, but they also revealed a certain ambivalence. As we have seen, DuBois defended Mencken's personal integrity, but he noted that Mencken does "not understand just where the shoe pinches."[34] The black artist is discriminated against in subtle ways by publishing houses, DuBois said; he is expected to write about "fools, clowns, prostitutes" and nothing else. Also, in his broad sweep of black artists, Mencken overlooked Dunbar, Toomer, McKay, and Hughes. "On the whole then," DuBois concluded, "despite a stimulating critic's opinion, we Negroes are quite well satisfied with our Renaissance. And we have not yet finished."

What is interesting about DuBois's appraisal of Mencken is that he did not hesitate to join those closing ranks against this white critic. In truth, DuBois himself around this time was beginning to feel uneasy about the direction of the Harlem Renaissance. In "Criteria of Negro Art," he feared that the literary movement might be headed toward a new kind of decadent aestheticism.[35] (He disagreed with Locke over what he called Locke's "search for disembodied beauty.")[36] Later, as he thought he saw the Negro artist following in Van Vechten's muddy footsteps, he arrived at a critical assessment far more pessimistic than Mencken's.[37]

Alain Locke also decided to joust with Mencken, though he too, eventually, came to recognize the justice of Mencken's views. Mencken, said Locke in *Ebony and Topaz* (1927), has suggested that "we would do well to page a black Luther and call up the Reformation."[38] Locke admitted that Mencken was right if one just looked at the bare facts; it was true that the Harlem Renaissance was short on goods, long on promises. Yet Mencken had made the mistake of limiting the idea of a renaissance to the Negro's contributions to it. The real aim of the Harlem Renaissance was "to infuse a new essence into the general stream of culture"; the Renaissance should not only be considered "an integral phase of contemporary American art and literature," but its purpose was also to make the American artist aware that Negro life is an untapped source for great art.

Locke was not being quite candid here, for the Renaissance as he defined it in *The New Negro* was a closed society. He did not exactly deny the white artist the opportunity to write about Negroes, but he made it quite clear that a "renaissance" presupposed an organic society in which the black artist spoke to and for a black audience. By 1927, his belief in such a society had been badly shaken, affecting his view of Harlem as the setting for the "Beloved Community." In attempting to answer Mencken's judgment upon the black artist, Locke pointed to the Negro's alienation from the South as one reason for his poor artistic showing.

> Indeed, if conditions in the South were more conducive to the development of Negro culture without transplanting, the self-expression of the "New Negro" would spring up just as one branch of the new literature of the South, and as one additional phase of its cultural reawakening. The common bond of soil and that national provincialism would be a sounder basis for development than the somewhat expatriated position of the younger school of Negro writers. And if I were asked to name one factor for the anemic and rhetorical quality of so much Negro expression to the present, I would cite . . . the pathetic exile of the Negro writer from his best material, the fact that he cannot yet get cultural breathing space on his own soil.

Words like "provincialism" and "soil" appear in a new context, and "transplanting" takes on a new meaning. The sense of community (Royce's "provincialism") now exists in the South; the "soil" is rural soil, and the Negro in being transplanted is uprooted. Living in the city has made an expatriate of him. His works are "anemic" because the city has not nourished him.

While deploring this situation, Locke tried to reduce the force of Mencken's criticism by turning his own weapons against him. The Negro artist, Locke continued, has recently pledged his allegiance to "a stridently self-conscious realism" in order to countermine a history of "sentimental partisanship," and yet this attitude of "studied . . . detachment" has robbed his work of "spiritual bloom." Thus the Negro artist is still ill at ease—real "Florentine ease and urbanity" continue to elude him, and Locke tacitly implied that Mencken's "realism" is as bad as all the other isms that have been foisted upon the Negro: "It is a fiction that the black man has . . . been naive: in American Life he has been painfully self-conscious for generations—and is only now beginning to recapture the naivete he once originally had." Locke could accept Mencken's paradox that "naivete" and "urbanity" were kindred virtues (belonging to the unself-conscious artist), but he argued that Mencken's insistence upon realism had deprived the Negro artist of his urbanity.

However, Locke never gave up his commitment to realism in literature, and after 1927 the idea of a "Reformation" began to concern him. He recognized the need for one in his "Reptrospective Review"[39] for Opportunity magazine (a series of reviews which he first began in January 1929), and throughout the later 1920s and early 1930s he could never quite decide whether the literary movement was progressing or retrenching. To a certain extent, the metaphors that Locke employed to describe the Harlem Renaissance had some relevance to himself as well. He saw himself as a prince of a small city-state, a prince whose power and authority had been firmly established by his editorship of The New Negro and by his academic position at Howard University. (Besides, he had been chosen for his regal role by Charles S. Johnson, editor of Opportunity.) Yet by 1927 his position had been seriously questioned, and Mencken's articles seemed to have given permission to the younger generation to challenge authority—not only that of Locke but of DuBois as well.

This shift in Mencken's influence upon the black writers of the 1920s is significant. Previously, James Weldon Johnson, W.E.B. DuBois, and Walter White—in short, the NAACP group—had been moved by Mencken's attacks upon the South and his espousal of the educated Negro. Now, however, Mencken implied that it was not enough to attack the South, that the inner life of the Negro was not being depicted adequately, and that the middle-class Negro lacked a sense of humor about himself. Mencken had already given license to the younger black writers to do sketches of Negro lowlife (his remarks on Odum's *Left Wing Gordon*),[40] and now he was giving them ammunition with which to attack the Old Guard.

There is still, of course, a legitimate question to ask: Which came first, Mencken or the black Menckenites? As Schuyler pointed out, he had himself been skeptical of the accomplishments of the literary movement long before Mencken had challenged them. Yet it is also clear that Schuyler, Theophilus Lewis, Wallace Thurman, and Eugene Gordon, the Young Wits who were dissatisfied with the bombast attached to Negro literature, had all learned their muck-raking from Mencken. Thus, in October 1926 Lewis could puncture the Renaissance balloon in a Menckenian style:

> I lead off with the cardinal heresy of denying that the spirituals are triumphs of art. I further depose and declare that I am aware of no Aframerican musician of the first order, barring a concert singer or two; that I do not concede the Aframerican any pronounced racial talent for dramatic or histrionic art; that not one of the expensive churches Negroes are building or buying indicates that the preacher has taste enough to prevent an architect or a passel of Jews from selling him a granite barn; that in the whole roster of colored prose writers under forty years old there are only two producing work which can be called literature without insulting the term: George S. Schuyler is a genuine humorist and Jean Toomer is the only story teller able to create a striking and original character; "promising" is the best you can say about the rest of the lot, and most of them are not promising very much. In fact, to make it snappy, the celebrazione of chocolate culture is 99.44-100 percent pale pink whoofle dust.[41]

Not only does Lewis have Mencken's flair for the sweeping roundhouse right, but he also has a few of his prejudices. Whatever their failings, Lewis continued, Negroes have produced some solid poets. Yet instead of dwelling upon these poets' individual virtues, he took away with one hand what he had given with the other, adding that the reason they are poets and not prose writers is that the culture is immature.

> Poetry is essentially the expression of emotion while prose is essentially a medium for the expression of ideas. Since in the common relations of life, anger, sadness, pity and the desire for revenge are feelings everybody experiences daily while only a few people either possess the ability or meet the necessity for sustained thinking it is inevitable that words and phrases packed with emotional meaning should multiply faster than terms invented to convey ideas. Thus the poet finds both the language and the habits of thought of a people prepared for him much earlier than the writer who wants to express himself in prose.

The problem with Negro culture, Lewis continued, is that it has failed to create an environment that nourishes the intellect.

> As for cultural ideas which grow out of a refined way of living the race has produced none at all, simply because there has been no refined way of living. With a background so saturated with feeling and so barren of ideas and refinement it is not at all surprising that we have swarms of respectable poets while we have not yet produced six fiction writers capable of consistently writing up to the standard of Snappy Stories.

Lewis's argument is essentially the same as Mencken's. Prose is the real barometer of a culture. When ideas flow freely, then the novelist can dip his bucket in the well; but when ideas dry up, as they do in a puritan culture like America's, then the novelist is cut off at the source. The function of criticism—and Mencken would have readily agreed to this Arnoldian view—is to stir up controversy, to motivate the free flow of ideas, so that the novelist can again slake his thirst.[42]

The Young Wits considered Mencken an ally because he sanctioned rebellion against stodginess and self-satisfaction. They saw a connection between his attack on the genteel tradition in American literature and their own warfare against genteel Negro culture. When Wallace Thurman said that the black people who rail against Langston Hughes "have their counterpart in those American whites who protest the literary upheavals of a Dreiser, an Anderson, or a Sandburg,"[43] he was appealing to those who remembered, and sympathized with, Mencken's early battles. Moreover, Thurman often used Mencken's weapons as well as his themes. "The truly sincere artist," said Thurman in the first and only issue of the magazine *Harlem* (1928), "does not take into consideration what the public might say if his characters happen to be piano movers." This artist, if he happens to be black, does not care what the "best people" in the Negro community think because it is perfectly clear that the "best people . . . do not think at all."[44] In short, being genteel does not necessarily mean that one is refined—quite the opposite. Those who are the most genteel are also the most fearful, the most moral, the most narrow-minded. For Thurman, DuBois became a symbol of this psychological paranoia. (Some author out there is trying to disgrace me!) For this reason, Thurman indirectly referred to him as the "Judge Landis of literature" (an updating of Mencken's Anthony Comstock).

Thurman (and others) kept up a constant sniper fire upon genteel Negro culture, and often the warfare spilled over to include the Renaissance itself. In one article, he said that the "results of the renaissance have been sad rather than satisfactory,"[45] and, on another occasion, he doubted if anyone could call it either new or unique.

Precisely the same thing is happening in Negro America as has already
happened in the far west (finding expression in Twain, Miller, Ward, and
Harte), in the middle west (note Norris, Dreiser, Sandburg, Anderson,
Masters, Herrick, et al.), and concurrently in the south (vide Peterkin,
Stribling, Heyward, Glasgow). It has also happened among the immigrant
minority groups. . . . And because the same nation-wide wind chanced
to stir up some dust in Negro America, whites and blacks deafen us with
their surprised and vociferous ejaculations. Renaissance? Hell, it's a backwash![46]

It was the Menckenian tone of this passage which took one by surprise —
that, and its sweeping judgment of a sacred cow. Locke too had recognized
the literary movement's debt to America's recent upheavals, but he had
always stressed the distinctive integrity of the Renaissance. Now here
was a young upstart calling the whole thing a "backwash."

Not only did Thurman question the racial origins of the Renaissance,
he added (via George Schuyler's "Negro Art Hokum") an additional
skeptical note. If the Negro was essentially American, how could he
produce "an individual literature"? "What he produces in the field of
letters," said Thurman, "must be listed as American literature, just as the
works of the Scotchman Burns or the Irishman Synge are listed as English
literature."[47] This last remark was probably meant to upset the Old
Guard (DuBois, James Weldon Johnson, and White), who had made a
special claim for the Negro's artistic contributions.

Thurman once said to Granville Hicks that "the wealthy, aristocratic
Negroes . . . are proud of us [the younger generation] unless we tread on
their toes by saying unkind things about them or by painting a realistic
and uncomplimentary picture of the race."[48] Thurman, it seems, did not
want to give them a chance to be "proud of us," and he took a special
opportunity to do some foot-stomping in *Fire*, another magazine like
Harlem which had a brief flare and then died after one issue. After the
magazine's failure, Thurman claimed that its only purpose had been to be
artistic, to deal with proletarian characters and not the "bourgeoisie."[49]
For these reasons, he said, the "best people" had become very upset over
the magazine's appearance. Yet he was not being very candid in this
instance. As editor he had put together the magazine in such a way that it
would upset the "best people." Moreover, *Fire* illustrated a confession he
made to Hicks about the split between the two generations of Negro intellectuals. Referring to the "older movement led by W.E.B. DuBois and
James Weldon Johnson," he said, "They tolerate us, and we laugh at
them."

When *Fire* made its short-lived appearance, Langston Hughes wrote
to Thurman and applauded his "laughter." Hughes's praise of Thurman's

satirical column, "Fire Burns," is indicative of the way most of the younger writers felt at this time. Hughes told Thurman that the column in the magazine "should be kept burning." What was needed was "clever, satirical comment on the vices and stupidities of the race. Make it hot."[50] As far as the Young Wits were concerned, heat, not cool decorum, was what the race needed, and the contents of *Fire* bear out Hughes's directive: The "vices and stupidities of the race" were indeed satirized.

In *Fire*'s opening story ("Cordelia the Crude"), written by Thurman, the narrator is an *ingénu*, a "respectable" Negro. Much to his surprise, he discovers that the innocent gesture of giving a young lady two dollars is the first step towards making her a prostitute. So much for the middle-class virtue of charity. In a languid sketch of a penniless, bohemian black artist ("Smoke, Lilies, and Jade"), Richard Bruce delights in shocking the bourgeoisie. At one point, the young man's reverie turns to his mother and her stuffy companions who "scoff at him for knowing such people as Carl [Van Vechten] . . . Mencken . . . Toomer . . . Hughes . . . Cullen . . . Wood [Clement] . . . Cabell. . . . Oh the whole lot of them."[51] The illusion that these people are his friends sustains his sense of importance, and although Bruce is ridiculing the young man because of his self-deception, he is also mocking the middle class for knowing nothing of the privileged world that the young man dreams he belongs to.

A kind of antiintellectualism ran throughout *Fire*, as if Thurman were reminding the "best people" that the world is often seamy and unpredictable. Zora Neale Hurston treated primal vengeance in "Sweat," and she delved into the realm of abnormal psychology in "Color Struck." The mental machinations of Hurston's heroine in "Color Struck" made a perfect introduction to Arthur Huff Fauset's short essay, "Intelligentsia." Here Fauset roasted everyone who pretended to the name, but his targets were so vague that readers could not tell whether the intellectuals he was attacking were black or white or both. One thing was sure, however; Mencken was not included. Said Fauset, "One can admire truly intellectual types like Sinclair Lewis, Dreiser, H.L.M., and Shaw," even though their followers were "carrion."[52]

In a sense, Alain Locke was caught in the middle of all this. He sympathized with the attack upon DuBois by the Young Wits; he had, in fact, published his well-known piece "Art or Propaganda?" in *Harlem*. Coming out on the side of art, he seemed to be fit company for the new iconoclasts. Yet there was a side to Locke which disturbed them. Despite his desire for realism, he shied away from what he called "Menckenian skepticism" (a "negative pole"),[53] and his own language tended toward a certain vagueness. More than one black intellectual would have agreed with Walter White's complaint to Claude McKay that Locke's "usual indefinite manner [of speaking] . . . did not amount to much when boiled down to words of less than two syllables."[54] Locke's problem was in trying to be all things to all men—interpreter of the Renaissance to the whites, defender of the decencies to the Old Guard, and rebel to the new men. Unfortunately, he ended by losing his credibility with young and old alike, but especially with the young, who saw Locke's celebration of the folk as being at odds with their desire to be self-critical. He called their self-criticism decadence, as did DuBois, and they called it satire.

By comparing J. A. Rogers's *From "Superman" to Man* with Schuyler's *Slaves Today*, one can easily see the difference between the satire at the beginning of the decade and at the end. Published in 1917, Rogers's work is a cross between *Gulliver's Travels* and *The Wizard of Oz*. Certainly its satiric strategy is indebted to Swift. A southern senator sits down next to a Pullman porter and begins a conversation in which he assumes intellectual superiority. He might as well be Gulliver attempting to present his "civilized" trinkets to a Houyhnhnm, for he soon meets the surprise of his life. Instead of being an ignorant darkey, Dixon is the embodiment of the Menckenian ideal: intelligent, educated, articulate, and well bred. The southerner, of course, is just the opposite: rude, emotional, unread, and provincial in the most negative sense. The comedy of the situation lies both in Dixon's unruffled demeanor as he faces the senator's anger and in his encyclopedic rebuttals as he challenges the senator's ignorance. The major thrust of the satire concerns the southern legislator's "education." Just as Gulliver discovers that the horses are not the inferior creatures he at first deemed, so too the senator finally sees himself and his countrymen in the mirror of reality.

Rogers, in the end, finally backs away from the bleaker implications of Swift's satire. It is true that twice in the story Dixon calls for a satirist of the extremest sort: "Juvenal, Voltaire, Swift nor any of the great masters of satire ever had so pregnant and suggestive a theme as this color situation." And, "Whom does the white American really worship, I ask? the fetish of color, or the Christ whose name he mouths? What material for a satirist. Voltaire nearly laughed the Pope off his throne in the Vatican for less than this."[55] Yet the book's conclusion suggests that the senator is not so bad that he cannot be saved. When the train arrives in Los Angeles, he is a new man—ready to give jobs to Negro actors in the Hollywood movie studio he owns and ready, in general, "to make our beloved America into a real republic." Appropriately, the final scene takes place in the West of Rogers's imagination; satire is a cleansing fire whereby a new America will be born from the ashes of the old.

By 1931, the world was not quite so rosy for George Schuyler. His second novel, *Slaves Today*, was originally to follow the satiric pattern of *Black No More*, published in the same year. However, the Juvenalian satire of the first novel becomes overwhelmingly grim in the second and completely dominates the occasional comedy. We get some sense of the original plan of *Slaves Today* in a letter Schuyler wrote to Mencken describing an article he wanted to do for the *Mercury*. In summarizing the history of Liberia, Schuyler said, "The American Colonization Society of Northern sentimentalists and Southern slaveholders [was] eager to get rid of troublesome freedmen. These freedmen went to establish a Valhalla for Zigaboos and perhaps your readers might like to know how the experiment has turned out."[56] Both the published article ("Uncle Sam's Black Step-Child")[57] and the letter to Mencken dwelled upon the ironic results of the "experiment." Since this experiment was so similar to the archetypal American experiment, we can easily imagine how this "Valhalla" turned out. An additional irony lay in the fact that just as England had kicked out our Pilgrim ancestors (and forced them to dress up necessity as a virtue), so too these Negro adventurers, having been thrown out of America (by "Sentimentalists," no less), were determined to put the best face on a bad situation. In short, the Republic of Liberia, which claimed to be a paradise, actually was run by thugs who were even worse than the white exploiters in America. In fact, they had taken their masters' lessons to heart, and did unto their brothers what had been done unto them.

In *Slaves Today*, a little of this satiric comedy is indeed present. The rulers of Liberia are not aristocrats (as one recent critic has asserted),[58] but low-caste blacks who behave like white trash. They ride roughshod over the country with all the finesse and political subtlety of a Clarence Snopes. It is as if President Johnson, Commissioner Jackson, and Captain Burns—characters who symbolize three levels of power in Liberia—had taken a correspondence course in civic government from the Imperial Wizard of the Ku Klux Klan. Yet never are these characters simply knaves; rather, they project the very irrationality of evil itself. Schuyler's depiction of their villainy is unrelenting, and often this villainy appears to be without motive.

Thus Schuyler found himself in *Slaves Today* creating a type of black character which had no place within the accepted boundaries of realistic portraiture. It had been easy at the beginning of the 1920s to justify satire's grotesques, since they were white characters who had been shaped by the racist society in which they lived. The Negro satirist sometimes assumed that his satire would reform these grotesques through the corrective power of laughter. By the end of the decade, Schuyler seemed to suggest both that the grotesques could be black and that they might be beyond humor's redemptive touch. Yet neither he nor the other black intellectuals of the decade could reconcile this possibility with realism (Mencken's "normalities"), and the possibility of reconciliation would remain unacknowledged until Richard Wright's *Native Son* (1940).

An intriguing question remains: Why did the object of Negro satire change color? That is, why did the satirists suddenly focus more attention on their own than on the master race? One possibility may be that the vices of white people had passed the point of being funny. Throughout the 1920s, racism was as virulent as it had been during the prewar period; the Dyer antilynching bill died time after time on the floor of Congress, and if such were the case, was it still possible to laugh at white Americans who were insensitive to ridicule? Was it possible to maintain an urbane voice of gentle cynicism in the face of nightmarish Yahoos? But perhaps an answer closer to home might explain why the black satirist now lampooned black people instead of white. Perhaps the real reason lay in the disillusionment with the very dreams of the Renaissance itself. For if the Renaissance did begin as an internal affair, as Alain Locke had argued, then it was only fitting that when disaster came, the black intellectuals would turn inward for an explanation of what went wrong.

In any event, at the end of the decade there existed a wealth of fine writing that fulfilled Mencken's demand for self-criticism. The short stories of Zora Neale Hurston, Claude McKay, and Rudolph Fisher, and novels such as *The Blacker the Berry, Infants of Spring, Quicksand, Passing, One Way to Heaven, Black No More, The Walls of Jericho*—these tackled such difficult subjects as self-hatred (*Quicksand, Gingertown*), prejudice within the race (*The Blacker the Berry*), racial chauvinism (*One Way to Heaven*), and the black confidence man (*Black No More*). To a certain extent, Mencken had paved the way for this sort of satire with his Ovington review. Yet the call to depict the inner life of the Negro was intended to produce the Great Negro Novel. By the end of the decade, looking at Negro life from the inside had degenerated (at least in some eyes) to a kind of irresponsible smartness.

This was the way it appeared to Allison Davis, who, writing for the *Crisis*, accused a whole generation of new "intellectuals" of being "Menckenites."[59] He focused specifically on George Schuyler and Eugene Gordon, "young critics, writing for magazines and Negro newspapers . . . largely inspired by their master's attack upon Negro preachers and 'misleaders,' and his heralding of the 'self-critical Negro.'" Davis accused both Schuyler and Gordon of dealing in "eccentricities." Trying to be original, they sacrifice truth for wit, he wrote; their cleverness is "without taste, their radicalism without intelligence, their contempt for Negro leaders and our upper class, uninformed by serious principles." These men—Mencken included—lack a "discriminating judgment." In contrast to Van Vechten's espousal of primitivism and sensationalism, both Schuyler and Gordon yield to a facile iconoclasm: "A sterile cynicism has driven our Menckenized critics into smart coarseness." He added that both men and "their imitators" ("at two removes from Mr. Mencken") are playing the clown for white folk. Self-respect, emphasized Davis, is an important quality for black people, and both Schuyler and Gordon have lost it. The real virtues of the race are "fortitude, irony, and a relative absence of self-pity," and yet these two pretend that these qualities do not exist in order that they might dance the cakewalk before a gaping multitude.

By 1928, however, when Davis's article appeared, many Negro intellectuals did not believe that these virtues were endemic to the race—at least not to the upper crust of the loaf. Fearful of disgrace, humorless, ready to run to the Wailing Wall at a moment's notice—these were some of the charges leveled by Langston Hughes in 1926. It was because Mencken seemed to stand behind the younger men that his reputation took on a new meaning. Now the black intellectual community no longer saw him as a defender of the people but rather as a disturber of the peace—not the peace of the southerners, as in the early 1920s, but the peace of the race itself. Why criticize Negro preachers, some wondered, when the Klan was still marching in Washington, D.C.? Why focus on something as problematical as Negro "self-satisfaction" when most Negroes in the South couldn't vote? This approach by a former friend did not make any sense to the *Crisis*, but it did make sense to those black intellectuals who were tired of a black audience that had criticized their shortcomings but had failed to support their best efforts. These intellectuals—bogus or not—believed with Mencken that in a sense the external racial situation did not matter. What mattered was a clean house in a disordered world. To these men, skepticism and self-criticism seemed to be the only ways out of the sticky mess created by the race itself. They were ready to write satire, to paint the Negro's portrait for the gallery of fools.

The change in the object of satire was only one manifestation of the new mood of the Negro intellectuals, young and old. By 1927, many felt that the Harlem Renaissance had simply come and gone, without much happening in between. The biggest disappointment lay not in the race's failure to write satire at the white man's expense, but in the race's inability to produce the Great Negro Novel. Mencken had stressed that such a triumph would herald the emergence of the race from immaturity to maturity. This view was consistent, of course, with the broader one that held that if the Negro could create great art, if he could prove to the world that Negroes were an artistic people and loved great art, then the race would be accepted into the pantheon of civilizations. And although satire was naturally considered to be a noble endeavor, having behind it such prestigious names as Swift, Shaw, and Mencken himself, it was not the noblest endeavor—at least not for the America of the 1920s. No, the literary form to excel in was not satire but the novel. If one could write the Great Negro Novel, then the race would have something to be really proud of.

CHAPTER SIX

The Negro Novel
and the Limits of Realism

In his book reviews for the *Smart Set*, Mencken gave the impression that although America was a cultural nullity, someone out there in the vast steppes of the hinterland was writing the Great American Novel. He had already startled his reading public in 1908 by proclaiming *Huckleberry Finn* to be the best novel ever written by an American, and when *Jennie Gerhardt* was published in 1911, he came close to pinning the honor on Dreiser's effort. Mencken called *Jennie* a "Novel of the First Rank," and he implied that it was a work of art in the same class with Beethoven's Fifth Symphony. Its major distinction was that it "depicts the life we Americans are living with extreme accuracy and criticises that life with extraordinary insight."[1] Thus Mencken clearly established the criteria for writing the Great American Novel: It had to be realistic, honest, about Americans (preferably those of non-Anglo-Saxon stock), and critical of American life.

Mencken's method of reviewing novels in the *Smart Set* was subtly didactic. In his monthly column, he would condemn books as trash, and he would often complain about the poor state of American letters and the even poorer state of American taste; at the same time he made one feel that the repair of this defect was of the utmost importance both to him and to the nation at large. His strategy here is reminiscent of Walter Lippmann's famous remark about him in 1926: "He calls you a swine, and an imbecile, and he increases your will to live."[2] Mencken called American writers hacks and increased their will to write, called the American public illiterate asses and increased their desire to read.

Mencken's negative attitude, then, was often a rhetorical ploy. Although he might sound pessimistic about America's literary future, his last word was rarely pessimistic. For instance, he told his readers in 1920 that he had a glass of "near beer" with Carl Sandburg at a dingy little bar in Chicago, and though the beer was bad, Sandburg's conversation was interesting. The poet argued, said Mencken, that in the next fifty years American letters would undergo a tremendous cultural renaissance. "I had heard the whole thing before," Mencken said skeptically, "but where?" Then he realized that this theme of the Great Awakening had been uttered by Emerson, Whitman, and even more recently by a man who ordinarily showed good sense, Van Wyck Brooks. Mencken the scoffer could only laugh: "Always the same gaudy vision, the same baroque and enchanting dream. Always the pot of gold at the foot of the rainbow."[3]

Yet three months after his amusement at Sandburg's expense, he was already changing his mind. Anderson's *Winesburg, Ohio* was a great novel, he said; its "true worth" would be appreciated "in the years to come." Then he added, "If the great American novelists visioned by Carl Sandburg ever escape from Chautauqua . . . they will learn much more from *Winesburg* than ever they learned from Howells and Henry James."[4] And a month after this, he was admitting that Emerson and Whitman might be right—"Maybe even Sandburg is right." And why? Mencken had just read Sinclair Lewis's *Main Street*, and "it is, in brief, good stuff."[5] Throughout the early 1920s, Mencken kept finding more "good stuff," such as *Babbitt* ("at least twice as good a novel as *Main Street*").[6] As he said in February 1921, "Good novels by Americans, once so rare, become plentiful. Month before last I told you of Sherwood Anderson's *Poor White*. Last month I hymned Sinclair Lewis's *Main Street*. This month I offer *Moon Calf* by Floyd Dell."[7] Mencken kept a running account of the batting averages of American authors, hinting that someday, someone was going to hit a home run and that he would be there to tell about it. No wonder Fitzgerald wrote *The Great Gatsby* hoping for Mencken's approval. No one did more than Mencken between 1908 and 1930 to sustain the illusion that the Great American Novel could be written— and perhaps by a week from Monday.

Mencken kept up a continuous search in newspaper articles, in the *Smart Set*, and in his *Prejudices* series for new novelists to explore the American scene. Where was the woman novelist who would write her version of *Main Street*? What we need, he said, is an "articulate Carol Kennicott."[8] Where the novelist who would describe New York? "It is astonishing that no Zola has arisen to describe this engrossing and incomparable dance of death."[9] Who, he asked, will do "the very *Ur-Amerikaner*—the malignant moralist, the Christian turned cannibal, the snouting and preposterous Puritan"?[10] Who will do the "university president of the new model, half the quack, half the visionary, and wholly the go-getter"?[11] Who will do the American politician, the American journalist, the American policeman, the American clergyman ("not to be confused with the brutal, dogmatic Puritan") who is a modern businessman as well as a soul-saver?[12]

Mencken never tired of throwing out these "hints" for novelists, and always he strongly implied that "de-Americanized Americans" were not capable of acting on them.[13] In imitating Henry James, they had lost their ties to the American scene, or, to borrow a phrase from Malcolm Cowley's *Exile's Return*, they had undergone a "process of deracination."[14] If there was any hope, it would come from writers of the Midwest (such as Anderson) or from the Plains (such as Willa Cather) or from the southern wasteland (such as Julia Peterkin or Howard Odum). And who knows what the pulp factories might spew forth? For "is it so soon forgotten that Willa Cather used to be one of the editors of *McClure's*," or "that Dreiser . . . was an editor of dime novels,"[15] or that Sinclair Lewis was once "a star of the magazines, and apparently unfit for anything better"?[16]

In December 1923, Mencken took his leave from the *Smart Set*, and he decided that an assessment of the literary scene was in order. Later, he thought so highly of this farewell piece that he included it as part of "The American Novel," an essay he wrote for *Prejudices, Fourth Series* (1924). This inclusion is significant because for Mencken the status of the novel was synonymous with the status of the American literary scene.

In these two essays, Mencken argued that the literary situation had improved considerably since 1908, the year he began with the *Smart Set*. Comstockery was in abeyance—if not dead, at least lying still; the school-marmish New Humanists were in hiding; and the publishers were hospitable to new novelists who followed in the wakes of Dreiser, Lewis, and Anderson. For Mencken, it was Dreiser who had set the pace: "They all try to write better than Dreiser, and not a few of them succeed, but they all follow him in his fundamental purpose—to make the novel true."[17]

Still, Mencken was not completely happy. The artist is now "free," he declared, but he still has not proved that he has earned his freedom. He is too easily lured by the promise of big money from the magazines or the movies; he is too easily conned by his own propensity to be a "reformer" and not an artist; and he is too easily tempted by the gaudy aesthetic experiments of Greenwich Village, so that he has forgotten about content for the sake of style. "Many of the White Hopes of ten or fifteen years ago perished in the war," he said, and Mencken feared that many of the new White Hopes were beguiled by the latest aesthetic cant, by the newest political or social solutions, or by the glittering silver dollar. There is a "group," however, "which says little and saws wood,"[18] and although Mencken was not thinking of the Negro writers when he said this, one can be sure that the Negro writers who read it saw themselves as replacing the White Hopes who had perished, saw themselves as the Black Hopes who would suddenly appear and revitalize the American novel.

For had not Mencken told them to come out of their closets in his review of Ovington's novel, and had he not said that if anyone could tell the truth about the South, it would be the "Aframerican novelist, now struggling heavily to emerge"? It is more than a coincidence that Mencken's encouragement of Negro writers from 1917 to 1924 came at a time when he was encouraging other American writers to write the Great American Novel. And it is more than a coincidence that their new assessment of the literary situation in America was occurring at the same time as his, and that it was held within the context of realism, the mode that American writers and critics had associated with Mencken's name for almost two decades.

❧

In the early 1920s, two ideas about the Negro novel appeared time and again: Somebody was going to write a great one, and it would probably be an epic[19] — possibly it would be the Great American Novel. By 1929, the cynical Albert Halper was only expressing a truism when he wrote for the *Dial* that "editors and other folk seem to believe that out of the negro will come the great American Novel, the epic poem of America."[20] By this time, the list of white novelists who wrote about Negroes or who wanted to write their "Negro novel" was lengthy: Edna Ferber, Joseph Hergesheimer, DuBose Heyward, Roark Bradford, Clement Wood, Vera Caspery, I.A.R. Wylie, Gertrude Sanborn, Maxwell Bodenheim, Waldo Frank, T. S. Stribling, Sherwood Anderson, Carl Van Vechten, and many others.[21] When Van Vechten's favorite character, Gareth Johns, "wistfully" says in *Nigger Heaven*, "I think I'd like to write a Negro novel," he is only repeating an urge that seemed to strike every white novelist of his generation. Even by 1925, this situation of "Whites writing up Blacks" had become such a cliché that Hemingway could make fun of it in *The Torrents of Spring:* "Could that be the laughter of the Negro?" Hemingway's hero wonders.[22] Hemingway is satirizing not only Sherwood Anderson's *Dark Laughter* but the tendency to romanticize blacks as if they were a Greek chorus and the key to discovering mysterious, inchoate America. (Of course, Hemingway was to do a bit of romanticizing himself in *The Sun Also Rises*; Bill Gorton's tale of the "splendid nigger" could quite easily have found its way into Claude McKay's *Banjo:* the natural man versus corrupt Western civilization.)

Yet the white novelist's romanticizing had less impact on the theory of the Negro novel than did Mencken's advice in his Ovington article. What black critic George Morse said in 1929 can be taken as an attitude that was present all through the 1920s among black writers: "Just as we await the great American novel, which we almost welcomed in *Main*

Street, we still await the novel that adequately satisfies our comprehension of the Negro and the problems that are peculiar to him."[23] The association that Morse makes for the Negro novel is not with Harriet Beecher Stowe but with Sinclair Lewis, and the approach he is asking for is not melodrama but attention to detail. This is not to say that the idea of an epic was dismissed; instead, it was redefined in more homely terms. Braithwaite could still talk about the "great epic novel of the South," but Alain Locke would add that if such a book were written, it would follow the "realistic fiction of Negro life" currently emerging in the New South. The model for the New Negro novelist was René Maran, who with his "daring realism" and "Latin frankness" was "educative and emancipating."[24] Thus, when Oswald Garrison Villard (editor of the prestigious *Nation*) said in 1923 that "the great Negro novelist has yet to appear on this side of the ocean as René Maran has appeared on the other," he was only foreshadowing the major premise of the Harlem Renaissance for the Great Negro Novel: Just as Maran had realistically treated the natives of French Africa in his prize-winning *Batouala* (1921), so too the Negro novelist must follow the same antiromantic approach to art.[25] Or as Arnold Mulder put it in "Wanted: A Negro Novelist" (1924), he must steer clear of sentimentalities—the folksy darkey, the lynched victim, the loyal mammy. He will have to take a clean hard look at himself and his people, for only he can do it—only he "can lay bare for us the inner life of a people nominally free but living all the time under the menace of the mob's rope. . . . It is quite likely that no white man can do it. It is reasonable to suppose that his white psychology will always be in the way."[26]

In the early 1920s, Alain Locke and W.E.B. DuBois began to outline a program of aesthetic realism for the Negro writer. In an article called "The Colonial Literature of France," which he wrote for the newly created *Opportunity* in 1923, Locke took the opportunity to make some cross-cultural connections. Calling René Maran the "Zola of Colonial literature," Locke singled out his treatment of native life for special commendation. Maran did not simply use this material "as an artistic foil" for delineating the characters and political machinations of the superior race. No, he was quite interested in this material for its own sake, and seeing African society from the inside, he painted it with colors taken from nature, not art. Locke strongly implied that Afro-American authors could learn a lesson from Maran. They were urged to take a "purely aesthetic approach" to black life, to create "art for its own sake combined with that stark cult of veracity—the truth, whether it hurts or not."[27]

DuBois too was making his pleas for "the truth, whether it hurts or not." In 1921, he chastised his readers for not being able to accept the truth about themselves. "We are so used to seeing the truth distorted to our despite, that whenever we are portrayed on canvas, in story or on the stage, as simply human with human frailties, we rebel." The metaphor of art as a mirror is crucial to DuBois's argument. We are "distorted," he said, in the stories of Octavus Roy Cohen; but although we recognize the falseness of Cohen's portraiture, we develop a paranoia about all forms of artistic representation. "When the artist paints us he has a right to paint us whole and not ignore everything which is not as perfect as we would wish it to be. The black Shakespeare must portray his black Iagos as well as his white Othellos." Yet, DuBois continued, "we shrink from this," and the effect of this fear is pernicious. It discourages our artists from painting the truth, and they end by portraying "a world of stilted artificial black folk such as never were on land or sea." However, in 1921 DuBois optimistically thought that both artist and audience could overcome their timidity: "We stand today secure enough in our accomplishment and self confidence to lend the whole stern human truth about ourselves to the transforming hand and seeing art of the Artist, white and black."[28]

Other black critics in the early 1920s began to play off their ideas about realism against recently published novels by white authors. In 1922, three novels of Negro life had been published by three southern writers: H. A. Shands, Clement Wood, and T. S. Stribling. Mencken's essays had undoubtedly influenced the writing of all three novels, for each depicted a southern landscape in a different stage of barbarism. Stribling's novel (*Birthright*) made perhaps the greatest impact on black intellectuals because of the author's conception of his black hero. Peter Siner leaves Hooker's Bend, Tennessee, to be educated at Harvard, but when he returns home, he finds his education of little use. Like both Wood and Shands, Stribling treats the poor whites who live in, and control, Hooker's Bend as only a notch above simians; yet Peter's dilemma turns out to be more complicated than racial discrimination. Still an innocent after four years at Harvard, he sets out to improve the relations between white and black in the small southern town. He is defeated—as much by the folkways of his own people as by the malice of the whites: "The ethical engine that Peter had patiently builded in Harvard almost ceased to function in this weird morality of Niggertown."[29] At the novel's end, he decides to stop fighting both the white and black worlds and simply accept himself as a Negro. He marries the compromised Cissie Dildine and leaves all his high ideals in Hooker's Bend; as he and Cissie board a boat for Chicago, Peter at last has "made the amazing discovery that although he had spent four years in Harvard, he had come out, just as he went in, a negro" (p. 309).

All three novels came under the scrutiny of Alain Locke and Jessie Fauset in the *Crisis*. Of Wood's *Nigger* and Shands's *White and Black*, Locke complained that the authors' realism was too objective, as if black people were being studied under a microscope. What was needed was self-analysis, a realism that humanized black lives through the author's ability to see things from the inside.[30] Jessie Fauset was especially irritated by the implications of *Birthright*'s conclusions, yet she (like Locke) admitted that no treatment of Negro life could afford to leave the strict bounds of realism. "The successful 'Negro' novel must limn Negro men and women as they really are with not only their virtues but their faults. If Mr. Stribling went too far in depicting shiftless, atavistic Peter Siner, care must be taken too to avoid the portrayal of a character too emasculate and 'too good for human nature's daily food.' After all, this is just a round about way of saying that the portrayal of black people calls increasingly for black writers."[31] Again we see Mencken's advice to the Negro novelist repeated: the privileged view, characters seen with compassion, and characters who are true to life—real men and women with faults and virtues. Yet Fauset's remarks about Peter Siner suggest that realism may present an artistic universe as self-limiting as any other. The troublesome phrase in Fauset's passage is that Stribling "went too far." What she meant is that it is improbable and hence unrealistic that a character having a Harvard education would experience such a fall from grace.

She was not alone in making this charge. The atavistic ending of *Birthright* upset other Negro intellectuals around this time (1922-23), though they had mixed feelings about the novel. Here is a middle-class Negro as a hero, said Charles S. Johnson, but he is "unnatural."[32] Johnson, Benjamin Brawley, Walter White, and William Stanley Braithwaite all agreed—in Braithwaite's words—that Stribling had broken "new ground," but that he had a "totally false conception of the character of Peter Siner." Said Braithwaite of Stribling, "His failure was in limiting . . . the capacity of the hero to assimilate culture, and in forcing his rapid reversion to the level of his origin after a perfect Harvard training."[33] Said Fauset of Stribling's hero, "Here is a boy brave and far-visioned enough to pick himself up out of the ruck and mire and to get away to the very best of intellectual and aesthetic life only to yield on his return to the worst features of it. This hardly seems likely."[34]

Yet would Peter Siner's fate have surprised Mencken, he who so loved *Heart of Darkness*? In one sense, Johnson, Braithwaite, Brawley, Fauset, and White all rallied to realism as a defense because Peter Siner was a stereotype that they wished to combat; realistically, however, if Kurtz could betray his high ideals in the Congo, why not Peter in Hooker's Bend? There is a paradox here which is centered in the whole notion of "truth" in black art. On the one hand, DuBois told his readers that "we can afford the truth," that we need realistic portrayal to ensure the recognition of our humanity. On the other hand, neither he nor the others wanted too much "truth"—certainly not the kind that would make the Negro seem inhuman. For no one wanted to recognize (as did Richard Wright in *Native Son*) that there might indeed be some reality behind the stereotypes in American literature (although Wright would give his own explanation for them). The black intellectuals of the 1920s were willing to go so far with the truth but shrank from going any further. One can see this avoidance in the language Braithwaite used about Peter Siner; a "perfect Harvard education" sounds like an immaculate conception that should remove all doubt about Peter's inability to fall. Similarly, Jessie Fauset's last words on Peter's atavistic behavior, "This hardly seems likely," simply remove the question by not thinking about it. More than one writer in Western civilization has seen it "likely" that man should betray his best self; why did the black intellectuals shrink from facing this truth?

The reason lies, I think, in a political issue that kept intruding upon the aesthetic province of realism. To face the real truth of black life, as Richard Wright would do in *Black Boy* and *Native Son*, meant dropping the frail facade of gentility. DuBois and others fought hard to escape the bottomless pit; they were all educated men and women, some of them having impressive degrees from eminent academic institutions.[35] They could sympathize with those lower down, but always on their own terms. DuBois, for instance, could speak most eloquently of the origin and meaning of the "Sorrow Songs" in *The Souls of Black Folk*, and Locke seemed preoccupied almost to the point of obsession with the "folk gifts" of the race. Nevertheless, they refused to recognize—in the 1920s at least—that poverty, suffering, and oppression could turn people into Bigger Thomases, for that recognition touched upon the fragility of their own tenuous position as members of an elite class.

After all, the class lines in black life were, for the most part, more clearly defined than in the white world, since the gap between those who had something and those who did not was great. Despite their rebellious demeanor, even the Young Wits could not quite break away from the idea of what being an intellectual meant to the older generation. It meant having a formal education, just as being a member of a real middle class meant having cash in one's pocket. Wallace Thurman may have turned bohemian in Harlem, but he went to the University of Southern California first. His white counterpart in Winesburg, Ohio, on the contrary, might go to Greenwich Village and call himself an intellectual, even though he had no formal education whatever. Mencken, of course, made fun of such pretentiousness, but then his own formal education, if he had been black, would have seemed woefully inadequate. He did not feel the need to go to Harvard or to any other university because, like the other white intellectuals of his time, he was in rebellion against academe and felt confident in that rebellion. The black intellectuals were not so secure. Even the incorrigible Claude McKay, the enfant terrible of the Harlem Renaissance, attended Kansas State College; and when Langston Hughes dropped out of Columbia University to pursue his travels, he took time off to get a degree from Lincoln University before he resumed them. Whatever his ostensible rebellion from the black middle class—and it was genuine enough—Hughes was not so rebellious as his white counterpart; he may have railed most vociferously against the obtuseness of the black middle class, but his return to a college community is symbolic of the insecurity that plagued all black intellectuals during the 1920s.

Thus, the political barrier between elites and nonelites (the masses) defined the kinds of questions about realism which would be asked by the black writers during the decade. Should the black middle class be given the primary consideration in the black novel, because it is the most "Real" (the best) in a Platonic sense? Or should lowlife be depicted because it represents the majority of the race? Locke would argue the latter view, always careful to make an important qualification: "The program of the Negro Renaissance was to interpret the folk to itself, to vitalize it from within."[36] The key word here of course is "interpret"; the writer is to tell the folk what the folk is. That only intellectuals use such a word as "folk" should have been hint enough that realism of this kind would go only part way.

Yet given the benefit of historical hindsight, we should not be too hard on the Renaissance's intellectuals. The aesthetic problems of realism were difficult enough without the added problem of class insecurity. Mencken grappled with the wild stallion called realism, and it managed to throw even him; following Mencken's lead, Walter White tried his hand at riding the beast, and although he too landed on a fleshy part of his anatomy, the ride itself had some twists and turns that are worth noting.

Mencken believed not only that the novelist was "half a scientist" (a careful observer), but that the novel itself was "representational"; that is, it presented "a genuine description and interpretation of life as human beings are living it in the world."[37] In short, it held the mirror up to nature. Although this definition of the novel, given as early as 1913, seems literal-minded, Mencken (like Aristotle) was quick to point out to the novelist that art was *not* life. As he told Walter White, "In fiction, it is not sufficient merely to convince the reader that an episode is possible, it is also necessary to convince him that it is probable. He will believe a story on the front page of a newspaper that would make him laugh even in the Argosy Magazine."[38] Thus, art reflects reality, but it is also more ordered than life. The artist's theme may be that life is meaningless, that it is chaotic flux without pattern, but the novel that presents such a theme must in itself be clearly patterned, observing the laws of probability and causality. Clearly, then, the novelist is only half a scientist; as an artist, he shapes his material, and he expresses an attitude toward it. Mencken berated Arnold Bennett, whom he ordinarily admired, for being too detached from his people—the opposite vice of someone such as H. G. Wells, he added, who had recently developed the bad habit of interjecting himself between his characters and our perceptions of them.[39]

Yet although Mencken did insist that art and life are distinct, his theory of realism as representational often caused him to blur the distinction. "Realism," he said, "is simply intellectual honesty in the artist. The realist yields nothing to what is manifestly not true, however alluring. He makes no compromise with popular sentimentality and illusion. He avoids the false inference as well as the bogus fact."[40] Because Mencken was in constant warfare with those people and forces who would stand in the way of "intellectual honesty" (the southern chauvinists, the puritan moralists, the weepy-eyed populace), he often overstated his case for realism. If the novel departs from "representational fidelity ever so slightly," he once warned, "it becomes to that extent a bad novel."[41] That a novel was "true" was sometimes the only standard he seized upon in judging a book's worth, and his espousal of this criterion could not but influence the black novelists' conception of their own work. Consider Walter White's remark to Rudolph Fisher in 1925, a published novelist writing to an unpublished one. Those black writers, said White, "who are writing about Negro life as it really exists are exploring a field which is as yet practically untouched. I remember a letter from Mr. Mencken shortly after I had been asked by a publisher to eliminate considerable portions of my own novel because of fear that it would offend the South. Mr. Mencken wrote me, 'the pussyfooting Southern novel is dead and the only hope in writing such fiction lies in complete honesty.'"[42] For White and others, seeing black life "as it really exists" and expressing that perception in art became the dominant concern of the 1920s. They were exploring virgin territory, and they had a moral obligation to explore it correctly—to tell the real truth about Negro life as only a Negro could tell it.

Yet telling the truth about Negro life "as it really exists" carried a burden that White did not quite understand when he wrote *The Fire in the Flint.* Whenever someone complained to him after the novel was published that he had loaded the dice against the South or that he had made all southerners into Genghis Khans, he would always return the answer that these events and people were true. Everything in his novel, he would say, was based upon actual fact, which he could verify from his own investigations of lynchings in the South. In reply to a person who had complained that *The Fire in the Flint* was "overdrawn," White said that he "could furnish [you] with hundreds, even thousands of cases far more terrible than anything that is pictured in my novel."[43] Although White here forgot Mencken's warning that art and life are not the same, Mencken himself sometimes talked as if art and life were one. As he said of Sinclair Lewis, "No other contemporary novelist . . . has dredged more memorable stuff out of the illimitable stock of what-everyone-knows. The joy of recognition is not the only joy that a work of art can engender, but it is surely one of the most agreeable and satisfying."[44]

In light of the background of lies about Negroes in fiction, White should not be blamed too harshly for thinking that the "joy of recognition" would be enough. His problem as a novelist was compounded, however, by trying to follow Mencken down too many side roads. White himself realized the extent to which he was indebted to the Sage of Baltimore, for he told one correspondent that to Mencken "more than to any other man I owe what little I have done in the way of writing."[45] In *The Fire in the Flint*, he had set two goals for himself: to tell the truth about the South and to be an objective novelist. At first glance, these two goals do not seem contradictory; the problem lay in what White considered to be the truth about the South, for he saw himself imitating Mencken in "The Sahara of the Bozart."

There is no doubt that White admired that essay tremendously. When it appeared in *Prejudices, Second Series*, White—though he had not yet met Mencken—wrote to him, praising him for his honesty and courage.[46] Soon the young man from Atlanta seemed to be quoting the essay everywhere. Naturally, it served as the major inspiration for writing *The Fire in the Flint*, and when Doran received the manuscript and hesitated about accepting it, White rushed to its defense by quoting Mencken's essay verbatim. "The South," White told Eugene Saxton, "is 'as sterile, artistically, intellectually, culturally, as the Sahara Desert.'"[47] On another occasion, he told Saxton that "in seeking to oppress the Negro the white South has created a Frankenstein monster that is all but devouring the South."[48] Unhappily, Mencken's essay all but devoured White's novel. What White failed to see was that "The Sahara of the Bozart" was not a realistic picture of the South, but a satire. Mencken had deliberately distorted the South for comic effect, and in so doing he had created a region that had more in common with Swift's Laputa than with Lewis's Gopher Prairie. Inevitably White misinterpreted Mencken's tone, translating it in his own novel into one of self-righteous stridency. Consequently, his polemic against the South in *The Fire in the Flint* did not fit comfortably with his aims of objectivity.

It is important to understand that White had intended to be objective. He had read Mencken's advice in the Ovington review, and he was determined to take a nondidactic approach to his material. A good indication of his desire for detachment appears in an unpublished letter of 1925, in which White explained his narrative method in *The Fire in the Flint*. "I tried, with the same scientific objectivity of the chemist in the laboratory, to place Kenneth Harper with certain ideas and ideals in the midst of a definite environment and then to present as fairly as I could his reactions to the environment and the environment's reaction towards him."[49] In this description, White was undoubtedly thinking of an earlier statement by Mencken about George Bernard Shaw. Paraphrasing Shaw, Mencken imagined the playwright saying, "Here . . . I have set down certain human transactions and depicted certain human beings brought face to face with definite conditions, and I have tried to show them meeting these conditions as persons of their sort would meet them in real life."[50] In both instances, one might say that the artist merely watches; he does not interfere with the workings of fate.

Ostensibly, White's story does follow the procedure he set down in his letter. *The Fire in the Flint* deals with a young doctor who returns to his hometown to practice medicine after being educated at a reputable university in the east.[51] He soon discovers that his desire to remain aloof from the racial problems of Central City, Georgia, is impossible. Distressed by the economic plight of the poor black tenant farmers in the area, he tries to start a farm cooperative despite white opposition, but before he can put this into effect, his sister is raped and his brother brutally murdered. Driven half-mad with grief, he avenges his brother's death and meets his own at the hands of a lynch mob. As White later described his hero's moral development, "A latent spark, covered over by a disinclination to do anything other than follow his profession, is struck into a flame of revolt."[52] Thus, he uses a metaphor from a laboratory experiment to explain the significance of the novel's title.

If White had written as he said he was going to, he might have produced a good novel—or at least a consistent one. Yet he also wanted to depict the South as a case of arrested development, a victim of a strange kind of psychological paralysis that had frozen everything in the Confederacy as solid as a granite statue left over from the Civil War. This was Mencken's thesis in "The Sahara of the Bozart," but, unlike Mencken, White could not attach this exaggeration to an aesthetic purpose; it became merely an excuse to preach.

White's defense of his novel as a kind of aesthetic laboratory experiment was not his last word on the subject. He knew he had been guilty of special pleading in *The Fire in the Flint*, and he had promised Mencken and other white friends that he was going to avoid the "Messianic delusion" in his next novel (*Flight*, 1926).[53] Nevertheless, he also developed an interesting argument for the "propagandist" in black fiction, and he did not hesitate to express it to his black friends. J. A. Rogers had told White that he had heard *The Fire in the Flint* called a "propaganda type" novel, and he further noted that most people have "such queer and stereotyped views" on the differences between art and propaganda.[54] White, of course, eagerly picked up on the subject.

> There is such a thing as preaching in a novel or poem or play or in any other art form which would spoil the thing from the viewpoint of pure art. On the other hand, however, there are a great many white people and even a number of colored people, who, it seems to me, lean over backwards in trying to dodge the imputation of spreading "propaganda." Some of these people fall down in adoration before the name of Swift who, to my mind, was one of the greatest propagandists who ever lived. Again, Flaubert is held up as a model for writers. Yet no person can read his *Sentimental Education* and fail to see his decided aversion for any liberal in politics or any other field.

And then he added the following significant observation: "I fail to see how any person can write honestly and intelligently about Negroes without making his characters discuss in one form or another this thing we call the race problem."[55]

Although White cleverly dodged the question of whether he in fact preached from a soapbox in *The Fire in the Flint*, his remarks on the artist as propagandist are perceptive. If we are going to treat *real* Negroes in our fiction, how can we ask them not to speak about social issues when these issues are crucial to their lives? We cannot simply abstract their humanity from their racial identity—to do so would be unrealistic. Hence, there is no such thing as "pure art" as far as Negroes are concerned, because if artists are to treat them realistically, they are going to have to place them in the context of racial tension and racial strife.

Of course, what White should have said was that there is no such thing as pure art in the novel. Every author, as Wayne Booth reminds us in *The Rhetoric of Fiction*, communicates his value system to his readers, no matter what kind of narrative method he uses. White's problem—and here he was not alone—was that he was not quite sure whether he should have in fact shown "aversion" in his fiction. On the one hand, he wanted to be as detached as a scientist, as detached as James Joyce's artist who pares his fingernails behind the scenes as his characters go about their business. On the other hand, he wanted to be Flaubert or Swift, the author who is unashamed of his aversion because it is just and is grounded in the fundamental truth of things. White's dilemma was that he could not quite decide which view represented the true artist, but in this he certainly was not alone. Wallace Thurman could find fault with himself for writing *The Blacker the Berry* because in this novel he felt he had betrayed his artistic detachment. His original plan was "to interpret some of the internal phenomena of Negro life in America," yet he saw that he had indirectly, but continually, brought up the presence of white people to explain the behavior of his own race.[56] That he had written a brilliant satire on this behavior seemed less important to him than that he had stooped to what he saw as propaganda. Ironically, both the position of aversion and that of detachment found their justification in a mimetic view of art, and the reason that many black intellectuals of the 1920s found themselves caught between art and propaganda is that no one reminded them of this fact. One could appeal to the supreme court of realism to defend whichever position one wished to hold, and Walter White is the perfect example of the artist who held both positions at the same time.

The blame for this confusion cannot be placed on the black intellectuals alone. Mencken himself had not always been consistent in his definition of realism. Frank Turaj has observed that Mencken's espousal of representational reality held an uneasy truce with aestheticism. He clapped with approval when Joel Spingarn said that poetry is no more moral or immoral than is "an isosceles triangle." He was always quick to point out to the moralists that art had its own kind of integrity, its own justification that defied the didactic. Yet Mencken the representational realist could pounce on a conception of beauty that existed *"in vacuo."* Although he praised Spingarn's liberation from "moralism," he hesitated to go all the way with what he considered Spingarn's art-for-art's sake position. He reminded the learned professor that art does have "its social, its political, even its moral implications." In other words, art is not just a product of the artist's imagination but is also an imitation of life, and hence it imitates all those nasty things that seem to stick to life.[57] Turaj further notes that what linked these two views of art was Mencken's belief in empiricism. Thus Mencken could argue that art is sui generis because it is created by the sense impressions of the author, but that it is also objectively verifiable because it is an imitation of reality. Says Turaj, these two views were knit together in Mencken's mind "with an unsightly seam."[58] One might argue that the seam was just as "unsightly" in the minds of the black intellectuals, and that before the Renaissance ended, it was to come apart more than once.

❦

In a sense, Walter White symbolizes the fulcrum of the art versus propaganda controversy that was fought with so much acrimony during the 1920s. The common view of this battle is that the lines were sharply drawn: Alain Locke standing coolly on one side of the trench with the word "art" emblazoned on his banner, and W.E.B. DuBois snarling on the other side with "propaganda" scrawled upon his fiery red shield. In truth, however, as we have seen in the case of White, the distinctions cannot be so easily perceived. Walter White, Jessie Fauset, and W.E.B. DuBois did not want soapbox oratory, and Locke admitted with Mencken that literature could not be void of "its social, its political, even its moral implications."

One can make sense out of this controversy, I think, by beginning with Mencken's basic premise about realism, that it is representational. The question inevitably arose, What section of the Negro people was the most representational, in the sense of the most representative? Although Jessie Fauset, Walter White, and W.E.B. DuBois would not admit it, they all made an unconscious assumption: They tacitly agreed that the race should be represented by its "best" element. Although all three knew that the "best" need not come from the middle class, they did make a distinction between "best" and "sordid." And because they associated the "best" with the "most real," they began to consider the sordid element in Negro life as unreal. As one might imagine, a conflict developed between their democratic desire to grant the artist his freedom to depict whatever he wants and their aristocratic prejudice that led them to spell "real" with a capital *R*. DuBois, in particular, let himself be trapped by this issue of representational reality, so that he often said things at odds with his more generous principles. From early on in the 1920s, he had waged war with white publishers and the white press against their depictions of Negroes in popular literature. He complained to the *Saturday Evening Post* about the mirror it held up to the Negro when it published only stories that showed the "lowlifer" as representative of the race. Could not the magazine publish stories about a better class of Negro, realistically rendered instead of distorted for the sake of slapstick comedy? "My chief criticism is not on what you *do* publish but rather on what you *do not* publish."[59]

Nevertheless, DuBois's concern for "what you *do* publish" led him to slant the mirror of art toward his own perspective. For instance, the questions that he asked in the *Crisis* symposium on Negro art reveal his bias for a certain kind of reality. He began by asking a seemingly innocuous question: Should the artist (black or white) be "under any obligations or limitations as to the sort of [Negro] character he will portray"? The answer to this question is obviously no—until one reads the remaining six questions:

2. Can any author be criticized for painting the worst or best characters of a group?

3. Can publishers be criticized for refusing to handle novelists that portray Negroes of education and accomplishment on the ground that these characters are no different from white folk and therefore not interesting?

4. What are Negroes to do when they are continually painted at their worst and judged by the public as they are painted?

5. Does the situation of the educated Negro in America with its pathos, humiliation and tragedy call for artistic treatment at least as sincere and sympathetic as "Porgy" received?

6. Is not the continual portrayal of the sordid, foolish and criminal among Negroes convincing the world that this and this alone is really and essentially Negroid, and preventing white artists from knowing other types and preventing black artists from daring to paint them?

7. Is there not a real danger that young colored writers will be tempted to follow the popular trend in portraying Negro character in the underworld rather than seeking to paint the truth about themselves and their own social class?[60]

The metaphor that frequently occurs here is one from actual portraiture: painting. How are Negroes to be painted? DuBois asks, and so the questionnaire seemingly espouses realism (mimesis) and gives the impression of being disinterested. Actually, however, his questionnaire to "the artists of the world" was subtly didactic. Its purpose was to convince black and white artists alike that they had an obligation to paint the educated Negro. Not only were questions six and seven rhetorical, they were meant to answer question two. In other words, yes, an author can be criticized for painting the worst side of his people. Question five was also rhetorical and also an answer to question two: No, an author cannot be criticized for painting the best elements in his group *if* those people have never received accurate portrayal in art. Question five was also an answer to question three: Since Negroes "of education and accomplishment" are obviously unique, then publishers are to be blamed for not printing works about them.

DuBois's essay "Criteria of Negro Art" (also published in 1926) further illustrates how his bias for a certain kind of reality affected his critical judgment. DuBois argued that "all art is propaganda," that is, that all art is a subjective presentation of the truth and therefore expresses a value system of the author's own making. Although DuBois was quite perceptive on this point, he let his own prejudice against white publishers lead him back to the issue of middle-class reality. Since he was convinced that white publishers would present only one perception of black life, he argued that black writers should commit themselves to expressing the real truth. The publishers are free to present their view of things, he claimed, "but I do care when propaganda is confined to one side while the other is stripped and silent."[61] There is a neat logical jump here, which DuBois did not realize he was making. Now the Negro's truth is confined to the race's "best" people, whereas Negro "lowlife" is simply a ploy by publishing houses to give white audiences what they want. As time went by, he actually began to think of Negro "lowlife" as a distortion of the truth, failing to distinguish between caricature and realistic portrayal. His critical judgments on seamy surroundings and seamy characters began to lose that "catholicity of temper" which he had so urged Negro audiences to develop. When he reviewed Van Vechten's *Nigger Heaven*, he saw his bête noire (Negro "nastiness") on every page,[62] when in truth Van Vechten was writing a rather complex social novel about the relationship between the classes on all levels. As time went by, DuBois became increasingly uncharitable to his own writers, reviewing *Home to Harlem* as if McKay had deliberately set out to wallow in the "untruths" that Van Vechten had made so popular.[63]

The aesthetic philosophy of Alain Locke was also committed to realism, but the trap that Locke fell into was different from DuBois's. Locke agreed with DuBois that realism liberated Negro portraiture from the stereotypes of the past. "By and large, the Negro as subject matter achieved artistic freedom and stature only as American literature itself crossed over into the domain of realism."[64] Still, Locke reacted so violently to the middle class's demand for the mirror of art to be held up to its face and its face alone that he went to another extreme: He suggested that art should divorce itself from all social significance. In "To Certain of Our Phillistines," he complained bitterly that the middle class could not make a purely aesthetic judgment of a work of art. They kept interjecting "irrelevant social values of 'representative' and 'unrepresentative,' 'favorable' and 'unfavorable'" into their responses to art, and thus they were destroying the possibility of creating a "truly racial art."[65] Locke urged the Negro artist to hold the mirror up to the "folk-spirit" of the race. Although this term was somewhat vague, he meant that the artist should try to paint the manners, mores, and customs of a people who have a distinct culture. Since that culture is distinct, the artist should focus on its inner machinery and avoid irrelevant issues. As one can see, there is temptation here to view all social issues outside the homogeneous culture as irrelevant, and it is not surprising that Locke sometimes yielded to it. Occasionally, he talked about "pure art values," as if a work of art were some kind of hermetically sealed test tube that would be contaminated by the foul air of social analysis.[66] Locke never intended to go to this extreme, but his hatred of propaganda sometimes pushed him over the edge. He began with the premise that special pleading in art is an admission of "group inferiority" (an argument that can hardly be faulted) and ended with the irrational conclusion that the "social problem" should not be included in art. Years later, he would praise Wright's *Native Son* for artistically rendering the social problem in the novel: "Bigger's type has the right to its day in the literary calendar."[67] Ironically, in *Home to Harlem*, Claude McKay had delineated "Bigger's type" with the same stark realism that Locke was to admire in Wright's novel. Yet in 1928, Locke refused to believe that Harlem turned people into wolves, as it had McKay's Zeddy.[68] Because he was committed to his golden dream of the city and to his pristine conception of "folk" culture, he accused McKay of ignoring the folk for the sake of seamy characters, of pandering to "decadent aestheticism" to please the tastes of white readers.[69] In making these statements, he seemed unaware of the irony that he had ended in the same critical camp as his arch enemy.

Actually, DuBois and Locke were much closer to one another in their essential views than their aesthetic positions implied. Both men believed that beauty and truth were one, and that realism was the way for the Negro artist to reveal (in Locke's words) "the beauty which prejudice and caricature have obscured and overlaid."[70] DuBois's emphasis on propaganda was actually a plea for Locke's "self-expression": The Negro's world would be revealed when the Negro artist told the truth about himself. And Locke's emphasis upon art was itself propagandistic: The truth in art, he kept saying, will set us free. Both men, in fact, tended to link realism in art with a kind of secular religion. Said DuBois, "Until the art of black folk compels recognition they will not be rated as human."[71] Locke was even more pious: "Negro things may reasonably be a fad for others; for us they must be a religion."[72]

One sad fact of the Harlem Renaissance is that each man came to think of the other as a heretic. Each man used realism as a club against his enemy. Locke accused DuBois of straying beyond the boundaries of mimesis, and DuBois hinted that Locke's conception of beauty was "disembodied." To a certain extent, both men were right in their accusations. Locke did gravitate toward a kind of deracinated realism, and DuBois did lose his urbanity as a critic. In his cooler moments, Locke certainly knew that including the social world in art was inescapable; in his calmer moments, DuBois knew that the milieu of whores and pimps was as real as that of doctors and lawyers. There is no doubt that the Harlem Renaissance was damaged by the failure of these two men to resolve their differences of opinion, which were not as irreconcilable as they seemed.

❦

Realism, Mencken had argued, involves a strong belief in the rational principle in man, no matter how irrational the gods might be. It involves the belief that what is "out there" is real and is objectively verifiable through the senses. It also involves the belief that what is real moves by certain immutable laws, which can be perceived, even explained. For Mencken and the generation that revered him, even the most bizarre behavior has some link to the rational. If such is the case, then experience, even the most private and personal, can be expressed in clear, simple, precise language. This view of art does not rule out the existence of oblique narration (the privileged view, the "unreliable narrator"), but it does exclude expression that is not clear and precise—expression that in fact depends upon myth and symbol because reality itself is unperceivable in any other terms.

Like Walter White, Jean Toomer had responded to the promise of realism, had recognized its value as a liberating force for the Negro author. Like Walter White, he had read Mencken's "Sahara of the Bozart," and it had started him thinking about the South and everything the region meant to black people. Yet unlike Walter White, he came to reject realism and Mencken's essay; the rejection led him to write *Cane*, a composite of prose, poetry, and even a drama ("Kabnis"), as well as an essay of his own about the South.

On the eve of *Cane*'s publication in 1923, Toomer wrote a piece that was to serve as an advertisement for both Waldo Frank's *Holiday* and his own book. It is unfortunate that his essay, "The South in Literature," was never published, for its themes foreshadowed those of Faulkner's fiction. Toomer asked the inevitable question: Compared with other sections of the country, why has the South not "contributed an equivalent achievement to our sectional art?" But instead of cataloging all the diseases that afflict the South, he focused on those elements of its spiritual terrain—normal or otherwise—that could inspire the artist.

> For surely no other section is so rich in the crude materials and experiences prerequisite to art. The South has a peasantry, rooted in the soil, such as neither the North nor West possess. Therefore, it has a basic adjustment to its physical environment (in sharp contrast to the restless mal-adjustment of the northern pioneer) the expression of which the general cultural body stands in need of. And, rising from its agricultural communities there spreads a Southern life of rich complexity. Factories, Main Streets, and survivals of the old plantations roughly chart these degrees. It has a strong theme of the black and white races. But above all, the South is a land of great passions: hate, fear, cruelty, courage, love, and aspiration. And it possesses a leisure by means of which these attributes might find their way into a significant culture.[73]

In brief, Toomer defined a world of exciting diversity, not one of deadening uniformity.

The difference between Jean Toomer and Walter White can be seen in how each interpreted Mencken's advice to young authors that the real South needed to be treated in American literature. White wrote to one correspondent in 1925 that "[Lawrence] Stallings was right in his review of my novel in which he spoke of Georgia as being full of the stuff of which novels and dramas are made. . . . It rests upon a few of us to use this material, not only because it is good dramatic stuff, but we have got to use it as a means of debunking the state and the South."[74] White primarily conceived of this "material" as a means of "debunking" the South, but Toomer wanted something more than a whip in his hand. Like White, Toomer told a story of an educated Negro who returns to Georgia (and like White too, he probably had *Birthright* in mind when he wrote it),[75] but his character, Kabnis, is not destroyed by southern racism or southern rot but by his own inability to come to terms with the South's rich complexities. As Toomer said in "The South in Literature," his hero, "a talented Negro," is "unequal to the task of winning a clear way through life." And it is the fecund life of Georgia that his "dissipated . . . forces" are unequal to.

Toomer puts it succinctly in *Cane:* "Things are so immediate in Georgia."[76] Kabnis's problem is that he cannot reconcile the spiritual and physical contradictions in this ever-present immediacy. He cannot reconcile the rednecks, red mud, rats, and hen coops—the ugliness of the small southern town—with the beauty of the natural world. "Kabnis is about to shake his fists heavenward. He looks up, and the night's beauty strikes him dumb" (p. 83). One character, Lewis, defines Kabnis's confusion: "Cant hold them, can you? Master; slave. Soil; and the overarching heavens. Dusk; dawn. They fight and bastardize you" (p. 107). Unable to harmonize the oppositions within southern life, past and present, Kabnis is also unable to reconcile the oppositions within himself.

For "Kabnis" tells a story about an artist manqué, about a black writer who fails to shape experience because he is overwhelmed by it—and not just by the experience of racial hostility. He is the artist become Cain, a cursed and alienated man. A crucial scene in the novel occurs when he rejects Father John, the spirit of the Negro past. The old man, living in Halsey's cellar, is the "dead blind father of a muted folk" (p. 105). The old man is also mute—except for one brief moment when he says something that has the terse ambiguity of an ancient oracle: "O th sin th white folks 'mitted when they made th Bible lie" (p. 115). Kabnis reacts to this platitude with disgust, and he calls Father John "you old black fakir." But he does not really hear what Father John has to say; perhaps the truth would be unbearable.

The lie that Father John speaks of is the American myth that Negroes are the descendents of Cain or of Canaan, Ham's son—Ham, who bears the curse of Noah's wrath: "Thou shalt be the servant of servants." Kabnis's tragedy is that he accepts the white man's lie. The curse placed upon him is not his Negro blood but his own self-hatred because he is part Negro. He has forgotten, or has never known, that the myth in Negro folklore works the other way. The white man is the Negro's Cain, the fratricide whose face blanched at the horror of what he had done.[77]

All of this meaning is present in Father John's speech, though Kabnis misses it. The meaning, reflecting the southern experience, is rich and multidimensional. There is no single way to view the South; and at the novel's end, Toomer implies that the South still awaits its interpreter. Kabnis is spiritually destroyed by his own weakness and the South's complexity, and Lewis, another educated visitor (and "what a stronger Kabnis might have been"), finds the "pain" of the black people in the small town too difficult to face (pp. 110-11). Both men want to be artists, but both ultimately fail in their attempts to render the South in artistic terms. Kabnis is swallowed up by it, and Lewis runs away from it. Although Carrie K embraces Father John at the novel's end (youth and age, past and present linked by her wordless grasp), there are no artists in this story to articulate their union. Only the natural world seems to respond to this spiritual embrace between the young girl and the old man, the morning sun sending "a birth-song slanting down gray dust streets and sleepy windows of the southern town" (p. 116).

A major theme in *Cane* is the theme of expression and its eternal elusiveness. In the "Song of the Son," Toomer, the narrator, the descendant of slaves, returns to the South to sing of his heritage before it fades forever into the daylight of modern times. Thus, the "son" returns before the "sun" can set on this generation of "song-lit" men and women. Yet despite the narrator's ambitions, he feels that he never entirely measures up to the complexities of his subject matter. Fern bewilders him ("Something I would do for her"—but he can't); and Carma he can only reveal in "the crudest melodrama"—her real character eludes him. Other women of the book also continue to haunt him—Avey, Karintha, Becky—because they cannot be contained by ordinary language. The elusiveness of their real lives accounts for his posturing and verbosity in "Avey" (as he realizes at the story's end) and a penchant for conjecture, as in the cases of Karintha and Becky. In any event, most of the people who inhabit *Cane* are as mysterious as the moon that shines through the factory door in "Blood-Burning Moon." Like the moon (and Louisa), the South casts its spell of enchantment over people. Africa and America, black and white, town and country—all exist side by side in the strange, surreal world, nothing ever quite fusing, nothing ever quite being understood. The only way Toomer can explain people like Karintha and Becky is through metaphor, symbol, and myth, and even these tools seem hardly adequate.

Since one can never quite understand the South in a rational sense, one can never quite depend on prose to reveal the whole truth. Realism is inadequate, because the South isn't quite rational. The very makeup of *Cane*, with its unorthodox structure, is part of Toomer's aesthetic strategy to approach the South from as many angles as possible. A world as complex as the South needs a complex literary form. It also needs a literary form that avoids the conventional plot format of a beginning, a middle, and an end. Toomer wrote his friend Waldo Frank before the novel was published and said that the design of *Cane* was a circle. He resorted to this metaphor because his aesthetic universe could not travel along a linear frame. Without beginning or end, the circle is a traditional symbol of eternity. For that reason, Toomer added that though his circle stops in "Harvest Song," it is only pausing there. "From the point of view of the spiritual entity behind the work, the curve really starts with Bona and Paul (awakening), plunges into Kabnis, emerges in Karintha etc. swings upward into Theater and Box Seat, and ends (pauses) in Harvest Song. . . . Between each of the three sections, a curve. These, to vaguely indicate the design." Toomer also indicated that the design was geographical as well as metaphysical: "Regionally, from the South up into the North, and back into the South again. Or, from the North down into the South and then a return North."[78]

Although Toomer seems a bit arbitrary when talking about actual landscape, he is making a very interesting point about the South's effect upon black people's lives. No matter where they are, this region never leaves them. In the first section of *Cane*, the narrator is a northerner drawn South because of an ancestral tug upon his soul, and in the second section, Washington is southern in atmosphere (though above the Mason-Dixon line) because of the presence of Negroes and their ties to their homeland. Thus, the South is a magnet silently, tenaciously, drawing people to it; or it is a spiritual presence that operates upon people in subtle ways even when they are lost in the northern cities. In Chicago, Paul ("Bona and Paul") senses its mysterious attraction as he stares at the "L" trains. It is not just his Negro blood that makes him "moony" (as his friend Art calls him); it is the South.

Although those characters whom Toomer admires never stray too far from the source of their strength (as does Muriel in "Box Seat" or John in "Theater"), Toomer does not sentimentalize the South. It is a killer as well as a life giver—as Becky, Mame Lamkins ("Kabnis"), and other portraits of southern cruelty show. However, the cruelty is not always racist. The immediacy of the South "ripens" things too soon, so that people like Karintha are as ephemeral as a "November cotton flower."

Because the South's meaning can never be expressed by any one voice, there are many "songs" in *Cane*. In fact, the singer with his song becomes an important metaphor throughout, each voice trying to reveal some aspect of the ineffable landscape. For instance, Dorris's dancing in "Theater" is described as "glorious songs" ("Her singing is of cane-brake loves and mangrove feastings"); the woman in "Calling Jesus" sings of her buried life at night ("Her breath comes sweet as honeysuckle whose pistils bear the life of coming song"). Paul "sings" to the doorman in "Bona and Paul," when he should be singing to Bona. And the dwarf's real song in "Box Seat" is not his literal song but the "words" that "form in the eyes," as he tries to tell Muriel that he is not grotesque. (So too the Negro's heritage is neither ugly nor beautiful but a strange mixture of the two which one must accept *in toto* if one is to be whole.)

Most voices in *Cane* only hint at reality. Fern sings to the narrator, but her song is separated from the identity of the singer: "Dusk hid her; I could hear only her song. It seemed to me as though she were pounding her head in anguish upon the ground." The tentative nature of Toomer's last sentence ("It seemed to me as though . . .") is commensurate with the image of the dusk. The narrator cannot see Fern clearly, just as he cannot see the South clearly. And this image of fading twilight appears over and over in *Cane*; it suggests not only the transitional world in which the "song-lit" people live but also the very obscurity of the metaphysical landscape. The complexity of the South makes it obscure, and only many voices, singing many songs, can approach an expression of its reality. Thus, Toomer's song in "Song of the Son" (the confident voice of the artist) is set against Kabnis's anguish in the cellar, against the reaper's "song" of suffering in the cotton field ("Harvest Song"), against Esther's mute song at Barlo's doorstep ("Esther").

Although no one song seems adequate, music is the only bastion against chaos. The reaper's song brings him solace, but it does not bring him "knowledge of [his] hunger" (p. 69). The "shouting" of the church members which Kabnis listens to with fear and loathing is poetry, though Kabnis is too blind to see this. The shouting is not merely an attempt to understand suffering, which perhaps will never be understood, but an attempt to control or to contain it. For this reason, Toomer includes the following refrain throughout "Kabnis":

> White-man's land.
> Niggers, sing.
> Burn, bear black children
> Till poor rivers bring
> Rest, and sweet glory
> in Camp Ground.

To sing goes beyond recognition. It is a positive act that makes life tolerable until the "poor rivers bring / Rest."

The "singing" in *Cane* does not bring ultimate wisdom. All its voices, taken individually, express partial truths. They are attempts to explain the mystery of existence and the mystery of the South. Toomer's own voice in *Cane*, poetic even in prose, is an attempt to capture the ineffable in the only way language can—through symbol, myth, and metaphor. Finally, the ends of Toomer's circle never meet, as he graphically demonstrates on the introductory page to the last section of *Cane*.

Because Toomer realized that language had to be used poetically if the truth was to be grasped, he broke away from the realistic side of Sherwood Anderson's influence. As a budding writer, he had been moved by *Winesburg, Ohio* (1919) and *The Triumph of the Egg* (1921), especially by Anderson's innovative experiments in aesthetic form. "It is hard to think of myself as maturing without them," he told Anderson in December 1922.[79] And since *The Triumph of the Egg* combines prose tales with three free-verse poems, Anderson may well have shown Toomer that poetry and fiction could be combined to create a new kind of novel. Nonetheless, Toomer later complained to Waldo Frank (who had also ended his friendship with Anderson) that Anderson not only ignored the dimensions of his writing "other than Negro," he could see in Toomer only the themes that he himself was preoccupied with: "a sense of the tragic separateness, the tragic sterility of people."[80] Although this theme appears in *Cane* ("Esther"), tragic waste was only half the story for Toomer.[81] Furthermore, Toomer believed that Anderson's muse was too pedestrian, too tied to the finite world of tangible objects. As he said to Frank, Anderson's "sweet narrative gift swings along like a carriage-dog nosing the dust and flowers of a mid-western roadside. Its paws are sensitive to the rocks and bumps beneath them. Its eyes register the passing of isolated farm houses. Its mind glimpses the tragedy of unpainted clapboards and closed doors. But its nose keeps to the dust and flowers of the road, and its heart beats regularly as it lopes along."[82] No wonder, then, that Toomer came to embrace Waldo Frank as his spiritual brother. A modernist, Frank wanted to write lyrical novels—books that caught the inner essences of people and things. Toomer did not want to travel on the surface with Anderson's realism, among the "dust and flowers of the road." (It is significant, too, that Toomer became close friends of both Georgia O'Keeffe and Alfred Stieglitz, modernists who were experimenting with aesthetic form in painting and photography, respectively.)

Frank and Toomer planned to write books about the South (*Holiday* and *Cane*) which would escape the confinements of realism. Unfortunately for Toomer, he was writing in the America of Mencken's Sherwood Anderson. Anderson the realist, not Anderson the experimenter in aesthetic forms, was the one Mencken admired. Although the expatriates in

Europe were exploring new avenues of narrative expression which would bear fruit in the future, for the moment it was Mencken's day in court. His judgment of Frank's style in *Holiday* could stand for an indictment of *Cane* as well: "Frank would be improved, I suspect, if he could be set to writing editorials for the *New York Times* for thirty days and thirty nights."[83] Obviously the "lyrical crystallizations" that revealed character, the oblique plot that set symbols in opposition to one another, and the poetic dialogue—all of which Toomer had admired[84]—made little impression upon the champion of realism.

Of course, *Cane* was not ignored by everyone. The black intellectuals especially recognized Toomer's genius, although they did not quite know what to make of Toomer's book. Few took *Cane* as something to be learned from; or if they did, they always held up a segment or a theme for imitation. For *Opportunity* critic Montgomery Gregory, Toomer was the new René Maran, a realistic portrayer of the peasant world of the South; for Langston Hughes, Toomer was both a satirist and a poet; and for Alain Locke, Toomer was primarily a poet and a celebrator of the "folk-spirit" of the race. The black critics all praised him highly (Braithwaite calling him the "morning star" of Negro literature), but the praise was often vague, and they made little attempt to investigate the thematic complexity of *Cane* or—an even more difficult task—its narrative complexity. Although Eric Walrond probably imitated Toomer's elliptical, poetical prose style in *Tropic Death* (1926), few in the 1920s, black or white, responded to his exciting use of symbol, myth, and metaphor as ways of giving organic unity to his work and of depicting the South.

Strange to say, Toomer's method of revealing the South's reality may be closer to Mencken's techniques in "The Sahara of the Bozart" than is White's realism. Mencken may have preached realism from his critical pulpit, but he practiced an aesthetic that often distorted reality for the sake of a higher, comic truth. Like Toomer, he wanted the South to be seen with fresh eyes, and so he blew it out of all proportion. After Mencken, it might be said, few authors could comfortably return to the old myth of the magnolia tradition; Mencken used one myth to destroy another, his "waste land" motif reminding us of T. S. Eliot rather than Dreiser. Despite his hard line on realism, Mencken had the imagination of a poet, and his "mythical method" in treating the South linked him with Toomer rather than White.

White's problem was that he saw neither the humor in Mencken's portrait of the South nor the mythological framework that he employed. In *The Fire in the Flint*, White fell between two stools. He wanted to illustrate Mencken's thesis in "The Sahara of the Bozart" (that the rednecks now ruled the South, that the region was a cultural wasteland), but he also wanted to write a realistic novel in the manner of Dreiser. Since he literalized the themes of Mencken's essay, leaving the art behind, his characters became stock figures in a tragic melodrama. This was not the fault of realism; rather, it reflected White's inability to perceive another kind of poetical reality. However, in one respect White's short-sightedness is typical of the Harlem Renaissance in general. He tended to see the depiction of the black character as an either-or proposition. As he asked Eugene Saxton of Doran, "Must we always conform to stereotypes created by those who know little or nothing of what the real facts are? . . . Or are we to be honest with ourselves and stand or fall by the one standard, 'Is it true?'"[85] As we shall see, this either-or approach often prevented the black writers of the 1920s from seeing other kinds of reality which a more flexible realism might have included.

✻

In June 1922, Jessie Fauset reviewed a short story by Don Marquis for the *Crisis*, and she admitted to being puzzled by it. Her reaction to "Carter" is perhaps indicative of the hold realism had on a whole generation of black writers. "Carter," she said, presents "an aspect of the Negro problem which I confess I never have seen manifested."[86] It is a tale, she continued, about a man seven-eighths white, who hates the one-eighth of himself which is black. In a crucial moment in the story, Carter tells his fiancée that he is part black, and her indifference shocks him: "By God. I can't have anything to do with a woman who'd marry a nigger."[87] Fauset thought that perhaps the story showed how much white people hated themselves—at least that was the reaction of a "colored school girl" to whom she told the story.

What Fauset left out of the description of "Carter" was the central paradox in Carter's confession to his fiancée. If the girl had shrieked in horror, Carter would have been equally unhappy. His "nigger" blood would have hated her, as much as his white blood had hated himself. In other words, he is damned whether she accepts or rejects him. Either way, her response is simply a manifestation of the warfare carried on inside him, a warfare that is psychological but also metaphysical: "His destiny was not a matter of environment so much as a question of himself." Like Faulkner's Joe Christmas, who beats up a prostitute because she is willing to fornicate with a "nigger," himself, Carter is a symbol of profound existential despair. As such, he cannot be explained by the vocabulary of realism.[88]

What Jessie Fauset did not see is in a sense what the Harlem Renaissance failed to see. One story by Hemingway which was completely overlooked by the black writers of the 1920s was "The Battler" (*In Our*

Time, 1925). The story is deceptively simple; its mythical reverberations, complex. Hemingway's *ingénu*, Nick Adams, drops off a freight train after being roughed up by the brakeman, and he meets a strange couple camping by the side of the railroad track. The white man is a famous ex-boxer, who was jilted by his wife and is now half-crazy, and the Negro is his friend, who looks after him. The two men live off the money the wife sends the boxer.

At first "Bugs" (the Negro) seems a perfect stereotype: polite (he calls Nick and the boxer "Mr."), solicitous, and smiling. Yet when the three sit down to eat a common meal around the campfire, the situation suddenly becomes surreal. The boxer asks Nick for his knife, and the Negro tells Nick not to give it to him. Instead of attacking Bugs, the boxer accuses Nick of being a "snotty bastard."[89] When he finally threatens Nick with violence, Bugs quietly but efficiently coldcocks the boxer with a concealed blackjack. He then tells Nick to leave before the boxer wakes up: "It might disturb him back again to see you."

The jolt Nick receives from this experience makes the black eye he got from the brakeman insignificant. At least the black eye is real, but he doesn't know what to make of Bugs; greed and malice now seem to be subtly hidden behind the mask of human compassion. And like our response to one of Hawthorne's tales, we are not quite sure what we have seen. Bugs seems genuinely concerned for the boxer, Hemingway even suggesting that Bugs has replaced the boxer's wife. But then this suggestion makes their relationship seem even more grotesque, as if both marriage and friendship were predatory arrangements. Further, Hemingway intimates that the story casts a weird light (as does *Benito Cereno*) on the diabolical nature of slavery itself. Who is slave? Who is master? And has the "peculiar institution" corrupted both slave and master, each capable of metamorphosing himself into his opposite, given the right circumstances?

No wonder, then, that Ralph Ellison looked to Joyce, Hemingway, and Faulkner as his godfathers and not to the black writers of the 1920s.[90] A character such as Bugs transcends realism. He is both the loyal retainer and a black widow. He is both a man and a myth, revealing only the ambiguous surface of reality. Surely Lucius Brockway in *Invisible Man* partakes of the same ambiguity. As chief engineer in the Liberty Paints factory, he is an Uncle Tom, a con man, and a rugged individualist, and to limit him to any one of these labels is to lose him. Apparently a victim of racist America, he, like Bugs, reminds us of Melville's "power of darkness" at the core of things. So too Richard Wright wanted more than realism when he came to write *Native Son*. He looked back to the Gothic stories of Poe and Hawthorne and to Dostoevsky's *Crime and Punishment*, not to the Harlem Renaissance.[91] Bigger Thomas is multidimensional, the meaning of his character spreading out like the colors of an opened fan. He is Prometheus who has stolen fire from the gods, or he is just a poor dumb brute who is driven to consciousness by a quirk of fate. Wright gives us as many views of him as possible, letting us see that his condition springs from the archetypal myths that govern America. He is a native son who pulls himself up by his own bootstraps, but his spiritual transcendence is achieved through a brutal murder. Like Jay Gatsby, Bigger is paradoxical because America is paradoxical—Gatsby, recall, has the romantic sensibility to respond to the possibilities of the New World and yet is just as easily corrupted by those possibilities.

Thus, post-Renaissance novelists such as Baldwin, Wright, and Ellison did not simply want to document black life. They wanted a perspective that would wring more truth out of existence than could the realism of the 1920s. Baldwin found the Old Testament and the myth of the city for *Go Tell It on the Mountain*; Ellison and Wright, the myths of American Negro folklore and antiquity for *Invisible Man* and *Native Son*. These writers did not look to their predecessors in the Harlem Renaissance because the latter were dominated by Mencken's conception of realism. Despite his own use of satiric distortion in such a piece as "The Sahara of the Bozart," Mencken as literary critic urged the black novelist to be an investigative reporter, not a myth maker. As perceptive as Mencken was as a literary critic, he had trouble responding to the new novelists of the 1920s who were exploring other kinds of realities than the ones uncovered by the quasi scientists. Frank Turaj observes that Mencken did not see the myth of America behind *The Great Gatsby* when he reviewed it.[92] (Mencken said that it did not have much of a story; and given the standards that he applied to the novel, he was quite right.) Also, Mencken did not seem to respond to Faulkner's mythopoetic treatment of the South, though he most certainly liked Faulkner as a comic storyteller.[93] As a critic, he was indifferent to T. S. Eliot's use of archetypes in *The Waste Land* and to Hemingway's use of symbol and myth in *The Sun Also Rises*.[94] (But again, it is a mistake to say that Mencken did not like Hemingway's work. When *A Farewell to Arms* was published in 1929, he praised it highly, although in his typical terms: He noted that at last people who actually had served in the Great War were writing about it.)[95] Appropriately, Mencken called James T. Farrell in 1947 "the best living American novelist," for Mencken's ideas about the novel had not changed since he first began writing reviews for the *Smart Set*.[96]

It is one of those ironies of American literary history that Mencken introduced Richard Wright to realism, but what Wright took from this introduction did not make him a realist. Wright saw that the South in "The Sahara of the Bozart" was not the real South but a mythical one, and a myth, not reality, was what Wright needed to shape *Black Boy*.

Wright took Mencken's essay and used it to create not a comedy but a Gothic tale based on the materials of his own life. Like Mencken's South, Wright's too is a topsy-turvy world in which sanity is an abnormal condition, in which paranoia and fear are the orders of the day. After one frightening experience with a group of white men, when he was punished for an impropriety he did not realize he had committed, Wright says, "It was like living in a dream, the reality of which might change at any moment."[97] The metaphysics of this universe had no logic that he could understand. "The words and actions of white people were baffling signs to me. I was living in a culture and not a civilization and I could learn how that culture worked only by living with it. Misreading the reactions of whites around me made me say and do the wrong things" (p. 171). Like Theseus, he needed a thread to lead him out of this labyrinth.

Wright's discovery in *Black Boy*, a discovery that in retrospect he knew he had been groping toward since he first learned to speak, is that the thread is language: He has to have a vocabulary to express the world that so confuses him. This was the other thing Mencken had taught him, that words can become a surrogate club. Heretofore, the South permitted him only two responses as a Negro, rebellion or docility, and both were self-destructive. Mencken showed him that words can be used as weapons, and that one need not be destroyed in the process. On the contrary, language is not just a way of getting even; it is a way of saving oneself from madness and spiritual suicide; it is a way of shaping that which threatens to destroy.

It is because his father has no vocabulary that he is doomed. "I tried to talk to him," Wright says of his father many years afterwards, but "we were forever strangers, speaking a different language, living on vastly different planes of reality" (p. 30). And it is not just that his father speaks a "different language"; he is largely inarticulate, lacking a culture, the "intangible sentiments which bind man to man." Wright's other relatives share the same fate; they are controlled and smothered by an insane world whose logic they cannot understand. Normal human impulses —love, friendship, trust—are stifled because these people live in a constant state of fear, of whites and of one another. Wright's grandmother becomes rigidly puritanical—not out of a love of morality but out of a fear that she will violate some southern taboo. And the black family in general closes its doors upon the human spirit of its members. Father and mother, uncle and aunt—all dam up the inquiring nature of the child because they do not want him hurt exploring the mysteries of the Gods.

This, then, is why Mencken and the other writers Mencken recommended meant so much to Wright, despite the fact that he could not accept their adherence to realism. They "seemed to feel," said Wright, "that America could be shaped nearer to the hearts of those who lived in it" (p. 227). They told Wright through their perceptions and their anger that he was not crazy to respond to the world the way he did. It was the world that was crazy: southern madness, as Mencken had defined it. Yet, like Toomer in *Cane*, Wright's spiritual life is intimately connected to the South. The two men could come to terms with themselves only after they had come to terms with the South. Once Wright could articulate what he saw, then he was free — free perhaps to return to the South in a new way, as an artist. Both *Black Boy* and *Cane* are finally portraits of the artist, the artist who needs first to create a myth in order to understand the real.

In 1926, the publishing house of Albert and Charles Boni offered a thousand-dollar prize to the Negro author who would write the best novel about Negro life for that year. The year came and went, and no prize money was given because the publishing house felt that no black novelist deserved the reward. Ironically, *Nigger Heaven* was published that year, and it turned out to be a tremendous best seller. Although Van Vechten was attacked mercilessly by the black press and by many black intellectuals, there was a touch of envy in the criticism. Charles S. Johnson spoke for more than one man when he said that "my extreme tribute to the book is that I wish a Negro had written it."[98] For around 1926, a wave of disillusionment had set in, a sense that perhaps the Great Negro Novel was not going to be written by a Negro. That this was more than just a passing mood was substantiated by a curious event. In 1928, Charles Waddell Chesnutt received the Spingarn Medal for his contributions to Negro literature. Chesnutt, of course, was a novelist, and a good one, but he had not published anything for over twenty years.[99] It was almost as if the Renaissance had decided that its time was past.

Yet it would be a mistake to suggest that the idea of the Great Negro Novel, to be written by a Negro, died a quick death. And it would be a mistake to insist that realism as a literary mode destroyed the Negro's chances for writing it. After all, if Dreiser could produce *An American Tragedy* in 1925, then why couldn't a Negro produce a comparable work? One difficulty may have been that the very idea of the Great Negro Novel seemed to presuppose that it would be written by a Negro, and for that reason it would have to supersede all other novels about Negroes. Hence, the pressure on the Negro novelist must have been enormous, as if with each effort he had to better previous efforts by white writers or he would be a failure. We get an inkling of that pressure if we look at the literary columns in the magazine *Opportunity*. Both Sterling Brown and Alain Locke kept a running account of novels published by and about Negroes. After one listing, Brown lamented, "But where, oh where is the Negro author?"[100] Locke thought that Langston Hughes had made a noble effort to win the garland in *Not Without Laughter* (1929). If the promise contained in Hughes's novel is ever "fulfilled," he continued, "we shall have a Negro novelist to bracket with Julia Peterkin and DuBose Heyward."[101]

Locke's tendency to rank novelists is especially telling, especially Menckenesque, and perhaps even especially American. Like Mencken, he was looking for a slugger, a black Babe Ruth who with the long clout could break into the big leagues. In reviewing a novel written by a white author which Locke admired, he used a metaphor that revealed his bias for the long ball. With Marie Stanley's *Gulf Stream*, he said, "the Negro sphinx has come nearer our literary Thebes. May some real genius, black or white, go blithely out of the walls to question her." The sphinx, we can safely assume, is black life, a mystery that is yet to be solved, but one that has a single answer. The youth who ventures from the city's walls must find the right key to the puzzle, or he dies just another unsuccessful quester. He may go down in history as a heroic failure, but he is a failure nonetheless. It should be noted, however, that Locke's metaphor contained an inherent fallacy—that one single novel was going to achieve perfection. Curiously, the one novel that did qualify for the role of the Great Negro Novel, *Cane*, made the point that perfection could not be achieved, that the artist had to be satisfied with partial truths about black life, inadequately grasped.

That the age did not see that *Cane* was the novel it sought is a measure of its aesthetic limitations. Toomer put together a book whose structure was based on myth, symbol, metaphor, and musical motif. It foreshadowed a similar narrative strategy that Hemingway was to use in *In Our Time* (1925), and it looked back to the unorthodox form of *Winesburg, Ohio* and *The Triumph of the Egg*. Since it had no conventional beginning, middle, and end, critics of the 1920s, black and white, were at a loss to categorize it. Hence, the 1920s ended with the feeling among black critics that the Great Negro Novel was yet to be written.

The failure of *Cane* to serve as an example perhaps points to the negative effect of Mencken's influence on the writers of the Harlem Renaissance. Toomer had solved a problem that they had not even seen, the problem of understanding a culture even though one is detached from it. Locke thought that he could understand black life by observing its folkways, yet he did not realize that his own intellectual background would prevent him from seeing them clearly. Toomer perceived the gap that separated him from his past (he in fact dramatized this dilemma in "Kabnis"); he solved this problem by developing techniques that Locke and others did not fully comprehend because of their commitment to realism.

Mencken's "sanity" carried the day because the major issue for the black writers of the 1920s was realistic portraiture. The most forceful expression of this supposed sanity often took the form of satire, the cleansing of the body politic and the private soul. The new man after the New Negro was to be free of all myths, superstitions, and atavistic urges; the new man was George Schuyler, the Voltaire of the Young Wits, who now wished to laugh all follies of the Negro race out of fashion. Thus, when Mencken in 1930 told George Schuyler that "in the next issue of the *Mercury*, I am printing an editorial calling on Negro intellectuals to put down Methodist preachers," such people as Nella Larsen and J. A. Rogers came running to join the new crusade. Yet not everyone was eager to be liberated from all illusion. Some such as Zora Neale Hurston, James Weldon Johnson, and Countee Cullen felt that Mencken had missed the complexity of the Negro preacher, the real poetical qualities in the man.[102] And indeed, if we had to point to one limitation of Mencken's outlook, it would be his propensity to allow no middle ground between his definitions of sanity and insanity.

Nevertheless, if Mencken was wrong about the Negro preacher, he was right to focus upon him, because the preacher had always been a central figure in black life and would continue to be so in black novels.[103] It might be noted that although Mencken did not, in general, care for Negro preachers "of the lower orders," he had enough flexibility as a critic to admire Johnson's portrait of the preacher in *God's Trombones*. At his best, Mencken was a flexible literary critic, knew black life intimately, and expressed an enthusiasm for literature which was contagious. All these qualities help to measure his positive influence upon the Harlem Renaissance. From 1917 to 1930, Mencken held center stage in American life, and no one man during this era had quite the audience he had. When Mencken published Negroes in the *Mercury*, it was as if he were telling white Americans that they had better wise up and take these people seriously—because he took them seriously. He found time to give them advice; he found time to praise them, berate them, and argue with them. And as the editor of the *Chicago Defender* implied, Negro intellectuals, old and young, were entranced. And why shouldn't they have been? Mencken kept reminding them that they were dignified men and women, and that the people oppressing them were Yahoos who thought the invention of Coca-Cola a sign of cultural progress; he kept reminding them not only that they had their tales to tell about America but that they damn well better tell them; he kept reminding them that telling these tales in an artistic form was the highest expression of which a race was capable, and that if they as a race were going to amount to anything, they had better let their voices be heard.

No wonder the black writers were excited by this arrogant curmudgeon. He was the great cham of American letters, and he had stooped to talk to them, man to man. Even his gruffness met their approval, for it simply implied that they had not achieved the standards he had set for them. These were not standards fit for bondsmen, but standards of the noblest kind, striven for by the likes of Conrad, Hardy, Zola, and Dreiser. That the black intellectuals stumbled, faltered, and contradicted themselves in their attempts to satisfy Mencken's definition of excellence was perhaps to be expected. How much critical attention can a person accept gracefully? That the Young Wits became as self-righteous as the Old Guard, whom they attacked as Mencken might have, was perhaps also to be expected. Who could have foreseen at this time that their attitudes would be narrowed by their reaction to their elders? Curiously, they behaved as maliciously as they did because the first generation of Renaissance intellectuals had broken ground for the second. Though not completely free from the curse of gentility themselves, Hughes, McKay, and others were beginning to make contact with the masses, which Locke, DuBois, Fauset, and White had never been able to manage.

Could we not say then that Mencken and the Harlem Renaissance made possible a Richard Wright? When he read Mencken that one night in Memphis, Wright was inspired in a way that James Weldon Johnson could not have been. Now words were to be clubs, not delicate rapier thrusts. Wright could produce a truer realism, could smash the delicate glass of gentility, because of the imperfect efforts of previous Negro intellectuals. They had never been completely free of the black man's burden; they had always talked about black culture in ways that would legitimize it in white eyes. Wright, however, talked about the cultural barrenness of his own people without fear of how his words would appear to a white reader. He swore after *Uncle Tom's Children* (1938), a collection of short stories, that he would never again write for "bankers' daughters."[104] And he never did—because the Renaissance had agonized its way through territory that Wright could now pass through without looking back.

And in a sense all black novelists since Wright have followed in his footsteps. They don't all write like him, but they imitate his fearlessness. One could argue, then, that Mencken's work was not in vain, for fearlessness was the very quality he had stressed and embodied. Whatever Mencken's limitations, what he predicted in 1920 has finally come to pass. A recent black novelist like Toni Morrison has investigated the inner life of her people without any special pleading, without even the slightest nod in the direction of white readers, and she has given her readers the privileged view of black life which Mencken had so clearly seen belonged to the Negro novelist alone. One cannot imagine a white novelist writing Morrison's novels; the little touches, such as the naming of Not Doctor Street in *Song of Solomon*, have the ring of authenticity to them. Whatever Morrison's critical stature in the future, she has already done what Mencken believed sorely needed to be done: She has given us a "realistic picture of this inner life of the Negro by one who sees the race from within."

Would he have applauded her, if he had lived to read her novels? Perhaps. But then, the works of Zora Neale Hurston passed him by without comment, and she too had depicted the inner life of the Negro. By the 1930s, however, Mencken had lost interest in literature, and even when he had been the literary firebrand of his day, many good books escaped his notice. The wonder is that he was right so often. In many ways, Mencken seems quite modern—he hated cant, admired craftsmanship, and encouraged a healthy distrust of all aesthetic fads and moral dogmas. Yet he refused to make an effort to understand modernism. He would probably not, for instance, have responded to the flying African story in *Song of Solomon*, just as he missed Gatsby's mythic significance in Fitzgerald's novel. In truth, part of Mencken still lived in Victorian America, despite his portrait of it as a prissy schoolmarm, for he did believe that the purpose of the artist or the critic was to raise consciousness. If only we could throw off the restraints of puritanism, if only we could create a culture of connoisseurs, of natural aristocrats, then we would have a real civilization. Moreover, although Mencken might resent the comparison, there was a side to him that reminds us of Emerson. Like Emerson, he wanted Americans to find that "infinitude of the private man," which always seemed just within reach. That this may be an impossible dream is a reflection of an innocence that Mencken (and the Harlem Renaissance) took such great pains to hide; and yet, in retrospect, it is a dream that remains peculiarly American.

CHAPTER SEVEN

Epilogue

One misconception about Mencken is still current — that his politics took a sharp turn toward the right in the 1930s.[1] An earlier and more accurate assessment, persuasively expressed by William Manchester, is that the country had changed but Mencken had not.[2] And because he essentially had not changed his views on either politics or life, we are in a position to see his strengths and weaknesses vis-à-vis black culture, especially if we observe the maturation of his friendship with George Schuyler during this decade. In the beginning of the 1920s, Mencken placed his hope for black writers in Walter White; at the end of the 1920s, we remember, he placed his hope for black political sanity in George Schuyler. This shift in emphasis from literature to politics is symbolic of Mencken's new interests in the mid-1920s. When he took over the *Mercury* in 1924, he did not give up his passion for the arts altogether, but he did focus his attention more directly upon the political and social scene. Ironically, despite this new political engagement, he found himself at odds with the *Zeitgeist* of the 1930s. This did not necessarily make him a bad social critic; gadflies in any age are always useful. For the first time in his long literary career, however, he found himself to be merely a fly; only a few people took his buzzing and bites seriously.

As Manchester reminds us, Mencken gave up his job as editor of the *Mercury* because of a declining readership.[3] He continued to hammer away at the Roosevelt administration in the *Baltimore Evening Sun*, even though that paper's editorial policy began to support the New Deal. The newspaper tolerated Mencken because in the days of his glory he had been a frontrunner, and though he had had temptations aplenty, he never abandoned the newspaper of his youth and favorite town. Similarly, George Schuyler found himself pushed off the editorial page of the *Pitts-*

burgh Courier and onto a page buried deep in the newspaper's interior. The *Courier* tolerated Schuyler because, like Mencken, he had given the paper considerable prestige during his heyday. However, by 1936 Robert L. Vann, the *Courier's* editor, had become a high-ranking member of the Roosevelt administration, and the newspaper had seen the New Deal as truly a better deal than any other that Negroes had received from an American president. Said the *Courier* in 1936,

> armies of unemployed Negro workers have been kept from the near-star-vation level on which they lived under President Hoover. . . . Armies of unemployed Negro workers have found work on the various PWA, CWA, WPA, CCC, FERA, and other projects. . . . Critics will point to discrimi-nation against colored sharecroppers, against Negro skilled and unskilled labor. . . . This is all true. It would be useless to deny it even if there were any inclination to do so, which there is not. . . . But what administration within the memory of man has done a better job in that direction consider-ing the very imperfect human material with which it had to work? The answer, of course, is none.[4]

The gist of the *Courier* article is not "civilization" but survival; the new dispensation of the 1930s is economics, not "culture."

Walter White had been one of the chief spokesmen for culture during the 1920s. He had written two novels, had helped many of the younger writers get published, and had even considered challenging Alain Locke for the position of Renaissance spokesman. In 1930, however, he was made head of the NAACP, and along with so many of the country's intellectuals, black and white, he became a political activist. True, the change for White was not that dramatic; as investigator of lynchings for the NAACP during the 1920s, he had never been politically disengaged. (Besides, for a black writer, politics and art are never really strange bed-fellows.) Yet in the 1920s, White did see himself primarily as one of the bright "New Negroes," and that term by 1925 had lost much of the political significance that it had had immediately before and after Ameri-ca's entry into the Great War. By 1925, the date of publication of Locke's anthology, "New Negro" meant artist, not angry young man.

White's metamorphosis from novelist to political activist contains a curious irony. In 1922, Mencken believed that White symbolized the hope for the Negro's literary future, but when it finally dawned upon him that the man from Atlanta had been ensnared by the same emotional pitfalls that had beset past black writers, he began to reconsider his op-timistic forecasts. Now black people should put their polis in order before they engaged in aesthetic activities; a strong dose of George Schuyler's satire was what the race needed. Yet White decided in the 1930s that the race needed more than self-criticism; he saw the opportunity to seize the political and economic day for black people. If Roosevelt was shaking up the country's social structure, could not the Negro insist upon equality?

Mencken and Schuyler were equally engaged; they too had made the switch from literature to politics, but their brand of engagement was always of an intellectual nature. They preferred to comment upon the political world from the sidelines, and the reason for this detachment lay in their basic ideas, inherited from the eighteenth century, concerning the individual's relationship to the polis. One can see the striking differences between White, on the one hand, and Mencken and Schuyler, on the other, by looking at a letter that Mencken wrote to White after the latter had had a brief confrontation with Roosevelt during World War II. White had alternately threatened and cajoled the president: Give Negroes good jobs in the factories, or do not depend upon our political support. Mencken did not approve of White's actions for practical reasons.

> All the frauds will promise you everything you ask for, and all the honest men, if any, will be daunted by the visible impossibility of doing anything effectual. Race relations never improve in war time; they always worsen. And it is when the boys come home that the Ku Klux Klans are organized. I believe with George Schuyler that the only really feasible way to improve the general situation of the American Negro is to convince more and more whites that he is, as men go in this world, a decent fellow, and that amicable living with him is not only possible but desirable. Every threat of mass political pressure, every appeal to political mountebanks, only alarms the white brother, and so postpones the day of reasonable justice.[5]

Yet Mencken's pragmatism, like his literary realism, had blind spots, although his stand here is very much in character. Typically, he wanted first things first. The answer to the racial problem, he continued, is not to get the right to enter posh hotels that only the rich frequent. There is no answer to the Negro problem, but one should at least choose life and limb before luxuries; one can try "to protect the Negro, if it can be done, against the inevitable attempt of white competitors on the lower levels to dispose of him by outrage and murder." Furthermore, Mencken wanted "reasonable justice"—not absolute justice, which he considered impossible to achieve for any human being, no matter what his color. These things can be won, he insisted, if the Negro can convince the American citizen that he is "a decent fellow."

Again Mencken's curious faith in the moral response of the common man comes to the fore—the belief that individuals cause the world to change, not laws or religious crusades[6] or large abstractions or even the capitalization of the word "negro." Of course, his view of the common man harked back to Thomas Jefferson, one of the few Americans Mencken admired, and this common man for Jefferson was not "common." He was the natural aristocrat, the good man and true who made the difference. The welfare of the Republic lay within his hands.

Now in theory this is a wonderful view of society, that individuals determine the welfare of the polis. But by 1932, the year of Roosevelt's election to office, the world did not seem that simple. For the first time in American history, the full impact of Marx's economic theories hit home: The individual, in whom Mencken and Jefferson had placed such faith, was often powerless in a system of forces beyond his control. For the moment, Marxism seemed to explain a point about racism which until now had been inexplicable. How could a man hate another man merely because his skin was black? Marxism gave a precise answer to this question: The man lowest down on the economic ladder is hated because he is in a condition of servitude, and serfs of all nations are hated with equal ferocity by members of the ruling class. Once the social structure is overhauled, once there is no more class struggle, then there will be no more racism. To Mencken and Schuyler, this explanation was simply another crackpot scheme offered up by visionaries and "jitney" Messiahs; they laughed at the idea that racism was going to be removed by taking a new overnight cure from Dr. Crookman.

Although I sympathize with their amusement over the utopian aspect of Marxism, neither one understood that if Marx was wrong about the world's being made anew, he was right about the possibility of the world's being changed through a realignment of economic forces. Because the world had been different in the past—different social structures, different class struggles—Marx assumed that the world could be different in the future, if the right measures were applied. This is what Franklin D. Roosevelt came to see, and this is what Walter White saw along with him, even though both men would have been shocked if someone had called them Marxists. White fought Roosevelt for every cent that the New Deal was sending to those lower down on the economic and social scale, because he realized that although there was not much chance of getting a square deal from the greedy whites who actually controlled the till, the very gesture of sending money lower down implied that the government knew that it was morally responsible for the welfare and humanity of all its citizens. It tacitly admitted that economic conditions determined the health of the polis. Furthermore, White understood that if blacks were to benefit from the New Deal, they would also have to exert, within limits, some influence over it. Their votes, shifted to the Democratic party for the first time, could act as leverage to change both their economic and human situations, and White saw that those situations were intimately tied together. And for the first time, a political party *did* begin treating Negroes as voters, as citizens, and in turn more blacks than ever before came to the polls to vote—to support Roosevelt.

Despite the social relevance of the new politics, Mencken and Schuyler remained myopic: They failed to see that the "mob" legitimately became the "masses" during the Depression. Locked into an eighteenth-century view of the mob, they could only look at those lower down as "simians," "gorillas," and "Yahoos," giving away their human potential and allowing themselves to be ruled by the emotion of the moment. Hence the "decent" man—the "forgotten man"—continued to be the citizen whose voice was lost in the welter of noise, "bugaboos," and hoopla which plagued American society. This forgotten man was not an economic creature but a moral one—he had a responsibility to remind others like himself that *boobus Americanus* was not the only bird in season.

Neither Schuyler nor Mencken wanted to recognize that social forces could create not only *boobus Americanus* but Bigger Thomas. For Mencken, the proletarian was "never a hero" because he was "by definition an incompetent and ignominious fellow." But Mencken's definition, again, is an eighteenth-century one, and it has little or nothing to do with the Marxist conception of a proletarian. Mencken could admire John Henry, because John Henry went his own way, but he could not admire someone who got lost in a crowd. That the Depression made the crowd larger and larger was a situation that Mencken and Schuyler steadfastly refused to see. No wonder that they grew closer to each other as the years went by.

Just as Mencken's brand of realism lost touch with modernism, so his brand of social criticism during the 1930s had little relevance to the real social scene. Ironically, the man whom he hated most during the decade, Franklin D. Roosevelt, did the same thing for the Negroes socially and politically which Mencken had done for them artistically—he gave them a sense of dignity. Like Mencken, he paid attention to them; like Mencken, he took them seriously. Thus, when Roosevelt told the students and faculty of Howard University, on the first occasion that an American president had ever addressed a black college, that "among American citizens there should be no forgotten men and no forgotten races,"[7] he was simply repeating Mencken's message to the black author, only in a new context. Moreover, in the 1930s Roosevelt hammered out one political change that Mencken had been fighting for in the 1920s: He enfranchised and brought to power the urban majorities. Like Mencken, Roosevelt was a city man, but in the 1930s Mencken was in no mood to perceive the irony. In letter after letter to Schuyler, Mencken took after the beast in the White House as if the 1920s had never ended. Mencken's old target had been the fundamentalists who lived in the countryside and inflicted rural values (such as they were) upon the city and the civilized few who lived therein. In the 1930s, the enemy changed its face but not its essential nature. Now it was the radical left who posed as the liberator of mankind but who in reality tried to rob the individual citizen of his freedom. The cause of this theft was Big Government and the huge bureaucracy that accompanied it. The propaganda that followed in the wake of this political takeover was quite similar to the "hokum" foisted upon the American public by the Comstockians and the Prohibitionists: All this is being done for your good.

The ease with which both Mencken and Schuyler shifted their guns to the new enemy reveals that neither perceived the essential differences between decades. To them, Roosevelt and Comstock were cut from the same cloth. If the country chose to worship a demagogue from the left instead of from the right, that was none of their business: A scoundrel was a scoundrel, no matter what his political orientation. Just as Wilson had manipulated the sympathies of the mob to get America into the Great War, so Roosevelt convinced the American public to give him dictatorial powers. Anyone who resisted the New Order instituted by Roosevelt was considered a traitor and was treated accordingly. Here was the democracy that Mencken had always deplored, the refuge of any scoundrel who is able to prey upon the low intelligence of the average citizen.

Faced with the prospect of Roosevelt's seemingly endless reign, the two men consoled each other during the 1930s and 1940s. For Mencken, Schuyler was the only truthful journalist now writing in the Republic; for Schuyler, he and Mencken were the last self-reliant men in a nation of goose-steppers. Mencken thought that Roosevelt planned to plunge the country "into the holy war," and referred to his domestic policies as the workings of the "Holy Ghost," adding sarcastically, "Utopia dawns."[8] "We are headed for a dictatorship,"[9] he told Schuyler, and thus he planned "to organize a society to be called The Friends of Despotism": "Its playform [sic] will contain three planks, to wit: the repeal of the Declaration of Independence, the withdrawal of the Emancipation Proclamation and the election of Roosevelt for life."[10] A month later he clarified his suggestion that the Emancipation Proclamation be withdrawn. He did not mean, he told Schuyler, that "the dark brethren alone be enslaved; the ofays deserve a massive dose out of the same bottle."[11] Occasionally, his pessimism hit rock bottom: "I am thoroughly convinced that the country is already lost. We are in the situation of the Romans who watched the decay of their great empire. They were quite unaware of it. The only thing they noticed was that the times were hard."[12]

Mencken's general gloominess can be overstressed, but his personal depression in the midst of the country's economic one was real enough. The untimely death of his wife in 1935 left its mark, for although Mencken outwardly was a stoical man, it is clear that he took his wife's death much harder than he let on. Certainly his disillusionment with America's future tended to influence the view that he now took toward the Negro's lot. When Senator Bilbo hatched his plan for colonizing Africa with black Americans, Mencken called it "magnificently idiotic,"[13] but then had second thoughts. Although Bilbo was "a master ass," he wrote to Schuyler, "there may be some sense in his scheme."[14] Mencken's cynicism in this respect reveals his "prejudices," his inability to perceive that blacks were actually benefiting from the New Deal. Of course, taking into account our own racially troubled times, we might hesitate before we reject outright his gloomy forecast: "I am thoroughly convinced that the future of the colored people in this country is far from rosy. No matter what progress they make they'll always find a vast horde of crackers against them."[15] It is characteristic of Mencken that, like Swift in "A Modest Proposal," he saw that the literal proposal was a reflection of a sad poetic truth: The situation in America is so bad for Negroes that maybe they should go back to Africa. Yet no matter how bleak things looked, Mencken's sympathy never wavered. When Kelly Miller wrote him that the next war would bring about those rights that were never realized in the previous one, Mencken smiled sadly. "I wish I could agree with you," he wrote Miller, "but I can't. My belief is that the patriotism of the black soldiers will be rewarded in the coming war precisely as it was rewarded in the last one."[16]

For Mencken, the more things changed, the more things stayed the same. His dilemma was that his view of the Negro's future was contingent upon the "decency" of the common man; yet he could not quite bring himself to believe in that decency. He wanted to believe in the human potential for responding to the Negro as an amiable fellow, but he was more often confronted with the human potential for Yahoo responses. Since he refused to recognize that operations of the government could change the Negro's economic status (and hence his human status), he was often left with a sense of fatality. His belief in the power of the *Übermensch*, which he had inherited from social Darwinism, Shaw, and Nietzsche, gave little comfort if the "superior" Negro was always going to be up against "a vast horde of crackers." Thus, he and Schuyler often retreated to the ivory tower and spoke in cathedral tones of the death of kings and other kindred matters. Often, of course, they were quite perceptive. Schuyler was right that Roosevelt personally did very little to help the Negro, and Mencken was right to note that man does not live on bread alone, that personal integrity, as well as a full stomach, has value. The trouble was, not many people in the 1930s had full stomachs.

We can get a sense of where Mencken and Schuyler went wrong in the 1930s by considering their views of human nature. For both, the world was made up of knaves, fools, and a few honest men. The fools comprised the bulk of mankind, and the knaves and the honest men were constantly at war over their souls. Usually the knaves prevailed, but the honest men never quite gave up, never quite despaired altogether. What Alexander Pope said of himself as a satirist might also apply to Mencken and Schuyler:

> Yes, I am proud; I must be proud to see
> Men not afraid of God, afraid of me.[17]

The satirist never wins. He never even keeps the knaves honest, but he does make them stand in fear. In their heyday, both Schuyler and Mencken made the enemy stand in fear, and they gave a lot of pleasure to others in doing so. But as they grew older, they could not always see the real enemy. Was it actually Roosevelt? Or Martin Luther King?

Schuyler's infamous conservatism loses much of its bad odor if we see it as a protest against human stupidity. His complaint against "Negro agitators" in the 1960s was based on the idea that these people knew not what they did.

> To elicit more sympathy for their cause, the radical Negro agitators operating on the white collar front have been engaging in a veritable campaign of Negro mass disparagement. They write theses on the "failure" of the Negro family, dwell on the "helplessness" of the colored community, emphasize the high incidence of crime, disease, narcotics addiction, and other social evils. The white sociologists and welfarists vie with them with a suspicious relish reminiscent of the Negrophobic propaganda of a half century before, when such hatemongers as Thomas Dixon held literary sway. The picture of Negro life that emerges is pessimistic and frightening, tending to make insistence on integration ridiculous.[18]

For Schuyler, the fools have played right into the hands of the knaves. To dwell on failures is to give ammunition to the enemy, who is only too willing to believe the worst that can be said about the Negro people. That Schuyler was wrong about Martin Luther King does not negate the force of his argument.

Yet even here we can see that his argument hinges upon an older world view, one that hasn't quite come to terms with power politics—the legacy of the New Deal. Schuyler is still grasping for an idea of "culture," for the idea of the *honnête homme*. He refuses to recognize, as did many of his compatriots during the Harlem Renaissance, that a sordid environment could debase a man so that he could resemble the portraits painted by the Negrophobes. To a lesser extent, Mencken also shied away from this reality when he gave his advice to the black novelists in the Ovington review. Of course the man who loved Conrad knew that a black Kurtz could exist, yet his aesthetic program for the black novelist was such that realism subtly precluded a type like Kurtz, because it was too similar to the distortions fabricated by the white racists such as Thomas Dixon (note Schuyler's antique reference). Moreover, Mencken also knew that economics often dictated political policy (he acutely saw that the existence of the "peculiar institution" was tied to economics), but he closed his eyes to the possibility that the mysterious workings of money could radically change the human personality. As sympathetic as he was to Negro life and culture, in the 1930s he did not understand (to use DuBois's phrase) "where the shoe pinches." Since he did not believe the Depression to be real, it is no wonder that he failed to perceive how the majority of black people lived—in soul-killing poverty. Thus Mencken kept calling for the "civilized point of view," without realizing that the most likely thing produced by Bigger Thomas's neighborhood was the uncivilized point of view.

Mencken and Schuyler continued to sing the old tunes, but few applauded. As far as black literature and black life were concerned, both men had outlived their times. The man who had once given black writers dignity did not comprehend the terrible economic conditions that could rob people of it. That he did so much for the Negro is only one reason, among many, why he will be remembered; that he could not do more for the Negro was the result of an intelligence as provincial as it was perceptive. Yet this man who refused to sympathize with modernism, who refused to come to grips with the true meaning of the expatriate experience—that it meant being liberated from the parochialism of being an "American" author—this man also refused to participate in the ostentation surrounding the Harlem Renaissance. At the same time, however, he clearly symbolized its major thrust, and he encouraged its best efforts. If he had not included Negro writers in his program to revitalize American literature, the Harlem Renaissance would have been less than it was, and if he had not written with such wit, rage, intelligence, and humor about America, Richard Wright might never have picked up a pencil. A bundle of paradoxes despite his claim that he never mixed metaphors, booze, or opinions, he was the genuine article, the quintessential American: vulgar, outspoken, salty, well meaning, and compassionate. Black literature improved after Mencken lost his influence upon black culture, but the whole notion of the black writer as we have come to know him might never have existed had it not been for Mencken. He helped make the idea that there could be black writers a real one to the Negroes themselves.

Notes

CHAPTER ONE

1. Walter Lippmann, "H. L. Mencken," *Saturday Review of Literature* 3 (11 December 1926): 413.

2. Bertrand H. Bronson, "The Double Tradition of Dr. Johnson," in *Johnson Agonistes and Other Essays* (Berkeley and Los Angeles: University of California Press, 1965), pp. 156-76. Also, see Charles Angoff, *H. L. Mencken, A Portrait from Memory* (New York: Yoseloff, 1956).

3. Robert Brustein, "The W. C. Fields of American Journalism," *New York Times Book Review* 81 (19 December 1976): 3. Even so excellent and sympathetic a biography of Mencken as William Manchester's *Disturber of the Peace: The Life of H. L. Mencken* (New York: Harper, 1951) helped to sustain the folk image. Here is Manchester's description of Mencken getting out a paragraph on his Corona typewriter: "Out it came, with a spasm; another long pause, an oath softly muttered, then with a grunt he was off on another paragraph, viciously punching the keys and squirming in the suffering and articulate swivel chair. Periodically he sprang to his feet and paddled into the bathroom, to indulge in a curious but very necessary writing habit: a complete and vigorous washing of the hands" (pp. 48-49). Mencken's character is that of an eccentric from the pages of a Dickens novel.

4. Frank Turaj, "H. L. Mencken and American Literature" (Ph.D. diss., Brown University, 1968), pp. 1, 2. Other recent works that discuss Mencken's formidable literary reputation in the teens and 1920s are William Nolte's *H. L. Mencken, Literary Critic* (Middletown, Conn.: Wesleyan University Press, 1966), William Manchester's *Disturber of the Peace*, Charles A. Fecher's *Mencken: A Study of His Thought* (New York: Knopf, 1978), Carl R. Dolmetsch's *The Smart Set: A History and Anthology* (New York: Dial Press, 1966), Fred C. Hobson's *Serpent in Eden: H. L. Mencken and the South* (Chapel Hill: University of North Carolina Press, 1974), Carl Bode's *Mencken* (Carbondale: Southern Illinois University Press, 1969), W.H.A. Williams's *H. L. Mencken* (Boston: G. K. Hall, 1977). This is by no means an exhaustive list of the work done on Mencken's literary criticism, but these critics do present convincing evidence that Lippmann was not exaggerating. Furthermore, the general consensus today is that Mencken's literary criticism continues to hold up, that he was a first-rate critic. No longer do critics believe in the post-1930s, pre-1960s attitude of Edgar Kemler, who argued that because "Mencken was a cynic," he does not qualify "as a truly professional critic." See Edgar Kemler, *The Irreverent Mr. Mencken* (Boston: Little, Brown, 1950), p. 123. As William Nolte and Frank Turaj have shown, Mencken was no cynic when he discussed literature. He brought to it a passionate intelligence, which not only punctured cant but also recognized and appreciated real merit.

5. Alfred Kazin, *On Native Grounds* (1942; reprint, Garden City, N.Y.: Doubleday, 1956), p. 160.

6. Frederick Hoffmann, *The Twenties* (1949; reprint, New York: Collier Books, 1962), p. 354.

7. John McCormick, *The Middle Distance* (New York: Free Press, 1971), p. 167.

8. Isaac Goldberg, *The Man Mencken* (New York: Simon & Schuster, 1925), p. 254.

9. See Robert A. Bone, *The Negro Novel in America* (1958; reprint, New Haven: Yale University Press, 1965), p. 89. Books or articles that treat the Harlem Renaissance at length and that bypass Mencken (or only touch on him tangentially) are *The Harlem Renaissance Remembered*, ed. Arna Bontemps (New York: Dodd, Mead, 1972), Arthur Davis's *From the Dark Tower: Afro-American Writers (1900 to 1960)* (Washington, D.C.: Howard University Press, 1974), Nathan Huggins's *Harlem Renaissance* (New York: Oxford University Press, 1971), Amritjit Singh's *The Novels of the Harlem Renaissance* (University Park: Pennsylvania State University Press, 1976), Margaret Perry's *Silence to the Drums: A Survey of the Literature of the Harlem Renaissance* (Westport, Conn.: Greenwood Press, 1976), David Levering Lewis's *When Harlem Was In Vogue* (New York: Knopf, 1981), and Darwin T. Turner's "The Harlem Renaissance: One Facet of an Unturned Kaleidoscope," in *Toward a New American Literary History* (Durham: Duke University Press, 1980), pp. 195-210. Many of the above works provide excellent examinations of the literary movement from many different angles. Lewis's exploration of the decade's social and intellectual history is especially fine, and Turner's plea that we open our eyes to the vast "kaleidoscope" of the age is well made. In a sense, this book is a response to his stimulating article. Recently, Chidi Ikonne's *From DuBois to Van Vechten* (Westport, Conn.: Greenwood Press, 1981) has also followed Turner's lead by looking at the intricate relationships between black and white authors. However, Mencken's connection with the Harlem Renaissance is again slighted.

10. See Charles F. Cooney, "Mencken's Midwifery," *Menckeniana* 43 (Fall 1972): 1-4; Robert C. Hart, "Black-White Literary Relations in the Harlem Renaissance," *American Literature* 44 (January 1973): 616; Edward E. Waldron, *Walter White and the Harlem Renaissance* (Port Washington, N.Y.: Kennikat Press, 1978), pp. 56-60; and Lewis, *When Harlem Was In Vogue*, pp. 132-36.

11. Fenwick Anderson, "Black Perspectives in Mencken's *Mercury*," *Menckeniana* 70 (Summer 1979): 2. The French critic Guy Forgue has a brief, intelligent discussion of Mencken's aid to black writers in the late teens and early 1920s. See his monumental *H. L. Mencken: l'Homme, l'Oeuvre, l'Influence* (Paris: Minard, 1967), pp. 342-43. Also, see Fecher, *Mencken: A Study of His Thought*, pp. 214-17, for a penetrating account of Mencken's racial attitudes.

12. Justin Kaplan, "Mencken at 100," *New York Times Book Review* 85 (7 September 1980): 26.

13. Alan Dundes, ed., *Mother Wit from the Laughing Barrel: Readings in the Interpretation of Afro-American Folklore* (Englewood Cliffs, N.J.: Prentice-Hall, 1973), p. 143.

14. Jervis Anderson, "That Was New York (Harlem—part III)," *New Yorker* 67 (13 July 1981): 64. Anderson's article was one of four articles which appeared in the *New Yorker* and were recently collected in the book *This Was Harlem: A Cultural Portrait, 1900-1950* (New York: Farrar, Straus, Giroux, 1982).

15. Typical of the attacks upon Van Vechten's influence are Harold Cruse, *The Crisis of the Negro Intellectual* (New York: William Morrow, 1967), p 35; and Addison Gayle, *The Way of the New World: The Black Novel in America* (Garden City, N.Y.: Doubleday, 1975), pp. 86-96. For a balanced view of Van Vechten's role during the Harlem Renaissance, see Bruce Kellner's introduction to *"Keep A-Inchin' Along": Selected Writings of Carl Van Vechten about Black Art and Letters*, ed. Bruce Kellner (Westport, Conn.: Greenwood Press, 1979), pp. 3-13.

16. Carl Van Vechten, *Nigger Heaven* (1926; reprint, New York: Harper, 1971),

pp. 222-25.

17. There may be some gentle satire directed at Mencken as well. In *Nigger Heaven*, white novelist Roy McKain (probably Jim Tully) writes a "capital yarn" (says Durwood) about a Negro pimp: "I don't suppose he even saw the fellow . . . but his imagination was based on a background of observation" (p. 226). Van Vechten depicts McKain as a man who can observe detail but who completely misperceives its moral implications. As we shall see, Mencken was associated with literary realism from his early days as a book reviewer for the *Smart Set*. On the other hand, Van Vechten's narrative propensities lay toward the comedy of manners, the light ironic touch. Hence, the latter may be underscoring the limitations of a literal-minded realism, one that Mencken was sometimes (but not always) guilty of espousing.

18. James Weldon Johnson, *Along This Way* (1933; reprint, New York: Viking, 1968), pp. 305-6.

19. HLM, "Gropings in Literary Darkness," *Smart Set* 63 (October 1920): 140. Reprinted in *H. L. Mencken's "Smart Set" Criticism*, ed. William H. Nolte (Ithaca: Cornell University Press, 1968), pp. 320-22.

20. HLM to Walter White, 7 October 1922, NAACP Executive Correspondence Files, Manuscript Division, Library of Congress, hereafter referred to as the NAACP Files.

21. Yet see William L. Andrews, "William Dean Howells and Charles W. Chesnutt: Criticism and Race Fiction in the Age of Booker T. Washington," *American Literature* 48 (November 1976): 327-39. Andrews acutely observes that Howells could never quite free his literary judgment of Chesnutt from his political one. Although he had praised Chesnutt as a realist in his reviews of Chesnutt's early fiction, he talked of *The Marrow of Tradition* (1901) as if it were a tract on racial relations. Since Howells believed in Booker T. Washington's accommodationist position, he essentially disapproved of Chesnutt's "bitter" novel. Thus, Howells's extra-aesthetic views triumphed over his realist principles, and, in retrospect, it seems that Mencken was quite right to ignore him as an important influence upon realism in Negro letters.

22. See Helen Chesnutt, *Charles Waddell Chesnutt* (Chapel Hill: University of North Carolina Press, 1952), pp. 57-59; HLM, "The Father of Them All," *American Mercury* 15 (December 1928): 506, hereafter referred to as *Mercury;* Turaj, "Mencken and American Literature," p. 76.

23. See Robert M. Henderson, *D. W. Griffith: His Life and Work* (New York: Oxford University Press, 1972), pp. 156-59.

24. *Publishers Weekly* 96 (20 September 1919), advertisement for Dodd, Mead; and p. 745.

25. Ibid., 94 (3 August 1918), cover. The same claim was made for Means on the cover of the 31 May 1919 issue of *Publishers Weekly.*

26. Van Vechten, *Nigger Heaven*, p. 223.

27. HLM to W.E.B. DuBois, 15 October 1935, H. L. Mencken Papers, Rare Books and Manuscripts Division, The New York Public Library, Astor, Lenox and Tilden Foundations, hereafter referred to as NYP.

28. HLM to Walter White, 16 October 1923, NAACP Files.

29. HLM, "The Southern Negro," *Mercury* 9 (October 1926): 252-53.

30. HLM, "Songs of the American Negro," *World Review* 1 (8 February 1926): 279.

31. HLM, "Black Boy," *Mercury* 15 (September 1928): 126.

32. W.E.B. DuBois, "The Negro in Art," *Crisis* 31 (March 1926): 219.

33. Arthur O. Lovejoy et al., eds., *A Documentary History of Primitivism and Related Ideas*, vol. 1 (Baltimore: Johns Hopkins Press, 1935), pp. 10, 11.

34. At least this is what Julia Peterkin thought had happened. She told Mencken that "Knopf did 'Green Thursday' without any enthusiasm for the book. I think, out of courtesy

for you." Julia Peterkin to HLM, 25 January 1927, NYP. Also, see *The Collected Short Stories of Julia Peterkin*, ed. Frank Durham (Columbia: University of South Carolina Press, 1970), p. 53.

35. HLM, "The Father of Them All," *Mercury* 15 (December 1928): 506.

36. See HLM, "Chiefly Americans," *Smart Set* 63 (December 1920): 138-40; HLM, "Consolation," *Smart Set* 64 (January 1921): 138-40; HLM, "Portrait of an American Citizen," *Smart Set* 69 (October 1922): 139.

37. HLM, "A City in Moronia," *Mercury* 16 (March 1929): 381.

38. Van Wyck Brooks, *The Confident Years: 1885-1915* (New York: Dutton, 1952), p. 471.

39. All her novels were published in the 1930s, but Hurston never left the fictional perspective that she had learned in the 1920s. Her fiction ignores the Depression altogether. See Robert Hemenway's excellent biography, *Zora Neale Hurston* (Urbana: University of Illinois Press, 1977).

40. See James O. Young, *Black Writers of the Thirties* (Baton Rouge: Louisiana State University Press, 1973), p. 134. Throughout his informative book, Young makes the mistake of assuming that realism in black literature was the particular property of the 1930s.

41. Wallace Thurman, *The Blacker the Berry* (1929; reprint, New York: Collier Books, 1970), p. 227.

42. HLM, *Prejudices, Fifth Series* (New York: Knopf, 1926), p. 233. All six volumes of *Prejudices* were published by Knopf, and the dates are as follows: *First Series* (1919); *Second Series* (1920); *Third Series* (1922); *Fourth Series* (1924); *Sixth Series* (1927). Hereafter, only title and series number will be listed.

43. See Nella Larsen's letter to Carl Van Vechten, 12 November 1926, James Weldon Johnson Memorial Collection of Negro Arts and Letters, Collection of American Literature, Beinecke Rare Book and Manuscript Library, Yale University, hereafter referred to as JWJ: "Pablo de Segovia is marvelous. A tale of a Negro ruffian told in this naive manner would be interesting. (I think someone, Mencken perhaps, has made this suggestion somewhere.)"

44. HLM, "Novels for Indian Summer," *Smart Set* 60 (November 1919): 139, reprinted in *Smart Set Criticism*, pp. 46-47.

45. See Huggins, *Harlem Renaissance*, chap. 6, "Personae: White/Black Faces—Black Masks."

46. Arna Bontemps to Langston Hughes, 19 November 1945, in *Arna Bontemps-Langston Hughes Letters: 1925-1967*, ed. Charles Nichols (New York: Dodd, Mead, 1980), p. 200.

47. HLM, "View of Literary Gents," *Chicago Tribune*, 29 November 1925, reprinted in *The Bathtub Hoax and Other Blasts and Bravos*, ed. Robert McHugh (New York: Knopf, 1958), pp. 110-14.

48. HLM, *Prejudices* 3, p. 71.

49. HLM, *A Book of Prefaces* (1917; reprint, Garden City, N.Y.: Garden City Pub. Co., 1927), p. 199.

50. HLM, *Prejudices* 4, p. 283.

51. HLM, "Observations Upon the National Letters," *Smart Set* 62 (July 1920): 144.

52. HLM, *Prejudices* 3, p. 27.

53. HLM, "The Mailed Fist and Its Prophet," *Atlantic Monthly* 114 (November 1914): 607, reprinted in *The Young Mencken*, ed. Carl Bode (New York: Dial Press, 1973), p. 441, hereafter referred to as *Young Mencken*.

54. HLM, *Prejudices* 4, p. 141.

55. James Weldon Johnson, ed., *The Book of American Negro Poetry* (1922; reprint, New York: Harcourt, Brace, 1959), p. 9.

56. See H. M. Kallen, "Alain Locke and Cultural Pluralism," *Journal of Philosophy* 54 (28 February 1957): 121.

57. Alain Locke, "American Literary Tradition and the Negro," *Modern Quarterly* 3 (May-July 1926): 221.

58. Alain Locke, "The Colonial Literature of France," *Opportunity* 1 (November 1923): 334.

59. HLM to Walter White, 2 August 1934, NYP.

60. Roy Wilkins to HLM, 9 August 1934, NYP.

61. HLM, "Notes on Negro Strategy," *Crisis* 41 (October 1935): 289, 304.

62. HLM, "The Common Negro," *Baltimore Evening Sun*, 2 August 1910, reprinted in *Young Mencken*, pp. 128-31.

63. HLM, "Gropings in Literary Darkness," p. 141, reprinted in *Smart Set Criticism*, p. 321.

CHAPTER TWO

1. Richard Wright, *Black Boy* (New York: Harper and Brothers, 1945), pp. 217-18.

2. Floyd Calvin, "Interview with Countee Cullen," *Pittsburgh Courier*, 18 June 1927.

3. James Weldon Johnson, "Views and Reviews," *New York Age*, 20 July 1918.

4. Ibid., 21 February 1920.

5. George Schuyler, "Views and Reviews," *Pittsburgh Courier*, 30 July 1927.

6. Walter White, "The Spotlight," *Pittsburgh Courier*, 19 June 1926, 17 April 1926.

7. J. A. Rogers, "Scratching the Surface," *Amsterdam News*, 29 February 1928.

8. Countee Cullen to HLM, undated letter, 1924, NYP.

9. Claude McKay to Arthur Schomburg, undated letter, 1925, NYP (Schomburg Collection).

10. Ibid., 3 August 1925.

11. HLM's article appeared in the *New York World*, 25 September 1927, in his weekly column, "Hiring a Hall."

12. W.E.B. DuBois, "Mencken," *Crisis* 34 (October 1927): 276.

13. Miller was so taken with his theme that he promised his readers another article on Mencken, but as far as I know, he never wrote it.

14. Editorial, *Pittsburgh Courier*, 24 September 1927.

15. HLM, *The American Language: Supplement II* (New York: Knopf, 1948), p. 264. Also, see HLM, *The American Language*, 4th ed. (New York: Knopf, 1936), p. 271.

16. George Schuyler to HLM, 15 March 1938, NYP.

17. For Negro slang, see *The American Language: Supplement II*, pp. 263-70, 704-12. George Schuyler introduced Mencken to Dan Burley's column on "Jive" in the *Amsterdam News*. See George Schuyler to HLM, 8 September 1943, NYP. Schuyler called Burley's column a "mire of Harlem slang." For Negro designations, see HLM, *The American Language: Supplement I* (New York: Knopf, 1945), pp. 618-39. This section of *AL* is based on an earlier article, "Designations for Colored Folk," *American Speech* 19 (October 1944): 161-74, reprinted in Dundes, *Mother Wit from the Laughing Barrel*, pp. 142-55. Mencken also published George Phillip Krapp's "The English of the Negro," *Mercury* 2 (June 1924): 190-95.

18. HLM, *The American Language: Supplement II*, pp. 509, 265.

19. See Johnson's letters to him in which he apologizes for not writing the article: 19 December 1923, 20 February 1925, NYP.

20. HLM to George Schuyler, 15 January 1941, JWJ; George Schuyler to HLM, 18 January 1941, NYP.

21. HLM to George Schuyler, 27 September 1934, NYP. On an earlier occasion, Mencken told Schuyler that somebody ought to provide a clipping bureau for Negro news-

papers: "If you know anyone who wants to make the venture, tell him I'd like to be his first customer" (19 October 1927). See *Letters of H. L. Mencken,* ed. Guy J. Forgue (New York: Knopf, 1961), p. 305, hereafter referred to as *Letters.* Three days later, Mencken again encouraged Schuyler to find "some enterprising young man in Harlem" to start this much-needed service. HLM to George Schuyler, 22 October 1927, JWJ.

22. See the categories of "Negro" and "Slavery" especially: HLM, *A New Dictionary of Quotations on Historical Principles from Ancient and Modern Sources* (New York: Knopf, 1942).

23. HLM, *Minority Report* (New York: Knopf, 1956), p. 135.

24. HLM, "The Curse of Prejudice," *Mercury* 23 (May 1931): 125.

25. McCormick, *The Middle Distance,* p. 167.

26. "The Invisible Empire," *Baltimore Evening Sun,* 4 December 1922. For other articles attacking the Klan, see "The South Rebels Again," *Baltimore Evening Sun,* 17 November 1924; "Sub-Potomac Agonies," *Baltimore Evening Sun,* 22 March 1926; and "Sport in the Bible Country," *Mercury* 17 (July 1929): 382-83. For an interesting and unorthodox study of the psychology of the Klan's members, see "The Nightshirt Passes," *Baltimore Evening Sun,* 28 June 1926. Mencken perceptively argues that the Klan's rise to power after the Civil War may be due in part to "a reaction against the growing regimentation of American thought." Again, although he roundly satirizes the Klan's benighted stupidities, he makes the seminal attempt to understand it as a product of a specific social environment.

27. HLM, "The Anti-Lynching Bill," *Baltimore Evening Sun,* 14 May 1934; "The Costigan-Wagner Bill," *Baltimore Evening Sun,* 15 January 1934.

28. HLM to Walter White, 28 January 1935, NYP.

29. See Arthur Schlesinger's rebuttal to Charles Angoff's charge that Mencken was a racist: "Correspondence," *New Republic* 137 (16 December 1957): 23.

30. See Forgue, *Letters,* p. 331. It is worth noting that Mencken added in his letter to Schuyler, "Just as many are to be found in the white race."

31. DuBois, "The Negro in Art," *Crisis,* p. 219.

32. *Minority Report,* p. 152. Mencken once illustrated this theme of "pawky shrewdness" in a short story he wrote in his nonage. In "The Cook's Victory," a lowly Negro servant cleverly gets his revenge upon an ill-tempered sea captain. Written in 1900, this story is reprinted in Goldberg's *The Man Mencken,* pp. 313-24.

33. DuBois, "The Negro in Art," *Crisis,* p. 219.

34. Wallace Thurman, "Book Reviews," *Messenger* 8 (May 1926): 154.

35. George H. Douglas, *H. L. Mencken: Critic of American Life* (Hamden, Conn: Archon, 1978), p. 97.

36. HLM, "The Curse of Prejudice," *Mercury* 23 (May 1931): 125-26.

37. HLM, "The Burden of Credulity," *Opportunity* 9 (February 1931): 40.

38. HLM, "The Curse of Prejudice," *Mercury,* p. 125.

39. HLM, "Notes on Negro Strategy," *Crisis* 41 (October 1934): 289.

40. *Minority Report,* p. 136.

41. Ibid., pp. 234-35.

42. Ibid., p. 224.

43. HLM to George Schuyler, 4 October 1927, JWJ.

44. N. H. Hall, "The Art of the Pullman Porter," *Mercury* 23 (July 1931): 331.

45. HLM, *Heathen Days* (New York: Knopf, 1943), p. 96.

46. HLM, *Happy Days* (New York: Knopf, 1940), p. 269.

47. HLM, *Heathen Days,* p. 104.

48. HLM, *Happy Days,* p. 279.

49. Ibid., p. 153. Langston Hughes has repeated Mencken's graveyard humor about Baltimore's medical students in one of his "Simple" tales. See Langston Hughes, *The Best of Simple* (New York: Hill and Wang, 1961), p. 105.

50. HLM, *Happy Days,* p. 154.

51. William H. Nolte, "The Enduring Mencken," *Mississippi Quarterly* 32 (Fall 1979): 656.

52. Angoff, *Mencken, Portrait From Memory*, pp. 89-90.

53. HLM, "Hiring a Hall," *New York World*, 17 July 1927.

54. See Forgue, *Letters*, p. 272. As Forgue notes, the "reminiscences" were probably the second edition of Johnson's novel, *The Autobiography of an Ex-Colored Man*, which Knopf did republish in 1927.

55. See HLM, "The Murray Case," *Baltimore Evening Sun*, 23 September 1935.

56. HLM to George Schuyler, 12 October 1933, JWJ.

57. HLM to editor, *Pittsburgh Courier*, January 1947, NYP. Mencken's letter was in response to a questionnaire from the *Courier*. Mencken also privately told Schuyler that Schuyler's "column was worth all the rest" and that he regarded it as "the best produced in this free Republic, regardless of the cutaneous hue of its producers." HLM to George Schuyler, 10 July 1947, NYP.

58. I have found Mencken's note concerning the reprinted article in his unpublished correspondence with George Schuyler in NYP. The date on the note is May 1945. Schuyler's article on Roosevelt was originally published in the *Pittsburgh Courier*, 25 April 1945. Mencken wrote to Schuyler at the time and praised him for telling "the whole and bitter truth" about Roosevelt's relationship to the Negro. See *The New Mencken Letters*, ed. Carl Bode (New York: Dial Press, 1977), p. 554—hereafter referred to as *New Letters*. The theme of Negro "superiority" was a favorite one with Mencken. At one time, he urged DuBois to write an essay on the subject—see DuBois's letter to HLM, 16 January 1923, NYP. Also, see HLM, "Treason in the Tabernacle," *Mercury* 23 (June 1931): 160: "In many obvious ways they [Negroes] are superior to the whites against whom they are commonly pitted. They are not only enormously decenter; they are also considerably shrewder."

59. Countee Cullen, "The Shroud of Color," *Mercury* 3 (November 1924): 306-7.

60. HLM to Countee Cullen, 13 August 1924, Amistad Research Center, New Orleans, Louisiana.

61. HLM to Countee Cullen, 5 May 1926, ibid. Cullen then wrote Mencken a long letter explaining the details of the event. Countee Cullen to HLM, 7 May 1926, NYP.

62. HLM, *The Philosophy of Friedrich Nietzsche*, 3d ed. (Boston: Luce, 1913), p. 167.

63. Cruse quotes Samuel Putnam to the effect that one manifestation of the cultural revolt of the 1920s was "a contempt for the arts of the people that with Mencken and his followers became a contempt for the people themselves." See Cruse, *Crisis of the Negro Intellectual*, p. 62.

64. HLM, *Prejudices* 6, pp. 51, 207.

65. HLM, *Notes on Democracy* (New York: Knopf, 1926), p. 172.

66. HLM, "Editorial," *Mercury* 16 (January 1929): 152.

67. HLM, *Notes on Democracy*, p. 153.

68. HLM, "What Ails the Republic," *Baltimore Evening Sun*, 17 April 1922.

69. HLM, *Notes on Democracy*, pp. 172-73.

70. HLM, "The Burden of Credulity," *Opportunity* 9 (February 1931): 40-41.

71. HLM, *Minority Report*, p. 188.

72. HLM, *Notes on Democracy*, p. 165. Also, see HLM, "Editorial," *Mercury* 1 (January 1924): 28-29.

73. Answer to questionnaire sent by Lionel White in 1934, found in Mencken correspondence, NYP.

74. W.H.A. Williams, *H. L. Mencken*, p. 62.

75. HLM, *The American Language*, p. 174.

76. HLM to George Schuyler, 16 December 1943, NYP.

77. See Forgue, *Letters*, p. 477.

78. James Fenimore Cooper, *The American Democrat*, with introduction by H. L. Mencken (New York: Knopf, 1931), p. xviii.

79. HLM, *Prejudices* 2, pp. 66-69.

80. HLM, "Songs of the American Negro," *World Review* 1 (8 February 1926): 279.

81. See *Prejudices: A Selection*, ed. James T. Farrell (New York: Random House, 1956), p. viii.

82. HLM, *Prejudices* 6, pp. 142-43.

83. HLM, "Treason in the Tabernacle," *Mercury* 23 (June 1931): 158.

84. HLM, "The Burden of Credulity," *Opportunity*, p. 41.

85. HLM, "Sub-Potomac Agonies," *Baltimore Evening Sun*, 22 March 1926.

86. HLM, "Hiring a Hall," *New York World*, 25 September 1927.

87. HLM, "Treason in the Tabernacle," *Mercury*, p. 160.

88. HLM to George Schuyler, 25 July 1931, JWJ. Mencken asked Schuyler to "accumulate some materials on the growth of anti-clericalism among American Negroes. . . . The facts whatever they are would make a good article."

89. George Schuyler, "Black America Begins To Doubt," *Mercury* 25 (April 1932): 423-30.

90. Letter of recommendation that Mencken wrote for Schuyler, for Harmon Foundation prize, 30 July 1930, NAACP Files.

91. HLM, *The American Language: Supplement I*, p. 619.

92. George Schuyler, "Black Art," *Mercury* 27 (November 1932): 335-42.

93. HLM, "Literary Notes," *Smart Set* 65 (July 1921): 141.

94. Forgue, *Letters*, p. 221.

95. HLM, *Minority Report*, p. 287.

96. HLM, "Hiring a Hall," *New York World*, 17 July 1927.

97. HLM to George Schuyler, 11 November 1930, JWJ. Mencken said that he was sorry Schuyler could not stop by when he had last visited Baltimore: "My cellar has a just reputation, and is at the disposal of visiting literati."

98. See W.H.A. Williams, *H. L. Mencken*, p. 45. Mencken's aesthetic advice may have been the source of Bill Gorton's satirical song about "irony and pity" in Hemingway's *The Sun Also Rises*. Williams does not mention this connection, but it seems fairly obvious, given Hemingway's dislike of Mencken.

99. HLM, "The Fruits of Go-getting," *Baltimore Evening Sun*, 22 June 1925.

100. I am combining two letters here: HLM to George Schuyler, 9 September 1943 and 13 September 1943, NYP.

101. See Bode, *New Letters*, p. 400.

102. HLM, *Minority Report*, p. 293.

103. HLM, "Si Mutare Potest Aethiops Pellum Suam," *Smart Set* 53 (September 1917): 138.

104. W.E.B. DuBois, "The Looking Glass," *Crisis* 14 (October 1917): 298.

105. See Zora Neale Hurston's unpublished MS "Harlem Slanguage" in JWJ, and Rudolph Fisher's "An Introduction to Contemporary Harlemese" at the end of his novel *The Walls of Jericho* (New York: Knopf, 1928).

106. Joseph Wood Krutch, *Samuel Johnson* (1944; reprint, New York: Harcourt, Brace, 1963), pp. 140-41.

107. HLM, "Hiring a Hall," *New York World*, 25 September 1927.

108. HLM to George Schuyler, 30 June 1934, JWJ.

109. HLM to George Schuyler, 9 September 1943, NYP.

110. See "Correspondence," *New Republic* 137 (18 November 1957): 23.

CHAPTER THREE

1. The story of Mencken's difficulties during World War I has been told many times.

See Goldberg, *The Man Mencken*, p. 208; Bode, *Mencken*, pp. 106-16; Manchester, *Disturber of the Peace*, pp. 98-111. For a description of Mencken's warfare with the New Humanists, see Nolte, *H. L. Mencken, Literary Critic*, pp. 148-78.

2. HLM, "The Curse of Prejudice," *Mercury* 23 (May 1931): 125.

3. HLM, "The Coroner's Inquest," *Smart Set* 69 (September 1922): 144.

4. HLM, "The Land of the Free," *Smart Set* 65 (May 1921): 138-39.

5. HLM, *A Book of Prefaces*, p. 203.

6. HLM, "The Monthly Feuilleton," *Smart Set* 69 (December 1922): 140-41.

7. *New York Evening Mail*, undated, 1917. Found in the newspaper clippings in the Mencken Collection, Enoch Pratt Free Library, Baltimore. Mencken told James Weldon Johnson that Miller's "letter made a great impression on me. It should be reprinted as a pamphlet." Undated letter, 1917, NYP.

8. Quoted from the *Crisis* 21 (April 1921): 267.

9. See Huggins, *Harlem Renaissance*, pp. 38-40; Lewis, *When Harlem Was In Vogue*, pp. 3-24.

10. Editorial, *Chicago Defender*, 2 March 1918.

11. Cartoon, ibid., 26 March 1921.

12. Ibid., 2 July 1921.

13. Editorial, ibid., 12 February 1921.

14. Grace Johnson to HLM, 25 August 1942, NYP. In this same letter, Grace Johnson made a perceptive observation about Mencken's letters to her husband: "They are an interesting and valuable part of your range of thought *when most people were inarticulate who held the power of influence that you represented*" (italics mine).

15. HLM to James Weldon Johnson, undated letter, 1917, NYP. Johnson sent Mencken songs by Harry Burleigh, and Mencken wanted to know more about him. "Is he a colored man?" Mencken asked. Undated letter, 1917, NYP.

16. HLM to James Weldon Johnson, undated letter (circa 1922), NYP. Mencken also wanted Johnson to expand the section of the preface dealing with Negro music into an article or book: "Why not go into the history of ragtime at length, establishing names and dates accurately? It ought to be done. . . . Then you might do similar essays on negro poets and negro painters and sculptors, and so have a second book on the negro as artist. . . . I think a preface to poetry should stick to poetry pretty closely. . . . The whole thing interests me immensely."

17. James Weldon Johnson, "Views and Reviews," *New York Age*, 20 July 1918.

18. Ibid., 21 February 1920.

19. Ibid., 14 October 1922.

20. In 1913, beginning in June, Mencken dissected this species of *Homo sapiens* with relish. Carl Bode has conveniently collected five of these six essays in his *Young Mencken*, and my references will be to this text.

21. Bode, *Young Mencken*, p. 297.

22. Ibid., p. 289.

23. Ibid., p. 288.

24. HLM, *Prejudices* 3, p. 11.

25. Ibid., p. 16.,

26. Hobson, *Serpent in Eden*, pp. 19-26.

27. James Weldon Johnson, "Views and Reviews," *New York Age*, 21 February 1920.

28. HLM to James Weldon Johnson, 8 August 1919, in Bode, *New Letters*, p. 111.

29. HLM, "The Confederate Pastime," *Smart Set* 61 (February 1920): 45-46. HLM, "The Confederate Mind," *Smart Set* 62 (May 1920): 30-31.

30. HLM, *Prejudices* 2, pp. 144, 142.

31. Ibid., p. 153.

32. Ibid., pp. 146-49.

33. Louis D. Rubin, *The Curious Death of the Novel* (Baton Rouge: Louisiana State University Press, 1967), p. 117.

34. Hobson, *Serpent in Eden*, p. 16.

35. HLM, *Prejudices* 2, p. 150. Also, see Joel Williamson's informative book, *New People: Miscegenation and Mulattoes in the United States* (New York: Free Press, 1980). Williamson argues that by the 1920s people of mixed blood no longer saw themselves as "new people," but rather called themselves Negroes. For example, such people as W.E.B. DuBois, James Weldon Johnson, Alain Locke, and Walter White became the leaders of a literary movement that stressed that "black is beautiful," though they themselves were light-skinned. Notice that Mencken in the passage quoted does not make a distinction between mulattoes and "negroes."

36. HLM, "Letters and the Map," *Smart Set* 63 (November 1920): 139-40, quoted in Hobson, *Serpent in Eden*, p. 26.

37. Undated letter, 1917, HLM to James Weldon Johnson, NYP. On 27 November 1917, Mencken wrote Johnson and apologized for spilling "the 'Uncle Tom's Cabin' beans. Why not announce the work, and so protect your priority?" NYP.

38. HLM, "Si Mutare," p. 141.

39. George Schuyler, *Black and Conservative* (New Rochelle: Arlington House, 1966), p. 142.

40. James Weldon Johnson, "Views and Reviews," *New York Age*, 19 April 1919.

41. Johnson, *Book of American Negro Poetry*, p. 21. Johnson quotes Mencken's "Sahara" as proof that "the white South, too, is consuming all of its intellectual energy in this lamentable conflict" (p. 22).

42. Montgomery Gregory, "Our Book Shelf," *Opportunity* 1 (December 1923): 374-75.

43. Arnold Mulder, "Wanted: A Negro Novelist," *Independent* 112 (21 June 1924): 342.

44. George Schuyler, "Our White Folks," *Mercury* 12 (December 1927): 388-91.

45. DuBois, "The Negro in Art," *Crisis*, p. 220.

46. J. A. Rogers, "Wanted: A Satirist," *Amsterdam News*, 21 July 1926.

47. Fenwick Anderson, "Black Perspectives in Mencken's *Mercury*," *Menckeniana*, p. 2.

48. W.E.B. DuBois, "The Dilemma of the Negro," *Mercury* 3 (October 1924): 179-85.

49. George Schuyler, "Keeping the Negro in his Place," *Mercury* 17 (August 1929): 476.

50. J. A. Rogers, "The American Negro in Europe," *Mercury* 20 (May 1930): 1-10.

51. HLM to George Schuyler, 4 May 1929, JWJ.

52. G. Peyton Wertenbaker, "A White Man in the South," *Mercury* 17 (July 1929): 257-62.

53. HLM to George Schuyler, 4 May 1929, JWJ.

54. L. M. Hussey, "Homo Africanus," *Mercury* 4 (January 1925): 87.

55. Edward Rosenheim, *Swift and the Satirist's Art* (Chicago: University of Chicago Press, 1963), chap. 1.

56. See Waldron, *White and the Harlem Renaissance*, p. 37.

57. James Weldon Johnson, "A Negro Looks at Race Prejudice," *Mercury* 14 (May 1928): 52-56.

58. HLM to George Schuyler, 25 August 1927, in Bode, *New Letters*, pp. 213-14.

59. Ibid., 30 August 1927, in Bode, *New Letters*, p. 214.

60. HLM to George Schuyler, 5 October 1932, JWJ. Also, see HLM to George Schuyler, 30 January 1933, NYP. Mencken advised Schuyler to present his "facts in a perfectly grave manner and without any moralizing upon them."

61. George Schuyler, "Our White Folks," *Mercury* 12 (December 1927): 387.

62. George Schuyler, "Blessed Are the Sons of Ham," *Nation* 124 (23 March 1927): 313-14.

63. George Schuyler, "Our Greatest Gift to America," in *The New Negro Renaissance: An Anthology*, ed. Michael W. Peplow and Arthur P. Davis (New York: Holt, Rinehart, 1975), p. 67. Schuyler's essay originally appeared in *Ebony and Topaz*. Schuyler's point is not merely satiric exaggeration; he seems to be defining the very foundation of *Herrenvolk* democracy in the Old South. See George Fredrickson, *The Black Image in the White Mind: The Debate on Afro-American Character and Destiny, 1817-1914* (New York: Harper, 1971), p. 61, passim.

64. Theophilus Lewis, "In Defense of A Vanishing Fiction," *Messenger* 10 (January 1927): 4.

65. See Peplow and Davis, *The New Negro Renaissance*, p. 55. Frazier's essay originally appeared in *Forum* 77 (June 1927): 856-62.

66. Walter White, "I Investigate Lynchings," *Mercury* 16 (January 1929): 77-84.

67. George Schuyler, "Traveling Jim Crow," *Mercury* 20 (August 1930): 429-30.

68. HLM, "Nordic Blond Art," *Smart Set* 71 (May 1923): 138.

69. See Franz Boas, "The Question of Racial Purity," *Mercury* 3 (October 1924): 163-69; Melville Herskovits, "What Is A Race," *Mercury* 2 (June 1924): 207-10; Raymond Pearl, "The Biology of Superiority," *Mercury* 12 (November 1927): 257-66.

70. Alain Locke, "The Legacy of the Ancestral Arts," *The New Negro*, ed. Alain Locke (1925; reprint, New York: Atheneum, 1969), pp. 254-67.

71. Langston Hughes, "Cora Unashamed," *Mercury* 30 (September 1933): 19-24; "Poor Little Black Fellow," *Mercury* 30 (November 1933): 326-35.

72. Eugene Gordon, "The Negro's Inhibitions," *Mercury* 13 (February 1928): 159-65.

73. Eugene Gordon, "The Negro Press," *Mercury* 8 (June 1926): 207-15.

74. Rudolph Fisher, "The Caucasian Storms Harlem," *Mercury* 11 (August 1927): 393-98.

75. George Schuyler, "Uncle Sam's Black Step-Child," *Mercury* 29 (May 1933): 147-56.

76. George Schuyler, "Black Warriors," *Mercury* 21 (November 1930): 288-97.

77. George Schuyler and Theophilus Lewis, "Shafts and Darts," *Messenger* 6 (April 1924): 108.

78. George Schuyler, "Shafts and Darts," *Messenger* 6 (October 1924): 315.

79. Ibid. (February 1924): 41.

80. George Schuyler, "The Negro and Nordic Civilization," *Messenger* 7 (May 1925): 198.

81. See George Schuyler, "The Negro Art Hokum," *Nation* 122 (16 June 1926): 662-63.

82. George Schuyler, "Shafts and Darts," *Messenger* 7 (February 1925): 91.

83. Ibid., 8 (October 1926): 307.

84. Ibid., 9 (November 1927): 230.

85. George Schuyler, "Seldom Seen," *Messenger* 8 (November 1926): 344.

86. George Schuyler, "At the Darktown Charity Ball," *Messenger* 6 (December 1924): 377-78.

87. George Schuyler, "The Yellow Peril," *Messenger* 7 (January 1925): 28.

88. George Schuyler, "These 'Colored' United States," *Messenger* 7 (October-November 1925): 346.

89. George Schuyler, "Shafts and Darts," *Messenger* 7 (August 1925): 295.

90. George Schuyler, "At the Darktown Charity Ball," *Messenger* 6 (December 1924): 377.

91. George Schuyler, "Shafts and Darts," *Messenger* 7 (May 1925): 205.

92. Eugene Kinckle Jones and Robert Russa Moton, Director of the Urban Leage and President of Tuskegee Institute, respectively.

93. George Schuyler, "Shafts and Darts," *Messenger* 8 (August 1926): 239. Schuyler also satirized white writers for exploiting the Negro fad. See "At the Coffee House," *Messenger* 7 (June 1925): 236-38.

94. The paradox that some Negroes would be made unhappy by the removal of the color problem is a theme that Mencken had touched on in the *Mercury*. See Editorial, *Mercury* 12 (October 1927): 159.

95. See Charles Larson's introduction to *Black No More* (1931; reprint, New York: Collier Books, 1971), pp. 9-15. Larson completely misperceives the purpose of Schuyler's satire, arguing that Schuyler has no sense of racial pride and that he advocates Crookman's solution, on a figurative level, for all blacks. Such a literal-minded response to the novel is comparable to that of many students of Swift, who thought the "message" of "A Modest Proposal" to be a new lesson in the culinary arts.

96. George Schuyler to HLM, 30 August 1930, NYP. As far as I know, Mencken's answer to Schuyler's request for an introduction has been lost. However, Schuyler refers to it in an unpublished letter that he wrote to Mencken, 18 September 1930, NYP. It is clear from Schuyler's remarks that Mencken refused to write the introduction because he did not want to be put in the position of patron. Although disappointed, Schuyler agreed: "One thing I am very anxious to avoid is patronizing. There has, I believe, been altogether too much of it, especially in work done by the darker brethren."

97. W.E.B. DuBois, review of *Black No More*, by George Schuyler, *Crisis* 38 (March 1931): 100, reprinted in *Book Reviews by W.E.B. DuBois* (Millwood, New York: KTO Press, 1977), pp. 153-54—hereafter cited as *Book Reviews*.

98. W.E.B. DuBois, review of *Slaves Today*, by George Schuyler, *Crisis* 39 (February 1932): 68-69, reprinted in *Book Reviews*, pp. 161-62.

CHAPTER FOUR

This chapter contains sections that were first published in a form now thoroughly revised. See Charles W. Scruggs, "'All Dressed Up But No Place to Go': The Black Writer and His Audience During the Harlem Renaissance," *American Literature* 48 (January 1977): 543-63.

1. For instance, see the chapter in HLM, *Happy Days*, entitled "Rural Delights."

2. Charles N. Glaab, "Metropolis and Suburb: The Changing American City," in *Change and Continuity in Twentieth-Century America: The 1920's*, ed. John Braeman, Robert H. Bremner, and David Brody (Columbus: Ohio State University Press, 1968), p. 399.

3. Burl Noggle, *Into the Twenties: The United States from Armistice to Normalcy* (Urbana: University of Illinois Press, 1974), p. 156. Also, see Blake McKelvey, *The Emergence of Metropolitan America: 1915-1966* (New Brunswick: Rutgers University Press, 1968), pp. 18-19.

4. See Ernest Boyd, *H. L. Mencken* (1927; reprint, Folcroft, Pa.: Folcroft Press, 1969), pp. 14-15. Boyd quotes at length from a *Baltimore Evening Sun* article called "On Living in Baltimore," 16 February 1925. Mencken also expressed similar views to those expressed in Boyd's book in "New York," *Smart Set* 72 (September 1923): 138-43, and in "New York," *Baltimore Evening Sun*, 26 July 1926. In this last article, we see a side of Mencken which is absent from the Mencken who writes for the *Smart Set* or the *Mercury*, the small-town lad who loathes the canned goods of the big city. "Who, indeed, can escape the race's ancient nostalgia for trees, green fields, cows, horseflies, the song of the thrush, the soft earth underfoot? When it comes on in New York it engenders only homicidal moods. The town is made solidly of steel and concrete. The only sweet scents that it knows come out of bottles. It is so artificial that even the grass in its so-called parks looks like embalmed sauerkraut."

5. James Weldon Johnson, "Harlem: The Culture Capital," in *The New Negro*, ed.

Alain Locke (1925; reprint, New York: Atheneum, 1969), p. 309. All references are to this edition and appear in the text.

6. Alain Locke, "The Negro in American Literature," *New World Writing* (New York: New American Library, 1952), p. 28.

7. Alain Locke, "Jingo, Counter-Jingo and Us," *Opportunity* 16 (January 1938): 9.

8. Douglas L. Wilson, ed., *The Genteel Tradition* (Cambridge: Harvard University Press, 1967), p. 9.

9. Santayana first used the expression "the genteel tradition" in a speech that he gave at the University of California at Berkeley on 25 August 1911. The title of his talk was "The Genteel Tradition in American Philosophy." See Wilson, *Genteel Tradition*, pp. 3, 4.

10. Randolph Bourne, "The Puritan's Will to Power," *Seven Arts* 2 (April 1917): 631-37.

11. Claire Sprague, ed., *Van Wyck Brooks: The Early Years* (New York: Harper, 1968), p. 55. Also, see Arthur Wertheim's excellent chapter, "Puritans, Provincials, and Pioneers," *The New York Little Renaissance*, pp. 3-15 (New York: New York University Press, 1976).

12. It was Bourne who pointed out this possibility to Brooks. See James Hoopes, *Van Wyck Brooks* (Amherst: University of Massachusetts Press, 1977), p. 124. After the Great War, Brooks began to lose his optimism concerning America's future—that it was soon to become a real culture, that it would no longer remain a "vast Sargasso Sea" of "unorganized vitality." In 1922, he published an essay called "The Literary Life"—it appeared in Harold Stearns's *Civilization in the United States* (New York: Harcourt, Brace, 1922)—and here he specifically attacked the American reading public whose unimaginative and unsympathetic response forced real artists into mediocrity. He quoted Dreiser's rebuke of Jack London, who never wrote to excel but only to sell, because "he did not feel that he cared for want and public indifference" (p. 82). In the 1920s, Brooks increasingly focused on the "ordeal" of the American writer who lived in an environment that failed to nourish him. See *The Ordeal of Mark Twain* (1920) and *The Pilgrimage of Henry James* (1925). Only in the 1930s, after a mental breakdown, did he begin in his books to celebrate America's literary past.

13. Randolph Bourne, "Trans-National America," *Atlantic Monthly* 118 (July 1916): 90.

14. Sherman Paul, *Randolph Bourne* (Minneapolis: University of Minnesota Press, 1966), p. 31. Also, see John E. Smith, *Royce's Social Infinite: The Community of Interpretation* (New York: Liberal Arts Press, 1950), chap. 5. Paul does not mention that the expression "the Beloved Community" had its origin with Royce, though I am very much indebted to his excellent pamphlet on Bourne. The phrase "the Beloved Community" was to become a favorite of Mumford's as well. See *The Story of Utopias* (New York: Boni and Liveright, 1922), pp. 50, 64, 298.

15. Mumford, *Story of Utopias*, pp. 32-33.

16. Lewis Mumford, "The City," in Stearns, *Civilization in the United States*, p. 5.

17. Mumford, *Story of Utopias*, see chap. 10.

18. Alain Locke, "Art or Propaganda?" *Harlem* 1 (November 1928): 12. Locke sometimes argued from another aesthetic position, however. In investigating his racial heritage, Locke once said that the Negro was reacting against the "colorless conformity" of American life. See Alain Locke, "A Decade of Negro Self Expression," preface to a bibliography, The Trustees of the John F. Slater Fund, Occasional Papers, no. 26 (Charlottesville, Va., 1928), p. 7.

19. Mumford, *Story of Utopias*, pp. 292-93.

20. See especially Mumford's two books *Sticks and Stones: A Study of American Architecture and Civilization* (New York: Boni and Liveright, 1924) and *The Golden Day: A Study in American Literature and Culture* (New York: Norton, 1926).

21. HLM, *A Book of Prefaces*, p. 283.

22. Ibid., p. 207.

23. Patrick J. Gilpin, "Charles S. Johnson: Entrepreneur of the Harlem Renaissance," in *The Harlem Renaissance Remembered*, p. 217. Also see *When Harlem Was In Vogue*, pp. 95, 125-26: David Levering Lewis argues that Johnson was the real power behind Locke's throne, that the editor of *Opportunity* magazine personally chose Locke to edit the *Survey Graphic* issue that became the genesis of *The New Negro*. Although all this is quite true, once Locke took on the mantle of royalty he put his own aesthetic stamp on the materials he assembled for *The New Negro*.

24. Robert E. Park, Ernest W. Burgess, and Roderick D. McKenzie, *The City* (Chicago: University of Chicago Press, 1925), pp. 2, 122; also see pp. 113-22.

25. The following discussion is a condensed version of a paper that I gave at an MLA meeting in December 1978.

26. Eunice Hunton, "Breaking Through," *Survey Graphic* 6 (March 1925): 684.

27. It is entirely possible that Jean Toomer introduced Mumford's writings to Locke. In late 1920 and early 1921, Toomer wrote two emotionally intense letters to Locke. He told Locke that he had been reading Van Wyck Brooks, Randolph Bourne, and Waldo Frank, and that these authors shed light upon specific problems that concern black people. Brooks's categories of puritan and pioneer seem to explain a certain kind of behavior among us, he said. We are so busy trying to lead both a utilitarian and a moral life that we don't see those forces that draw us together as a people. "We need something to cement us," he said prophetically, "and that something can only spring out of a knowledge, out of certain fundamental facts which we share in common. It is to the lack of such a basis that I largely attribute our failure to get together in the past." After *Cane*'s publication (1923), Toomer came to reject the need for racial cohesion that he so eloquently outlined to Locke. His own attitude toward himself as a Negro took an ambiguous turn, resolved only, if then, by his adopting the mask of the "American" artist. (See Charles W. Scruggs, "Jean Toomer: Fugitive," *American Literature* 47 (March 1975): 84-96.) Nonetheless, around the time that he wrote Locke (circa 1920), as he said in his unpublished autobiography, he met Lewis Mumford ("the first flesh-and-blood writer to enter my life"), and since Mumford's theories about the city sprang from the Brooks-Bourne-Frank platform, Toomer may later have passed Mumford's writings on to Locke as he had those of the other members of the "little American renaissance." See Jean Toomer to Alain Locke, 23 August 1920, 26 January 1921, in Alain Locke Papers, Moorland-Spingarn Research Center, Howard University. For Toomer's memory of Mumford, see Toomer Collection, Fisk University Library, hereafter referred to as TC.

28. In this light, it is significant that Locke also deleted from the *Survey Graphic* a sketch by Rudolph Fisher which shows a Negro peasant terrified by the chaos of Harlem. The story focuses on a migrant worker, Jake Crinshaw, who leaves the rural South to find work in Harlem, there to meet one frustration after another. The story ends with Jake juxtaposed against the vast backdrop of the city. "He looked up at the buildings. They were menacingly big and tall and close. There were no trees. No ground for trees to grow from. Sidewalks overflowing with children. Streets crammed full of street-cars and automobiles. Noises, hurry, bustle—fire engines" (p. 646). The last scene hardly shows the Negro to be at one with his new environment.

29. HLM, *Prejudices* 2, p. 89; HLM, *Prejudices* 5, p. 180.

30. HLM, *Prejudices* 2, pp. 88, 101.

31. HLM, "On American Letters," *Baltimore Evening Sun*, 25 October 1920.

32. HLM, *Prejudices* 4, p. 282.

33. HLM, "What Is Civilization?" *Mercury* 16 (January 1929): 123.

34. HLM, *Prejudices* 2, p. 87.

35. HLM, *A Book of Prefaces*, p. 25.

36. HLM, "Art and the Mob," *Baltimore Evening Sun*, 8 May 1922.

37. Raymond Williams, *Culture and Society, 1780-1950* (1958; reprint, Harmondsworth, Middlesex: Penguin, 1976), pp. 53, 146.

38. Locke, "Art or Propaganda?," p. 12.

39. Alain Locke, "The Ethics of Culture," *Howard University Record* 17 (February 1923): 182.

40. Josiah Royce, "Provincialism," *The Basic Writings of Josiah Royce* (Chicago: University of Chicago Press, 1969), 2:1081.

41. Alain Locke, "The Negro in American Culture," in *Anthology of American Negro Literature*, ed. V. F. Calverton (New York: Modern Library, 1929), p. 249.

42. Paul Oliver, *Screening the Blues: Aspects of the Blues Tradition* (London: Cassell & Company, 1968), pp. 6, 7. These statistics are no doubt underestimated because they don't include Paramount's mail-order line with its large sales to southern rural blacks. It is also significant that when the Depression hit in the 1930s, it hit the poor blacks the hardest, and hence the bottom dropped out of the Race Record business. Now people were so desperate that even music was no longer considered a necessity. See Giles Oakley, *The Devil's Music: A History of the Blues* (London: British Broadcasting Corporation, 1976), p. 172.

43. Editorial, *Seven Arts* (November 1916), as quoted in Warner Berthoff, *The Ferment of Realism: American Literature, 1884-1919* (New York: Free Press, 1965), pp. 289-90.

44. See Berthoff, *Ferment of Realism*, pp. 287-98. Berthoff suggests that the best writers of the 1920s freed themselves from the cultural provincialism of the previous decade. They no longer asked, "How can I be American and real?" but "How would Flaubert have done it, or Balzac, or Jules Laforgue, or Mann or Joyce or . . . Dante or Shakespeare or Catullus?" (p. 298). In this sense, the Great War and the European experience liberated the American artist from being too preoccupied with his audience. On the other side of the ledger, Malcolm Cowley has amusingly described the aesthetic squabbles that followed in the wake of his generation's return from Europe. Instead of doing battle with the American public, they fought among themselves, often over the most petty principles. The "little American renaissance" had degenerated into a kind of civil war in Lilliput. See *Exile's Return* (1934); reprint, New York: Viking Press, 1961), pp. 171-96.

45. Lasch argues that this sense of alienation existed before the Great War and in fact created the idea of the "intellectual" in American culture. See Christopher Lasch, *The New Radicalism in America, 1889-1963: The Intellectual as a Social Type* (New York: Knopf, 1965), xii-xvii; Marcus Klein, *After Alienation: American Novels in Mid-Century* (Cleveland: World Publishing Co., 1964), pp. 17-21. Also see Henry May, *The End of American Innocence: A Study of the First Years of Our Own Time, 1912-1917* (New York: Knopf, 1959), pp. 279-301, 322-86. The conflict between the "Custodians of Culture" and the "Young Intellectuals," which May describes as one crack in the surface of the late nineteenth-century complacency, developed into an irreconcilable conflict between America's intellectuals and its middle class after World War I.

46. Alain Locke, "To Certain of Our Phillistines," *Opportunity* 3 (May 1925): 155-56.

47. Larzer Ziff, *The American 1890s: The Life and Times of a Lost Generation* (New York: Viking Press, 1966), pp. 126-27.

48. See Richard Wright, "Blueprint for Negro Writing," *New Challenge* 2 (Fall 1937): 53-65.

49. E. Franklin Frazier, "The New Negro Middle Class," *The New Negro Thirty Years Afterward*, ed. Rayford W. Logan, Eugene C. Holmes, and G. Franklin Edwards (Washington, D.C.: Howard University Press, 1955), p. 26.

50. James Weldon Johnson, "The Dilemma of the Negro Author," *Mercury* 15 (December 1928): 477, 480.

51. James Weldon Johnson, "Negro Authors and White Publishers," *Crisis* 36 (July 1929): 228.

52. Walter White to E. R. Merrick, 8 May 1924, NAACP Files.

53. HLM to Walter White, 16 October 1923, NAACP Files.

54. Walter White to HLM, 17 October 1923, NAACP Files.

55. Walter White to Eugene Saxton, 19 August 1923, NAACP Files.

56. Walter White to HLM, 17 October 1923, NAACP Files.

57. Walter White to L. Golden of Alfred A. Knopf, 26 September 1925, NAACP Files. Walter White sent Knopf a check for $3.20 and told Golden to keep the $114.00 he had coming to him from the sale of the novel. Thus, his total loss was $117.20. In his other dealings with the branches, he worked out an arrangement whereby he would not be liable if the novel failed to sell.

58. Walter White to L. Golden, 31 July 1925, NAACP Files. White told Golden that the only thing to be done with the Des Moines branch was to turn its account over to an attorney. White had written all three branches, asking them to pay for the copies they received, but to no avail. They simply could not sell White's novel even at the discount (50 cents off the $2.50 list price) that Knopf gave them.

59. W.E.B. DuBois, "Criteria of Negro Art," *Crisis* 32 (October 1926): 297.

60. Claude McKay to James Weldon Johnson, 30 April 1928, JWJ.

61. Jean Toomer to Mae Wright, 4 August 1922, TC. A few months earlier Toomer had dramatized this theme in his unpublished play "Natalie Mann."

62. Jean Toomer to Sherwood Anderson, 29 December 1922, TC.

63. See Langston Hughes, "The Negro Artist and the Racial Mountain," *Nation* 122 (23 June 1926): 694.

64. Langston Hughes, "These Bad New Negroes: A Critique on Critics," *Pittsburgh Courier*, 9 April 1927. His second article appeared in the *Courier* a week later, 16 April 1927.

65. George Schuyler, "Views and Reviews," *Pittsburgh Courier*, 31 July 1926.

66. Ibid., 4 May 1929.

67. Ibid., 31 July 1926.

68. Ibid., 13 October 1928.

69. Theophilus Lewis, "New Year's Message to Big Shroud-and-Coffin Men," *Messenger* 9 (January 1927): 27-28.

70. Walter White, "The Spotlight," *Pittsburgh Courier*, 15 May 1926.

71. George Schuyler, "Shafts and Darts," *Messenger* 6 (May 1924): 145-46.

72. Ibid., 8 (December 1926): 380.

73. Theophilus Lewis, "The Theatre," *Messenger* 8 (July 1926): 214.

74. Ibid., 9 (July 1927): 229. My analysis draws from both this article and the previous one.

75. Lewis, "New Year's Message," p. 27.

76. Lewis, "The Theatre," *Messenger* 6 (September 1924): 291.

77. Ibid., 7 (June 1925): 230.

78. Wallace Thurman, *Infants of Spring* (New York: Macaulay, 1932), p. 266. All references are to this edition and appear in the text.

79. "It was a matter of experience," Thurman wrote in his unpublished autobiography, "that he had and would suffer from the hands of the black mob as much if not more than he had and would suffer from the hands of the lily whites." Wallace Thurman, "Notes on a Stepchild," JWJ.

80. Countee Cullen, *One Way to Heaven* (1932; reprint, New York: Harper, 1975), p. 148. All references to this novel are to this edition and appear in the text.

81. Claude McKay to Walter White, 15 June 1925, NAACP Files.

82. Sterling Brown, "Our Literary Audience," *Opportunity* 8 (February 1930): 46.

CHAPTER FIVE

1. HLM, *Prejudices* 3, p. 162.

2. In an unpublished article called "The Negro in Contemporary Literature," White singled out Mencken's "Sahara" as one of four factors responsible for a revolutionary change in recent American literature—that of seeing "the Negro in a new light." NAACP Files.

3. HLM, *Prejudices* 2, p. 142.

4. Walter White, *A Man Called White* (New York: Viking Press, 1948), p. 65.

5. Walter White to HLM, 13 April 1922, NYP.

6. Eugene Saxton to Walter White, 16 August 1923, NAACP Files.

7. Walter White to Eugene Saxton, 23 August 1923 and 19 August 1923, NAACP Files.

8. White, *A Man Called White*, p. 67.

9. Walter White to Robert Kerlin, 26 December 1923, NAACP Files.

10. Walter White to HLM, 11 October 1923, NAACP Files.

11. Ibid., 5 October 1923.

12. HLM to Walter White, undated letter (circa October or November 1923), NAACP Files. Knopf has admitted that Mencken played a strong role in the firm's editorial decisions. See Alfred Knopf, "H. L. Mencken: A Memoir," in *On Mencken*, ed. John Dorsey (New York: Knopf, 1980), p. 287.

13. See Waldron, *White and the Harlem Renaissance*, p. 47; Lewis, *When Harlem Was In Vogue*, p. 135.

14. Knopf was Hugh Wiley's publisher, and Doran had just published Cobb's *J. Poindexter, Colored* (1922), a novel about the ubiquitous clever servant.

15. HLM to Walter White, 19 December 1923, NAACP Files.

16. Ibid., 24 December 1923 and 19 December 1923.

17. Walter White to HLM, 2 September 1924, NAACP Files.

18. Walter White to Carl Van Doren, 14 December 1923, NAACP Files.

19. As quoted from Charles F. Cooney, "Walter White and Sinclair Lewis: The History of a Literary Friendship," in *Prospects: An Annual Journal of American Cultural Studies*, ed. Jack Salzman, vol. 1 (New York: Burt Franklin, 1975), pp. 64-65.

20. Jim Tully, "The American Negro Enters Literature," *International Book Review* (March 1926); White referred to Tully's praise in a letter to R. F. Wood, 11 March 1926, NAACP Files.

21. I have discussed this side of White's character in my article "Alain Locke and Walter White: Their Struggle for Control of the Harlem Renaissance," *Black American Literature Forum* 14 (Fall 1980): 91-99.

22. HLM, "The Aframerican: New Style," *Mercury* 7 (February 1926): 254-55.

23. HLM, "Hiring a Hall," *New York World*, 17 July 1927, syndicated in the *Chicago Tribune* as "The Colored Brother," 17 July 1927.

24. HLM, "Hiring a Hall," *New York World*, 25 September 1927, syndicated in the *Chicago Tribune* as "The Dark American," 25 September 1927.

25. Editorial page, *Chicago Defender*, 30 July 1927.

26. Kelly Miller, "Kelly Miller Speaks," *Baltimore Afro-American*, 7 October 1927.

27. George Schuyler, "Views and Reviews," *Pittsburgh Courier*, 30 July 1927.

28. We have discovered only in the last two decades that black musical forms, be they spirituals, folk songs, or the blues, are quite sophisticated in both their meanings and the responses they evoke from their audience. See Lawrence W. Levine, *Black Culture and Black Consciousness: Afro-American Folk Thought from Slavery to Freedom* (New York: Oxford University Press, 1977); Charles Keil, *Urban Blues* (Chicago: University of Chicago Press, 1966); and Imamu Amiri Baraka, *Blues People* (New York: Morrow, 1963).

29. Editorial page, *Amsterdam News*, 27 July 1927.

30. Ibid., 28 September 1927.

31. Editorial page, *New York Age*, 30 July 1927.

32. Quoted on editorial page, *Chicago Defender*, 8 October 1927.

33. George Schuyler, "Views and Reviews," *Pittsburgh Courier*, 15 October 1927. Even Heywood Broun took up the cudgels against Mencken. See "It Seems to Heywood Broun," *Nation* 125 (19 October 1927): 416-17.

34. W.E.B. DuBois, "Mencken," *Crisis* 34 (October 1927): 276.

35. W.E.B. DuBois, "Criteria of Negro Art," *Crisis*, pp. 290-97.

36. W.E.B. DuBois, "Our Book Shelf," *Crisis* 31 (January 1926): 141.

37. See especially DuBois's review of Claude McKay's *Home to Harlem* and Taylor Gordon's *Born to Be*, in *Crisis* 35 (June 1928): 202; *Crisis* 37 (April 1930): 129.

38. Alain Locke, "Our Little Renaissance," *Ebony and Topaz: A Collectanea*, ed. Charles S. Johnson (New York: Opportunity, 1927), p. 117.

39. Alain Locke, "This Year of Grace," *Opportunity* 9 (February 1931): 51.

40. The success of DuBose Heyward's *Porgy* (1925) inspired many of these sketches, as did *Nigger Heaven*. A partial list of them follows: Jake in *Home to Harlem* (1928); Jimboy in *Not Without Laughter* (1930); Little Augie in *God Sends Sunday* (1931); Gabriel Prosser in *Black Thunder* (1936); Sam in *One Way to Heaven* (1932); the Reverend Pleasant Green (a Mencken portrait if there ever was one) in *Quicksand* (1928); Shine and Linda in *The Walls of Jericho* (1928); Banjo in *Banjo* (1929); Bita in *Banana Bottom* (1933); Emma in *The Blacker the Berry* (1929); the Reverend John Pearson and Lucy in *Jonah's Gourd Vine* (1934); and Janie and Tea Cake in *Their Eyes Were Watching God* (1937).

41. Theophilus Lewis, "Pre-'Renaissance' Poetry," *Messenger* 8 (October 1926): 312.

42. Mencken often insisted that criticism was not "constructive," but see "The Embattled Literati," *Mercury* 20 (June 1930): 154, in which he admits to holding the view mentioned above.

43. Wallace Thurman, "Negro Artists and the Negro," *New Republic* 52 (31 August 1927): 38.

44. Wallace Thurman, "High, Low, Past, and Present," *Harlem* 1 (November 1928): 31.

45. Wallace Thurman, "Nephews of Uncle Remus," *Independent* 119 (24 September 1927): 296.

46. Wallace Thurman, "This Negro Renaissance," unpublished MS, JWJ, pp. 1-2; probably the first draft of "Negro Artists and the Negro."

47. Thurman, "Nephews of Uncle Remus," pp. 296-97.

48. Granville Hicks, "The New Negro: An Interview with Wallace Thurman," *Churchman* (30 April 1927): 11.

49. Thurman, "Negro Artists and the Negro," p. 37.

50. Langston Hughes to Wallace Thurman, undated letter (circa 1926), JWJ.

51. Richard Bruce, "Smoke, Lilies, and Jade," *Fire* 1 (November 1926): 35.

52. Arthur Huff Fauset, "Intelligentsia," *Fire* 1 (November 1926): 46.

53. Locke, "Art or Propaganda?," p. 12.

54. Walter White to Claude McKay, 6 November 1924, NAACP Files. Thurman dramatizes White's generalization in his portrait of Locke (Dr. Parkes) in *Infants of Spring*.

55. J. A. Rogers, *From "Superman" to Man*, 4th ed. (New York: Lenox, 1924), pp. 70, 112.

56. George Schuyler to HLM, 16 June 1931, NYP.

57. George Schuyler, "Uncle Sam's Black Step-Child," *Mercury* 29 (June 1933): 147-56.

58. Singh, *Novels of the Harlem Renaissance*, p. 119.

59. Allison Davis, "Our Negro 'Intellectuals,'" *Crisis* 35 (August 1928): 268-69; 284-86.

CHAPTER SIX

1. HLM, "A Novel of the First Rank," *Smart Set* 35 (November 1911): 155.

2. Walter Lippmann, "H. L. Mencken," *Saturday Review of Literature* 3 (11 December 1926): 414.

3. HLM, "Notes and Queries," *Smart Set* 63 (September 1920): 138-39.

4. HLM, "Chiefly Americans," *Smart Set* 63 (December 1920): 138.

5. HLM, "Consolation," *Smart Set* 64 (January 1921): 138.

6. HLM, "Portrait of an American Citizen," *Smart Set* 69 (October 1922): 138.

7. HLM, "The Anatomy of Ochlocracy," *Smart Set* 64 (February 1921): 141.

8. HLM, "Reflections on Prose Fiction," *Smart Set* 68 (May 1922): 141.

9. HLM, "New York," *Smart Set* 72 (September 1923): 140.

10. HLM, "Yet More Hints for Novelists," *Chicago Tribune*, 27 June 1926, reprinted in *Bathtub Hoax*, p. 72.

11. HLM, "Hints for Novelists," *Chicago Tribune*, 27 December 1925, reprinted in *Bathtub Hoax*, p. 69.

12. Ibid., p. 70.

13. HLM, "Observations on American Letters," *Smart Set* 62 (July 1920): 138.

14. Cowley, *Exile's Return*, p. 28.

15. HLM, "Consolation," *Smart Set*, p. 138.

16. HLM, "Taking Stock," *Smart Set* 67 (March 1922): 143.

17. HLM, *Prejudices* 4, p. 288.

18. Ibid., p. 292.

19. Benjamin Brawley had made this point as early as 1916; see "The Negro in American Fiction," *Dial* 60 (11 May 1916): 445-50. Also see his "The Negro in American Literature," *Bookman* 56 (October 1922): 140.

20. Albert Halper, "Whites Writing Up Blacks," *Dial* 86 (January 1929): 29.

21. This list does not include playwrights such as Ridgely Torrence, Eugene O'Neill, and Paul Green, who were using the Negro as the central figure in their dramas. A still useful bibliography for white authors who wrote about blacks during the 1920s is Elizabeth Lay Green's *The Negro in Contemporary American Literature* (Chapel Hill: University of North Carolina Press, 1928). When *Nigger Heaven* was published in 1926, Joseph Hergesheimer wrote Van Vechten and confessed his desire to write "a short novel" about Negroes, and other American writers such as F. Scott Fitzgerald and Ellen Glasgow also wrote to Van Vechten to express their theories on the impact of urban civilization upon the Negro. See Joseph Hergesheimer to Carl Van Vechten, 23 August 1926, NYP; F. Scott Fitzgerald to Carl Van Vechten, undated (circa August 1926), NYP; Ellen Glasgow to Carl Van Vechten, 28 July 1926, NYP.

22. Ernest Hemingway, *The Torrents of Spring* (1926; reprint, New York: Scribner's, 1972), p. 41.

23. George Morse, "The Fictitious Negro," *Outlook and Independent* 152 (21 August 1929): 649.

24. Locke, *New Negro*, pp. 41, 50, 51.

25. Oswald Garrison Villard, "Negro Literature," *Literary Review* 3 (30 June 1923): 798.

26. Mulder, "Wanted: A Negro Novelist," pp. 341, 342.

27. Locke, "The Colonial Literature of France," pp. 331-35.

28. W.E.B. DuBois, "Opinion," *Crisis* 22 (June 1921): 55-56.

29. T. S. Stribling, *Birthright* (New York: Century Co., 1922), p. 302. All references to *Birthright* are from this edition and appear in the text.

30. Alain Locke and Jessie Fauset, "Notes on the New Books," *Crisis* 25 (February 1923): 162.

31. Jessie Fauset et al., "The New Books," *Crisis* 27 (February 1924): 177.

32. Charles S. Johnson, "*Nigger*—A Novel by Clement Wood," *Opportunity* 1 (January 1923): 30.

33. William Stanley Braithwaite, "The Negro in Literature," *Crisis* 28 (September 1924): 206.

34. Jessie Fauset, "As to Books," *Crisis* 24 (June 1922): 67.

35. DuBois and Locke had Harvard Ph.D.'s; Brawley, an M.A. from Harvard; Fauset, an M.A. from the University of Pennsylvania; and White, a B.A. from Atlanta University. In addition, Fauset had studied at the Sorbonne, and DuBois and Locke had attended the University of Berlin.

36. Alain Locke, "Spiritual Truancy," in *Voices from the Harlem Renaissance*, ed. Nathan Huggins (New York: Oxford University Press, 1976), p. 406.

37. HLM, "Again the Busy Fictioneers," *Smart Set* 39 (January 1913): 153.

38. HLM to Walter White, 13 March 1922, in Forgue, *Letters*, p. 235.

39. See HLM, *Prejudices* 1, pp. 22-51.

40. HLM, "On Realism," *Chicago Tribune*, 15 August 1926, reprinted in *Bathtub Hoax*, p. 109.

41. HLM, *Prejudices* 3, p. 205. I am indebted to Frank Turaj for this insight and for these two quotations from Mencken. See his excellent "Mencken and American Literature," pp. 61, 132.

42. Walter White to Rudolf Fisher, 12 March 1925, NAACP Files. Also, see HLM to Walter White, 7 October 1923, NAACP Files. This is the letter to which White refers.

43. Walter White to A. S. Frissel, 20 September 1924, NAACP Files.

44. HLM, "Escape and Return," *Mercury* 16 (April 1929): 507.

45. Walter White to W. P. Dabney, 19 January 1925, NAACP Files.

46. Walter White to HLM, 22 November 1920, NAACP Files.

47. Walter White to Eugene Saxton, 19 August 1923, NAACP Files.

48. Ibid., 23 August 1923.

49. Walter White to Professor Webster, 14 April 1925, NAACP Files. White made a similar defense of his novel to Eugene Saxton in his letter of 23 August 1923, NAACP Files.

50. HLM, *George Bernard Shaw: His Plays* (1905; reprint, New Rochelle, N.Y.: E. V. Glaser, 1969), p. xx.

51. White was clearly indebted to Charles Chesnutt's *The Marrow of Tradition* (1901) for this element of the plot, though he was also thinking of Stribling's *Birthright*. Unlike Peter Siner, Kenneth Harper will not have a spiritual relapse when he returns home.

52. Walter White, *The Negro's Contribution to American Culture: The Sudden Flowering of a Genius-Laden Artistic Movement*, Little Blue Book no. 1306, ed. E. Haldeman-Julius (Girard, Kan.: Haldeman-Julius Publications, 1928), pp. 50-51.

53. Walter White to HLM, 30 August 1924, NAACP Files.

54. J. A. Rogers to Walter White, 9 January 1925, NAACP Files.

55. Walter White to J. A. Rogers, 12 January 1925, NAACP Files.

56. Wallace Thurman, "Notes on a Stepchild," unnumbered page, JWJ.

57. Turaj, "Mencken and American Literature," p. 111. The essay referred to here is Mencken's "Criticism of Criticism of Criticism," in *Prejudices* 1, p. 18.

58. Turaj, "Mencken and American Literature," pp. 82-84.

59. W.E.B. DuBois, "Opinion," *Crisis* 25 (April 1923): 247.

60. DuBois ran this symposium through the months of March, April, May, and June 1926.

61. DuBois, "Criteria of Negro Art," p. 296.

62. W.E.B. DuBois, "Books," *Crisis* 33 (December 1926): 81-82.

63. W.E.B. DuBois, "Two Novels," *Crisis* 35 (June 1928): 202.

64. Alain Locke, "The Negro in American Literature," *New World Writing* (New

York: New American Library, 1952), p. 28. Locke uncharitably does not mention Mencken at all, either in the context of realism in American literature or in the context of the southern renaissance. Locke is not unusual in this respect; by 1952, most critics belittled Mencken's influence.

65. Locke, "To Certain of Our Phillistines," p. 155.

66. Locke implied a preference for "pure art values" in *The New Negro* (see p. 52) and made his implication explicit in "Art or Propaganda?" See p. 12.

67. Alain Locke, "Of Native Sons: Real and Otherwise," *Opportunity* 19 (January 1941): 4.

68. In his novel, *Home to Harlem* (1928; reprint, New York: Pocket Books, 1965), McKay was constantly reminding his reader of Harlem's capacity to turn men into beasts:

"Who's the Wolf?" timidly Zeddy's girl asked.

Zeddy pointed out Billy.

"But why Wolf?"

. . . Zeddy laughed. "'Causen he eats his own kind" (p. 49).

At the end of the novel, Zeddy figuratively tries to devour his best friend Jake, and at that point, Jake knows that it is time to leave town.

69. See Locke, "Spiritual Truancy," pp. 404-6.

70. Locke, "To Certain of Our Phillistines," p. 155.

71. DuBois, "Criteria of Negro Art," p. 297.

72. Locke, "Art or Propaganda?," p. 12.

73. Jean Toomer, "The South in Literature," TC.

74. Walter White to A. Bernd, 24 March 1925, NAACP Files.

75. On 23 July 1922 Toomer wrote to Frank about the latter's intended revision of *Our America*, in which Frank planned to include the Negro: "Those unspeakable palefaces who have been championing *Birthright*, and who have been clamoring for the black folk in our literature, will hate you for it." TC.

76. Jean Toomer, *Cane*, ed. Darwin Turner (1923; reprint, New York: Liveright, 1975), p. 84. All references to *Cane* are from this edition and appear in the text. The following discussion of *Cane* is a thoroughly revised version of an article that I published in 1972. See Charles W. Scruggs, "The Mark of Cain and the Redemption of Art: A Study in Theme and Structure of Jean Toomer's *Cane*," *American Literature* 44 (May 1972): 276-91.

77. That the color of the black man's skin was the mark of Cain is part of American folklore. See Winthrop Jordan, *White over Black: American Attitudes Toward the Negro, 1550-1812* (1968; reprint, Baltimore: Penguin, 1969), pp. 242, 416. On the other hand, as James Baldwin has noted, "In the same way that we, for white people, were the descendants of Ham, and were cursed forever, white people were, for us, the descendants of Cain." See *The Fire Next Time* (1963; reprint, New York: Dell, 1964), p. 59. Also, see Levine, p. 85-86.

78. Jean Toomer to Waldo Frank, 12 December 1922, TC.

79. Jean Toomer to Sherwood Anderson, 18 December 1922, TC.

80. Jean Toomer to Waldo Frank (circa 1923), TC.

81. Esther does bear a remarkable resemblance to Alice Hindman ("Adventure") and Kate Swift ("The Teacher") in *Winesburg, Ohio*.

82. Jean Toomer to Waldo Frank (circa 1923), TC.

83. HLM, "Holy Writ," *Smart Set* 72 (October 1923): 144.

84. Jean Toomer, "Waldo Frank's Holiday," *Dial* 75 (October 1923): 383-85.

85. Walter White to Eugene Saxton, 19 August 1923, NAACP Files.

86. Jessie Fauset, "As to Books," *Crisis* 24 (June 1922): 68, 69.

87. Don Marquis, *Carter and Other People* (New York: Appleton, 1921), p. 10.

88. Fauset herself was to create characters who shared Carter's racial makeup. Peter Bye in *There Is Confusion* (1924) discovers a blood link to an aristocratic white family who used to be the owners of his ancestors. Anthony Cross bears the cross of mescegenation in

Plum Bun (1929), and Laurentine Strange (*The Chinaberry Tree*, 1931) is a product of a liaison between a white Southern colonel and a mulatto mistress. In *Comedy, American Style* (1933), the tragedies of Teresa and Oliver are due to their mother's obsession with whiteness. Yet while skeletons appear in the closets of these fictional families, there is no sense, as there is in Faulkner, that the sorrows are irrevocable. In three of her four novels, the dilemma is neatly solved by a happy ending. Peter Bye waves goodbye to his white inheritance; Anthony Cross forgets his troubled ancestry when he finds true love with Angela Murray, and Laurentine is no longer "strange" when she marries Dr. Denleigh. Fauset always gave the impression that even the most irrational of situations look better in the light of day. Only in *Comedy, American Style* did she leave the warmth of sunlight for the power of darkness, but even here people are what they are, and they can be explained in rational terms.

89. Ernest Hemingway, *In Our Time* (1925; reprint, New York: Scribner's, 1930), p. 59.

90. Ralph Ellison, *Shadow and Act* (1953; reprint, New York: New American Library, 1966), p. 169. Also, see Michael Allen, "Some Examples of Faulknerian Rhetoric in Ellison's *Invisible Man*," in *The Black American Writer*, ed. C.W.E. Bigsby (Baltimore: Penguin, 1969), pp. 143-51.

91. Richard Wright, "How 'Bigger' Was Born," in *Black Voices*, ed. Abraham Chapman (New York: New American Library, 1968), p. 563.

92. Turaj, "Mencken and American Literature," p. 241.

93. See Joseph Blotner, *William Faulkner: A Biography* (New York: Random House, 1974), vol. 1, p. 670; vol. 2, p. 924. Mencken called "That Evening Sun" (published in the *Mercury* in 1931) "a capital story," and he later described Faulkner to a friend as "a wonderful comedy writer."

94. Turaj, "Mencken and American Literature," p. 240.

95. HLM, "Fiction by Adept Hands," *Mercury* 19 (January 1930): 127.

96. Turaj, "Mencken and American Literature," p. 228.

97. Richard Wright, *Black Boy* (New York: Harper, 1945), p. 159. All references are to this edition and appear in the text.

98. Charles S. Johnson to Carl Van Vechten, 10 August 1926, JWJ.

99. To Carl Van Vechten must go the credit of resurrecting Chesnutt during the 1920s. In his review of Locke's *The New Negro* and in his own *Nigger Heaven*, he held up the older writer as a model for the present generation of black writers. See *"Keep A-Inchin' Along,"* p. 59; *Nigger Heaven*, pp. 104, 176-79.

100. Sterling Brown, "The Literary Scene: Chronicle and Comment," *Opportunity* 9 (January 1931): 20.

101. Alain Locke, "This Year of Grace," *Opportunity* 9 (February 1931): 49.

102. One might argue that John Pearson in Hurston's *Jonah's Gourd Vine*, the preacher in Johnson's *God's Trombones*, and Reverend Johnson in *One Way to Heaven* were all written with Mencken's criticism in mind. Each portrait is of a man more complicated than he appears to be. Pearson is both a womanizer and a man of God; Johnson's preacher is a myth maker and a teacher of homely truths; the Reverend Johnson, a tough fighter and a kindly Christian. As Zora Neale Hurston told Johnson, "being a good man is not enough to hold a Negro preacher in an important charge. He must also be an artist. He must be both a poet and an actor of a very high order, and then he must have the voice and the figure. . . . the light that shone from GOD'S TROMBONES was handed to you, as was the sermon to me in *Jonah's Gourd Vine*" (quoted from Robert Hemenway's *Zora Neale Hurston* [Urbana: University of Illinois Press, 1977], p. 194).

103. Three portraits of the Negro preacher that fit the Menckenian mold are James Baldwin's puritanical Gabriel Grimes (*Go Tell It on the Mountain*), Ralph Ellison's blind

Homer Barbee (*Invisible Man*), and Richard Wright's complacent preacher in Bigger's cell (*Native Son*).

104. Wright, "How 'Bigger' Was Born," p. 557.

EPILOGUE

1. Young, *Black Writers of the Thirties*, p. 93.

2. Manchester, *Disturber of the Peace*, pp. 256-57.

3. Ibid., p. 265.

4. Quoted from Raymond Wolters, "The New Deal and the Negro," in *The New Deal: The National Level*, ed. John Braeman, Robert H. Bremner, and David Brody (Columbus: Ohio State University Press, 1975), vol. 1, pp. 210-11.

5. HLM to Walter White, 6 December 1943, in Forgue, *Letters*, p. 479.

6. Mencken attacked Christianity's relationship to slavery in two books that he wrote in the 1930s. He argued that slavery was not abolished by Christians; on the contrary, institutional religion was often the chief supporter of the "peculiar institution." It took men of the Enlightenment, most of them non-Christians and many of them atheists, to lead the charge for freeing the bondsmen. The muddle-headed Christians only followed the lead of these men (who had acted as morally responsible individuals) when the attack on slavery could be made into a "cause." Mencken's reasoning on this matter explains why he could be against both slavery and the Abolitionist movement. See HLM, *Treatise on Right and Wrong* (London: Kegan Paul, 1934), pp. 30-35, 48, 49. Also, see HLM, *Treatise on the Gods* (New York: Knopf, 1930), p. 29. In *Treatise on Right and Wrong*, Mencken typically took an unsentimental attitude toward slavery; it was primarily an economic affair, and when it was no longer profitable, slavery ended. However, he never squared this observation with his strong implication that if it had not been for the moral promptings of the Englightenment men, slavery might have continued.

7. Wolters, "New Deal and the Negro," p. 209.

8. HLM to George Schuyler, 8 November 1939, 18 November 1940, JWJ.

9. Ibid., 10 May 1939, NYP.

10. Ibid., 15 January 1945.

11. Ibid., 5 February 1945, in *New Letters*, p. 550.

12. Ibid., 15 January 1945, NYP.

13. Ibid., 7 May 1935, *Letters*, p. 390.

14. Ibid., 10 May 1939, *Letters*, p. 434.

15. HLM to Kelly Miller, 5 December 1939, NYP. Mencken wrote this letter to Miller three weeks before the latter's death (29 December 1939). Mencken had obviously been upset by Bilbo's scheme, because he mentioned it to Miller as well as Schuyler.

16. Ibid., 22 September 1939.

17. Alexander Pope, "Epilogue to the Satires, Dialogue II," *The Poems of Alexander Pope*, ed. John Butt (New Haven: Yale University Press, 1963), p. 701.

18. Schuyler, *Black and Conservative*, p. 351.

Index

The Johns Hopkins University Press

THE SAGE IN HARLEM
H. L. Mencken and the Black Writers
of the 1920s

This book was composed in Palatino text
by David Lorton and Bodoni and
Palatino display by The Composing Room,
from a design by Gerard A. Valerio
It was printed on 50-lb. Sebago paper
and bound in Holliston Kingston cloth
by The Maple Press Company.